# THE FAMILIAR
# ESSAY

# THE FAMILIAR ESSAY

MARK CHRISTENSEN
*Bemidji State University*

HEINLE & HEINLE
THOMSON LEARNING

Australia Canada Mexico Singapore Spain
United Kingdom United States

**HEINLE & HEINLE**

**THOMSON LEARNING**

English Editor: John Meyers
Marketing Manager: Katrina Byrd
Project Manager, Editorial Production:
Angela Williams Urquhart
Print/Media Buyer: Elaine Curda
Permissions Editor: Beverly Wyatt
Production Service: Impressions Book
and Journal Services, Inc.

Copy Editor: Natalie Bakopoulos
Cover Designer: Jane Tenenbaum
Cover Image: PhotoDisc
Cover Printer: Lehigh Press
Compositor: Impressions Book and
Journal Services, Inc.
Printer: Quebecor Printing Fairfield

For more information about
our products, contact us at:
Thomson Learning
Academic Resource Center
1-800-423-0563

For permission to use material
from this text, contact us by:
Phone: 1-800-730-2214
Fax: 1-800-730-2215
Web: http://www.thomsonrights.com

Library of Congress Control Number:
2001092289
ISBN: 0-15-505810-X

**Asia**
Thomson Learning
60 Albert Street, #15-01
Albert Complex
Singapore 189969

**Australia**
Nelson Thomson Learning
102 Dodds Street
South Melbourne, Victoria 3205
Australia

**Canada**
Nelson Thomson Learning
1120 Birchmount Road
Toronto, Ontario M1K 5G4
Canada

**Europe/Middle East/Africa**
Thomson Learning
Berkshire House
168-173 High Holborn
London WC1 V7AA
United Kingdom

**Latin America**
Thomson Learning
Seneca, 53
Colonia Polanco
11560 Mexico D.F.
Mexico

**Spain**
Paraninfo Thomson Learning
Calle/Magallanes, 25
28015 Madrid, Spain

# CONTENTS

## PART 2: POPULAR PRESS ESSAYS

PART 3: STUDENT ESSAYS

# PREFACE

This small book is designed to startle prospective writers into realizing that they can do what real writers do and have done in the professional world and in school: produce interesting essays. It assembles classic essays, essays of the modern press, and student essays in the hope of provoking emerging writers to realize that writing doesn't have to be stiff, impersonal, cold, and distant. Instead, writing essays can be a satisfying process of discovery, and reading essays can be entertaining and provocative.

The familiar essay is both a common reading experience and a common genre. As a genre, the familiar essay exhibits the personality of an individual writer, requires little or no specialized knowledge from the reader, and is unpredictable in content and form. In fact, the content often surprises the writer as it emerges in the process of writing.

Familiar essays are sometimes contrasted with themes, which are specifically thesis driven, and with arguments, which can be thought of as extensions or formal complications of themes. Familiar essays often are arguments, but without predetermined argument form. They can be found in many current popular magazines and are also some of the classic and often anthologized essays that are familiar to students and teachers.

In one sense, writing familiar essays as opposed to themes is analogous to educating writers as opposed to training them. In training a writer and in writing a theme, the writer's process is one of repetition and reproduction; in educating a writer and in writing familiar essays, the writer's process is one of adaptation to the evolving contexts of the piece and the initial creation of those contexts.

In their first drafts, familiar essays tend to emerge in the order that their ideas occurred to their writers. The root of the familiar essay is the writer's creativity at the moment of composing. This is in contrast to the practice of writing to produce a given outlined form. The discovery phase is much more exciting and spontaneous than is true in drafting pieces to fit a mold or mode. The first essay in this book is a description of what it can be like to write the first draft of a familiar essay.

All of the essays in this book were chosen for their singularity of voice, their accessibility, and their variety. The essays by professional writers were chosen for sheer quality. The essays by student writers are all competently written, but are also chosen for the interesting decisions made by their authors about form and voice.

Each essay is followed by questions on content and rhetoric, vocabulary, and writing prompts. The questions on content are just that—a quick check to make sure you, as a reader, stayed with the essay and can recall simple facts or ideas. The rhetorical questions give you an opportunity to analyze writing strategies the authors used. Because English is a flexible language, vocabulary words will keep your own vocabulary active, helping you to use language more effectively. The writing prompts are designed not only to stimulate ideas for writing, but also to generate active discussions of issues. These strategies will enable you to stay intellectually engaged in the process of critical reading, helping you to bridge the reading-writing connection.

This book is organized into three parts. Part 1 consists of classic essays and includes pieces by authors such as Mark Twain, George Orwell, E. B. White, and Loren Eiseley. Part 2 consists of modern popular press pieces by authors such as Judith Viorst, Ellen Goodman, Donald Hall, and Paul Gruchow. There is necessarily some overlap between Part 1 and Part 2, as some modern essayists' works have become so well known that they have reached the level of modern classic. Part 3 consists of essays written by college students in just the two or three years prior to this book's publication, whose names we hope will reappear in other venues.

I would like to thank the following instructors for their helpful comments and suggestions: Dan Butcher, Southwestern Louisiana University; Faye D. Christensen, Mobile Bay Writing Project; Robert Croft, Gainesville College; Michael Marx, Skidmore College; and Harry Phillips, Central Piedmont Community College.

I would like to acknowledge the following graduate assistants for helping with the selection of essays: Julie Altiero, Kelly Hagemeister, Corina Londo, Albin Polanyi, Lois Templin, Melissa Vene, and Joel Wolleat. I would also like to thank my colleagues, Susan Hauser and Mark Vinz, for their advice. Beyond that, I want to thank Jim Ertl, Julie McBurney, and Jessica Swigger for their help in making the book happen.

# INTRODUCTION:
# COMPOSING YOURSELF

## FROM ONE WRITER TO ANOTHER

Part of the excitement of writing familiar essays is that the writing keeps revealing new things. You might discover new things about yourself—new dimensions to explore. You might discover thoughts or opinions you didn't know you had before you wrote them. You might create thoughts or opinions you didn't have before you wrote them. You might even discover versions of yourself you didn't know were in you until the writing brought them out.

You are and can choose to be many versions of you—versions that can come out through writing. I've discovered a part of me that is an entertainer, poking fun at myself for my own pleasure and for the readers'. I've discovered a part that is a reporter, imparting the news I've noticed. There is a childlike part, marveling and wondering at ice on a lake or the funny way herons look when standing and the grace they assume when flying. There is a social commentator, bemused by gender politics, children shooting children, leaders lying. I have found more parts of me, too, and so can you. To get there, writers go into a composing zone.

*It is concentrated mindlessness, the space where athletes and children excel. You know that you are going to write something—*

*at least, a draft of something—and sometimes you have a notion of how you're going to start, but almost never do you know what is coming. You only go with it. You start and continue. You allow everything but the writing to disappear.*

*This zone is brutal. It has no tact. What comes, comes, and the writer self allows no concessions. That people will think what you write is silly or offensive or pompous or any other bad thing is irrelevant. It is a time of impersonal solitude—an indifference to the attitudes of others. It has a beautiful clarity, though the product, the piece, is a mystery still in the process of being revealed.*

Writing is a zone of its own. It is open to everyone. Sometimes we see someone in a café, or laundromat, or coffee shop hunched over a tablet, scribbling furiously, or their eyes frozen in a middle-distance stare. That someone has found a writing zone. Sometimes we see whole classrooms of students absorbed in their production of writing. Their bodies are tensed, their eyes are focused. They can find a writing zone, too. It's in their heads.

*Shades of jeans, sweatpants, a couple of baseball caps—one on backward. Hard tile floors and fluorescent lights belying the beauty of brilliant blue sky and greening grass outside the window. Inside, we write. We work in the ultimate consciousness of now, the moment of hope. Something good might happen. That is the affirmation of the writer—a statement of faith that when we write, something will happen. We will find our material or it will be sent to us. We will craft or we will be conduits. Craft or conduit.*

Writers commonly face a block that can prevent finding the ruthlessness of the so-called right writing zone. They are wary of audiences, especially teachers, and so often they do not enter that place of cold clarity as they write. That place is indifferent to the status of an audience.

The willingness to go to that place in the head is the precursor to writing passionate pieces. Passionate writing is written dispassionately. It demonstrates the writer's willingness to see and to be without embellishment or pose. In the moment of composing there is no room for agendas other than the piece. No gripes, no pettiness, no revenge, no swooning. Just the page and the piece and the moving hand.

*The delight and puzzlement and surprise. The moment by moment sense that something is coming, that I'm going to match words to some sense inside my head, some preverbal consciousness that isn't graspable until I match words to it. It is more surprise because the match is never perfect—the words never quite accurately and completely satisfy the meaning I'm fitting them too. That leaves me feeling that there is and was stuff in my head that didn't get said. It's still there, waiting.*

*Language leads me, too. While matching words to ideas in my head, the words that I've already written lead me to places, to meanings, other than the first word-to-meaning match I started. The words change my head, and I'm off following them on a mapless trip, a journey without predetermined destination, following until I have some sense of arrival.*

*I keep looking back to see where I've been writing and sometimes make changes in where I've been that cause me to shift where I'm going. I know the need for closure, and so as I'm writing, I'm also listening for possible pullings-together, for cadences and codas, and write with the sense of where I started and the knowledge that I want to pull together whatever comes out on the way.*

*When I started this little contemplation, I knew that I wanted to write about how the act of writing feels and that I wanted it to come to some end that feels like an end. I didn't know what would come out along the way between those points. I didn't know that I would use travel references (trip, journey, destination, arrival) or musical terms (cadence, coda), I only knew that something would come out. That's another beauty of writing—the mind comes through. It isn't empty or static, like some forgotten attic in an abandoned house, it is the living room, the place where I live. Minds resist emptiness. Writing is the opposite of emptiness. Writing heightens consciousness.*

Inside each of us is a silent watcher, an inner teacher. Writers talk about the ghost or monster on their shoulder, the critic that tells them whatever they are writing is junk. That inner critic worries about sounding stupid, which blocks the writing. That critic can also be harnessed, tamed, put to good use, or even set free.

The writing that feels strongest is the writing that feels closest to that interior watcher. It isn't about how I look, or whether I wear a tie, or what I do for a living, or my gender or race. It's that inner ear that listens to what I write and knows whether it is true and clean or not.

I think to tap into the strength of the silent watcher we have to give up worrying about image—that can come later. The good writing taps the internal voice, the mind as it works when it isn't junked up with fears or insecurities. It is fearless writing, willing to take on or face anything. Some of it can then be adapted for public consumption, so audiences can benefit from it, but first it has to be edgily right for the writer alone. That means we have to learn to trust that inner ear, and we can't muck up that ear by filling it full of worries.

*Writing is present tense.*

# I

---

# CLASSIC
# ESSAYS

# WHO KILLED BENNY PARET?

## NORMAN COUSINS

Sometime about 1935 or 1936 I had an interview with Mike Jacobs, the prize-fight promoter. I was a fledgling newspaper reporter at that time; my beat was education, but during the vacation season I found myself on varied assignments, all the way from ship news to sports reporting. In this way I found myself sitting opposite the most powerful figure in the boxing world.

There was nothing spectacular in Mr. Jacob's manner or appearance; but when he spoke about prize fights, he was no longer a bland little man but a colossus who sounded the way Napoleon must have sounded when he reviewed a battle. You knew you were listening to Number One. His saying something made it true.

We discussed what to him was the only important element in successful promoting—how to please the crowd. So far as he was concerned, there was no mystery to it. You put killers in the ring and the people filled your arena. You hire boxing artists—men who are adroit at feinting, parrying, weaving, jabbing, and dancing, but who don't pack dynamite in their fists—and you wind up counting your empty seats. So you searched for the killers and sluggers and maulers—fellows who could hit with the force of a baseball bat.

I asked Mr. Jacobs if he was speaking literally when he said people came out to see the killer.

"They don't come out to see a tea party," he said evenly. "They come out to see the knockout. They come out to see a man hurt. If they think anything else, they're kidding themselves."

Recently a young man by the name of Benny Paret was killed in the ring. The killing was seen by millions; it was on television. In the twelfth round he was hit hard in the head several times, went down, was counted out, and never came out of the coma.

The Paret fight produced a flurry of investigations. Governor Rockefeller was shocked by what happened and appointed a committee to assess the responsibility. The New York State Boxing Commission decided to find out what was wrong. The District Attorney's office expressed its concern. One question that was solemnly studied in all three probes concerned the action of the referee. Did he act in time to stop the fight? Another question had to do with the role of the examining doctors who certified the physical fitness of the fighters before the bout. Still another question involved Mr. Paret's manager; did he rush his boy into the fight without adequate time to recuperate from the previous one?

In short, the investigators looked into every possible cause except the real one. Benny Paret was killed because the human fist delivers enough impact, when directed against the head, to produce a massive hemorrhage in the brain. The human brain is the most delicate and complex mechanism in all creation. It has a lacework of millions of highly fragile nerve connections. Nature attempts to protect this exquisitely intricate machinery by encasing it in a hard shell. Fortunately, the shell is thick enough to withstand a great deal of pounding. Nature, however, can protect man against everything except man himself. Not every blow to the head will kill a man—but there is always the risk of concussion and damage to the brain. A prize fighter may be able to survive even repeated brain concussions and go on fighting, but the damage to his brain may be permanent.

In any event, it is futile to investigate the referee's role and seek to determine whether he should have intervened to stop the fight earlier. This is not where the primary responsibility lies. The primary responsibility lies with the people who pay to see a man hurt. The referee who stops a fight too soon from the crowd's viewpoint can expect to be booed. The crowd wants the knockout; it wants to see a man stretched out on the canvas. This is the supreme moment in boxing. It is nonsense to talk about prize fighting as a test of boxing skills. No crowd was ever brought to its feet screaming and cheering at the sight of two men beautifully dodging and weaving out of each other's jabs. The time the crowd comes alive is when a man is hit hard over the heart or the head, when his mouthpiece flies out, when blood squirts out of his nose or eyes, when he wobbles under the attack and his pursuer continues to smash at him with poleax impact.

Don't blame it on the referee. Don't even blame it on the fight managers. Put the blame where it belongs—on the prevailing mores that regard prize fighting as a perfectly proper enterprise and vehicle of entertainment. No one doubts that many people enjoy prize fighting and will miss it if it should be thrown out. And that is precisely the point.

## QUESTIONS ON CONTENT

1. How did Benny Paret die?
2. What is the most important element in successful promoting?
3. Name three proposed causes of Paret's death.
4. According to Cousins, who has the primary responsibility for Paret's death?

## QUESTIONS ON RHETORIC

1. When and how does the author establish his credibility for writing about this event?
2. Why do you think paragraph 4 is so short?
3. List the images in paragraph 9. What is Cousins trying to do with this descriptive writing?
4. Look at the repetition in paragraph 10. What impact does this repetition have?

## VOCABULARY

(2) colossus
(3) adroit
(8) hemorrhage
(9) poleax
(10) mores

## WRITING PROMPTS

1. Discuss the quote in paragraph 8: "Nature, however, can protect man against everything except himself."
2. Respond to this statement: Everyone needs to imagine being violent and being treated violently.
3. What makes people enjoy what they do?
4. Think of something you like doing. Describe whatever it is and what you think about while doing it. Figure out what causes you to like doing this thing.

# Two Ways of Seeing a River

## Mark Twain

Now when I had mastered the language of this water and had come to know every trifling feature that bordered the great river as familiarly as I knew the letters of the alphabet, I had made a valuable acquisition. But I had lost something, too. I had lost something which could never be restored to me while I lived. All the grace, the beauty, the poetry, had gone out of the majestic river! I still kept in mind a certain wonderful sunset which I witnessed when steamboating was new to me. A broad expanse of the river was turned to blood; in the middle distance the red hue brightened into gold, through which a solitary log came floating, black and conspicuous; in one place a long, slanting mark lay sparkling upon the water; in another the surface was broken by boiling, tumbling rings that were as many-tinted as an opal; where the ruddy flush was faintest was a smooth spot that was covered with graceful circles and radiating lines, ever so delicately traced; the shore on our left was densely wooded, and the somber shadow that fell from this forest was broken in one place by a long, ruffled trail that shone like silver; and high above the forest wall a clean-stemmed dead tree waved a single leafy bough that glowed like a flame in the unobstructed splendor that was flowing from the sun. There were graceful curves, reflected images, woody heights, soft distances, and over the whole scene, far and near, the dissolving lights drifted steadily, enriching it every passing moment with new marvels of coloring.

I stood like one bewitched. I drank it in, in a speechless rapture. The world was new to me and I had never seen anything like this at home. But as I have said, a day came when I began to cease from noting the glories and the charms which the moon and the sun and the twilight wrought upon the river's face; another day came when I ceased altogether to note them. Then, if that sunset scene had been repeated, I should have looked upon it without rapture and should have commented upon it inwardly after this fashion: "This sun means that we are going to have wind tomorrow; that floating log means that the river is rising, small thanks to it; that slanting mark on the water refers to a bluff reef which is going to kill somebody's steamboat one of these nights, if it keeps on stretching out like that; those tumbling 'boils' show a dissolving bar and a changing channel there; the lines and circles in the slick water over yonder are a warning that that troublesome place is shoaling up dangerously; that silver streak in the shadow of the forest is the 'break' from a new snag and he has located himself in the very best place he could have found to fish for steamboats; that tall dead tree, with a single living branch, is not going to last long, and then how is a body ever going to get through this blind place at night without the friendly old landmark?"

No, the romance and beauty were all gone from the river. All the value any feature of it had for me now was the amount of usefulness it could furnish toward compassing the safe piloting of a steamboat. Since those days, I have pitied doctors from my heart. What does the lovely flush in a beauty's cheek mean to a doctor but a "break" that ripples above some deadly disease? Are not all her visible charms sown thick with what are to him the signs and symbols of hidden decay? Does he ever see her beauty at all, or doesn't he simply view her professionally and comment upon her unwholesome condition all to himself? And doesn't he sometimes wonder whether he has gained most or lost most by learning his trade?

## Questions on Content

1. What is Twain describing on the river?
2. What is the "friendly old landmark" that Twain writes about?
3. Who does Twain pity?

## Questions on Rhetoric

1. List the descriptive words and phrases in the first paragraph.
2. How does Twain's use of color affect the mood of this piece?
3. Find examples of personification.
4. Why does Twain say the romance and beauty have disappeared from the river?

## Vocabulary

(1) conspicuous

(2) shoaling

(3) compassing

## Writing Prompts

1. Write about seeing.
2. Write about a relationship you've had that is over. Show why the relationship matters.
3. How has change affected your life recently?
4. Write about a place from your childhood that you revisited as an adult.

---

# WE MAY BE BROTHERS

## CHIEF SEATTLE

Yonder sky that has wept tears of compassion upon my people for
centuries untold, and which to us appears changeless and eternal,
may change. Today is fair. Tomorrow it may be overcast with clouds.
My words are like the stars that never change. Whatever Seattle says
the great chief at Washington can rely upon with as much certainty
as he can upon the return of the sun or the seasons. The White Chief
says that Big Chief at Washington sends us greetings of friendship
and goodwill. That is kind of him for we know he has little need of
our friendship in return. His people are many. They are like the grass
that covers vast prairies. My people are few. They resemble the scattering trees of a storm-swept plain. . . . I will not dwell on nor mourn
over, our untimely decay, nor reproach our paleface brothers with
hastening it, as we too may have been somewhat to blame. . . .

Your God is not our God. Your God loves your people and hates
mine. He folds his strong and protecting arms lovingly about the
paleface and leads him by the hand as a father leads his infant son—
but He has forsaken His red children—if they really are His. Our
God, the Great Spirit, seems also to have forsaken us. Your God
makes your people strong every day. Soon they will fill the land. Our
people are ebbing away like a rapidly receding tide that will never
return. The white man's God cannot love our people or He would
protect them. They seem to be orphans who can look nowhere for

help. How then can we be brothers?... We are two distinct races with separate origins and separate destinies. There is little in common between us.

To us the ashes of our ancestors are sacred and their resting place is hallowed ground. You wander far from the graves of your ancestors and seemingly without regret. Your religion was written upon tables of stone by the iron finger of your God so that you could not forget. The Red Man could never comprehend nor remember it. Our religion is the traditions of our ancestors—the dreams of our old men, given them in solemn hours of night by the Great Spirit; and the visions of our sachems; and it is written in the hearts of our people.

Your dead cease to love you and the land of their nativity as soon as they pass the portals of the tomb and wander way beyond the stars. They are soon forgotten and never return. Our dead never forget the beautiful world that gave them being.

Day and night cannot dwell together. The Red Man has ever fled the approach of the White Man, as the morning mist flees before the morning sun. However, your proposition seems fair and I think that my people will accept it and will retire to the reservation you offer them. Then we will dwell apart in peace.... It matters little where we pass the remnant of our days. They will not be many. A few more moons; a few more winters—and not one of the descendants of the mighty hosts that once moved over this broad land or lived in happy homes, protected by the Great Spirit, will remain to mourn over the graves of a people once more powerful and hopeful than yours. But why should I mourn at the untimely fate of my people? Tribe follows tribe, and nation follows nation, like the waves of the sea. It is the order of nature, and regret is useless. Your time of decay may be distant, but it will surely come, for even the White Man whose God walked and talked with him as friend with friend cannot be exempt from the common destiny. We may be brothers after all. We will see....

Every part of this soil is sacred in the estimation of my people. Every hillside, every valley, every plain and grove, has been hallowed by some sad or happy event in days long vanished. The very dust upon which you now stand responds more lovingly to their footsteps than to yours, because it is rich with the blood of our ancestors and our bare feet are conscious of the sympathetic touch. Even the little children who lived here and rejoiced here for a brief season will love these somber solitudes and at eventide they greet shadowy returning spirits. And when the last Red Man shall have perished, and the memory of my tribe shall have become a myth among the White Men, these shores will swarm with the invisible dead of my tribe, and when your children's children think themselves alone in the field, the store, the shop, upon the highway, or in the silence of the pathless woods, they will not be alone. At night when the streets of your cities and villages are silent and you think them deserted, they will throng with the returning hosts that once filled and still love this beautiful land. The White Man will never be alone.

Let him be just and deal kindly with my people, for the dead are not powerless. Dead, did I say? There is no death, only a change of worlds.

## RESPONDING TO READING

1. The point is made in paragraph 2 that Native Americans and whites are "two distinct races with separate origins and separate destinies." What differences are then identified? Are there any similarities?
2. Is the speech's tone primarily hopeful, resigned, conciliatory, angry, or bitter? What dreams, if any, does the speech suggest for Chief Seattle's people?
3. Paragraph 5 offers the observation, "We may be brothers after all. We will see." What do you suppose Chief Seattle means? Do you agree?

## QUESTIONS ON CONTENT

1. Why is Seattle making this speech?
2. Does Seattle agree to go to the reservation?

3. What it the relationship of the Red Man to the earth?
4. What does Seattle call the President of the United States?

## Questions on Rhetoric

1. The speech is filled with similes and metaphors. Find several and discuss the images they evoke.
2. There are many short sentences in the speech. What impact do these sentences have on the reader?
3. What is tone of the speech? Why do you think that?
4. How does Seattle use comparison and contrasts? Is it effective? Why?
5. What impact does the fact that a white person transcribed this speech have on the content?

## Vocabulary

(3) hallowed
(3) sachems
(4) portals
(5) destiny

## Writing Prompts

1. Write about Seattle's statement: "There is no death, only a change of worlds." (6)
2. Can opposites live in harmony?
3. Who does the earth really belong to?

# A Hanging

## George Orwell

It was in Burma, a sodden morning of the rains. A sickly light, like yellow tinfoil, was slanting over the high walls into the jail yard. We were waiting outside the condemned cells, a row of sheds fronted with double bars, like small animal cages. Each cell measured about ten feet by ten and was quite bare within except for a plank bed and a pot for drinking water. In some of them brown, silent men were squatting at the inner bars, with their blankets draped round them. These were the condemned men, due to be hanged within the next week or two.

One prisoner had been brought out of his cell. He was a Hindu, a puny wisp of a man, with a shaven head and vague liquid eyes. He had a thick, sprouting mustache, absurdly too big for his body, rather like the mustache of a comic man on the films. Six tall Indian warders were guarding him and getting him ready for the gallows. Two of them stood by with rifles and fixed bayonets, while the others handcuffed him, passed a chain through his handcuffs and fixed it to their belts, and lashed his arms tight to his sides. They crowded very close about him, with their hands always on him in a careful, caressing grip, as though all the while feeling him to make sure he was there. It was like men handling a fish which is still alive and may jump back into the water. But he stood quite unresisting, yielding his arms limply to the ropes, as though he hardly noticed what was happening.

Eight o'clock struck and a bugle call; desolately thin in the wet air, floated from the distant barracks. The superintendent of the jail, who was standing apart from the rest of us, moodily prodding the gravel with his stick, raised his head at the sound. He was an army doctor, with a grey toothbrush mustache and a gruff voice. "For God's sake, hurry up, Francis," he said irritably. "The man ought to have been dead by this time. Aren't you ready yet?"

Francis, the head jailer, a fat Dravidian in a white drill suit and gold spectacles, waved his black hand. "Yes sir, yes sir," he bubbled. "All is satisfactorily prepared. The hangman is waiting. We shall proceed."

"Well, quick march, then. The prisoners can't get their breakfast till this job's over."

We set out for the gallows. Two warders marched on either side of the prisoner, with their rifles at the slope; two others marched close against him, gripping him by arm and shoulder, as though at once pushing and supporting him. The rest of us, magistrates and the like, followed behind. Suddenly, when we had gone ten yards, the procession stopped short without any order or warning. A dreadful thing had happened—a dog, come goodness knows whence, had appeared in the yard. It came bounding among us with a loud volley of barks and leapt round us wagging its whole body, wild with glee at finding so many human beings together. It was a large woolly dog, half Airedale, half pariah. For a moment it pranced around us, and then, before anyone could stop it, it had made a dash for the prisoner, and jumping up tried to lick his face. Everybody stood aghast, too taken aback even to grab the dog.

"Who let that bloody brute in here?" said the superintendent angrily. "Catch it, someone!"

A warder detached from the escort, charged clumsily after the dog, but it danced and gambolled just out of his reach, taking everything as part of the game. A young Eurasian jailer picked up a handful of gravel and tried to stone the dog away, but it dodged the stones and came after us again. Its yaps echoed from the jail walls. The prisoner, in the grasp of the two warders, looked on incuriously, as though this was another formality of the hanging. It was several minutes before someone managed to catch the dog. Then we put my handkerchief through its collar and moved off once more, with the dog still straining and whimpering.

It was about forty yards to the gallows. I watched the bare brown back of the prisoner marching in front of me. He walked clumsily with his bound arms, but quite steadily, with that bobbing gait of the Indian who never straightens his knees. At each step his muscles slid neatly into place, the lock of hair on his scalp danced up and down, his feet printed themselves on the wet gravel. And once, in spite of the men who gripped him by each shoulder, he stepped lightly aside to avoid a puddle on the path.

It is curious; but till that moment I had never realized what it means to destroy a healthy, conscious man. When I saw the prisoner step aside to avoid the puddle, I saw the mystery, the unspeakable wrongness, of cutting a life short when it is in full tide. This man was not dying, he was alive just as we are alive. All the organs of his body were working—bowels digesting food, skin renewing itself, nails growing, tissues forming—all toiling away in solemn foolery. His nails would still be growing when he stood on the drop, when he was falling through the air with a tenth-of-a-second to live. His eyes saw the yellow gravel and the grey walls, and his brain still remembered, foresaw, reasoned—even about puddles. He and we were a party of men walking together, seeing, hearing, feeling, understanding the same world; and in two minutes, with a sudden snap, one of us would be gone—one mind less, one world less.

The gallows stood in a small yard, separate from the main grounds of the prison, and overgrown with tall prickly weeds. It was a brick erection like three sides of a shed, with planking on top, and above that two beams and a crossbar with the rope dangling. The hangman, a greyhaired convict in the white uniform of the prison, was waiting beside his machine. He greeted us with a servile crouch as we entered. At a word from Francis the two warders, gripping the prisoner more closely than ever, half led, half pushed him to the gallows and helped him clumsily up the ladder. Then the hangman climbed up and fixed the rope round the prisoner's neck.

We stood waiting, five yards away. The warders had formed in a rough circle round the gallows. And then, when the noose was fixed, the prisoner began crying out to his god. It was a high, reiterated cry of "Ram! Ram! Ram! Ram!" not urgent and fearful like a prayer or cry for help, but steady, rhythmical, almost like the tolling of a bell. The dog answered the sound with a whine. The hangman, still standing on the gallows, produced a small cotton bag like a flour bag and drew it down over the prisoner's face. But the sound, muffled by the cloth, still persisted, over and over again: "Ram! Ram! Ram! Ram! Ram!"

The hangman climbed down and stood ready, holding the lever. Minutes seemed to pass. The steady, muffled crying from the prisoner went on and on, "Ram! Ram! Ram!" never faltering for an instant. The superintendent, his head on his chest, was slowly poking the ground with his stick; perhaps he was counting the cries, allowing the prisoner a fixed number—fifty, perhaps, or a hundred. Everyone had changed colour. The Indians had gone grey like bad coffee, and one or two of the bayonets were wavering. We looked at the lashed, hooded man on the drop, and listened to his cries— each cry another second of life; the same thought was in all our minds; oh, kill him quickly, get it over, stop that abominable noise!

Suddenly the superintendent made up his mind. Throwing up his head he made a swift motion with his stick. "Chalo!" he shouted almost fiercely.

There was a clanking noise, and then dead silence. The prisoner had vanished, and the rope was twisting on itself. I let go of the dog, and it galloped immediately to the back of the gallows; but when it got there it stopped short, barked, and then retreated into a corner of the yard, where it stood among the weeds, looking timorously out at us. We went round the gallows to inspect the prisoner's body. He was dangling with his toes pointed straight downwards, very slowly revolving, as dead as a stone.

The superintendent reached out with his stick and poked the bare brown body; it oscillated slightly. "*He's* all right," said the superintendent. He backed out from under the gallows, and blew out a deep breath. The moody look had gone out of his face quite suddenly. He glanced at his wrist-watch. "Eight minutes past eight. Well, that's all for this morning, thank God."

The warders unfixed bayonets and marched away. The dog, sobered and conscious of having misbehaved itself, slipped after them. We walked out of the gallows yard, past the condemned cells with their waiting prisoners, into the big central yard of the prison. The convicts, under the command of warders armed with lathis, were already receiving their breakfast. They squatted in long rows, each man holding a tin pannikin, while two warders with buckets marched around ladling out rice; it seemed quite a homely, jolly scene, after the hanging. An enormous relief had come upon us now that the job was done. One felt an impulse to sing, to break into a run, to snigger. All at once everyone began chattering gaily.

The Eurasian boy walking beside me nodded towards the way we had come, with a knowing smile: "Do you know, sir, our friend (he meant the dead man) when he heard his appeal had been dismissed, he pissed on the floor of his cell. From fright. Kindly take one of my cigarettes, sir. Do you not admire my new silver case, sir? From the boxwallah, two rupees eight annas. Classy European style."

Several people laughed—at what, nobody seemed certain.

Francis was walking by the superintendent, talking garrulously: "Well, sir, all has passed off with the utmost satisfactoriness. It was all finished—flick! Like that. It is not always so—oah, no! I have known cases where the doctor was obliged to go beneath the gallows and pull the prisoner's legs to ensure decease. Most disagreeable!"

"Wriggling about, eh? That's bad," said the superintendent.

"Ach, sir, it is worse when they become refractory! One man, I recall, clung to the bars of his cage when we went to take him out. You will scarcely credit, sir, that it took six warders to dislodge him, three pulling at each leg. We reasoned with him, 'My dear fellow,' we said, 'think of all the pain and trouble you are causing to us!' But no, he would not listen! Ach, he was very troublesome!"

I found that I was laughing quite loudly. Everyone was laughing. Even the superintendent grinned in a tolerant way. "You'd better all come out and have a drink," he said quite genially. "I've got a bottle of whisky in the car. We could do with it."

We went through the big double gates of the prison into the road. "Pulling at his legs!" exclaimed a Burmese magistrate suddenly, and burst into a loud chuckling. We all began laughing again. At that moment Francis' anecdote seemed extraordinarily funny. We all had a drink together, native and European alike, quite amicably. The dead man was a hundred yards away.

## QUESTIONS ON CONTENT

1. Describe the setting of this essay.
2. What time of day is it? Why is it significant?
3. What stops the procession momentarily?
4. What story does the Eurasian boy tell after the hanging?

## QUESTIONS ON RHETORIC

1. List the characters and discuss Orwell's descriptions of them. What differences do you note?
2. Why is the use of dialogue important in this essay? Cite examples.
3. How does Orwell establish the mood for this essay?
4. What is the purpose of paragraph 19?
5. Why do you think Orwell ends his essay with the sentence he did?

## VOCABULARY

(8) gambolled
(11) servile
(13) abominable
(17) lathis, pannikin
(20) garrulously

## WRITING PROMPTS

1. Have you ever had to do something out of duty that you really wished you did not have to do? Write about the mixed feelings you had.
2. Write about something minor that happened that later turned out to be very significant for you.
3. Write about the morality of one country or group imposing its laws and customs on another country or group.
4. How do you feel about capital punishment? How did you come to have these feelings?

# THE DEATH OF THE MOTH

## VIRGINIA WOOLF

Moths that fly by day are not properly to be called moths; they do not excite that pleasant sense of dark autumn nights and ivy-blossom which the commonest yellow-underwing asleep in the shadow of the curtain never fails to rouse in us. They are hybrid creatures, neither gay like butterflies nor sombre like their own species. Nevertheless the present specimen, with his narrow hay-coloured wings, fringed with a tassel of the same colour, seemed to be content with life. It was a pleasant morning, mid-September, mild, benignant, yet with a keener breath than that of the summer months. The plough was already scoring the field opposite the window, and where the share had been, the earth was pressed flat and gleamed with moisture. Such vigour came rolling in from the fields and the down beyond that it was difficult to keep the eyes strictly turned upon the book. The rooks too were keeping one of their annual festivities; soaring round the tree tops until it looked as if a vast net with thousands of black knots in it had been cast up into the air, which, after a few moments sank slowly down upon the trees until every twig seemed to have a knot at the end of it. Then, suddenly, the net would be thrown into the air again in a wider circle this time, with the utmost clamour and vociferation, as though to be thrown into the air and settle slowly down upon the tree tops were a tremendously exciting experience.

The same energy which inspired the rooks, the ploughmen, the horses, and even, it seemed, the lean bare-backed downs, sent the moth fluttering from side to side of his square of the windowpane. One could not help watching him. One was, indeed, conscious of a queer feeling of pity for him. The possibilities of pleasure seemed that morning so enormous and so various that to have only a moth's part in life, and a day moth's at that, appeared a hard fate, and his zest in enjoying his meagre opportunities to the full, pathetic. He flew vigorously to one corner of his compartment, and, after waiting there a second, flew across to the other. What remained for him but to fly to a third corner and then to a fourth? That was all he could do, in spite of the size of the downs, the width of the sky, the far-off smoke of houses, and the romantic voice, now and then, of a steamer out at sea. What he could do he did. Watching him, it seemed as if a fibre, very thin but pure, of the enormous energy of the world had been thrust into his frail and diminutive body. As often as he crossed the pane, I could fancy that a thread of vital light became visible. He was little or nothing but life.

Yet, because he was so small, and so simple a form of the energy that was rolling in at the open window and driving its way through so many narrow and intricate corridors in my own brain and in those of other human beings, there was something marvellous as well as pathetic about him. It was as if someone had taken a tiny bead of pure life and decking it as lightly as possible with down and feathers, had set it dancing and zig-zagging to show us the true nature of life. Thus displayed one could not get over the strangeness of it. One is apt to forget all about life, seeing it humped and bossed and garnished and cumbered so that it has to move with the greatest circumspection and dignity. Again, the thought of all that life might have been had he been born in any other shape caused one to view his simple activities with a kind of pity.

After a time, tired by his dancing apparently, he settled on the window ledge in the sun, and, the queer spectacle being at an end, I forgot about him. Then, looking up, my eye was caught by him. He was trying to resume his dancing, but seemed either so stiff or so awkward that he could only flutter to the bottom of the window-

pane; and when he tried to fly across it he failed. Being intent on
other matters I watched these futile attempts for a time without
thinking, unconsciously waiting for him to resume his flight, as one
waits for a machine, that has stopped momentarily, to start again
without considering the reason of its failure. After perhaps a seventh
attempt he slipped from the wooden ledge and fell, fluttering his
wings, on to his back on the window sill. The helplessness of his attitude roused me. It flashed upon me that he was in difficulties; he
could no longer raise himself; his legs struggled vainly. But, as I
stretched out a pencil, meaning to help him to right himself, it came
over me that the failure and awkwardness were the approach of
death. I laid the pencil down again.

The legs agitated themselves once more, I looked as if for the
enemy against which he struggled. I looked out of doors. What had
happened there? Presumably it was midday, and work in the fields
had stopped. Stillness and quiet had replaced the previous anima-
tion. The birds had taken themselves off to feed in the brooks. The
horses stood still. Yet the power was there all the same, massed outside, indifferent, impersonal, not attending to anything in particular. Somehow it was opposed to the little hay-coloured moth. It was
useless to try to do anything. One could only watch the extraordi-
nary efforts made by those tiny legs against an oncoming doom
which could, had it chosen, have submerged an entire city, not merely
a city, but masses of human beings; nothing, I knew, had any chance
against death. Nevertheless after a pause of exhaustion the legs flut-
tered again. It was superb this last protest, and so frantic that he succeeded at last in righting himself. One's sympathies, of course, were
all on the side of life. Also, when there was nobody to care or to
know, this gigantic effort on the part of an insignificant little moth,
against a power of such magnitude, to retain what no one else valued or desired to keep, moved one strangely. Again, somehow, one
saw life, a pure bead. I lifted the pencil again, useless though I knew
it to be. But even as I did so, the unmistakable tokens of death
showed themselves. The body relaxed, and instantly grew stiff. The
struggle was over. The insignificant little creature now knew death.
As I looked at the dead moth, this minute wayside triumph of so

great a force over so mean an antagonist filled me with wonder. Just as life had been strange a few minutes before, so death was now as strange. The moth having righted himself now lay most decently and uncomplainingly composed. O yes, he seemed to say, death is stronger than I am.

## QUESTIONS ON CONTENT

1. What scene is Woolf describing?
2. What does she compare the rooks to?
3. What does she do when she realizes the moth is dying?
4. What time of day does the moth die? Is this significant?

## QUESTIONS ON RHETORIC

1. Woolf changes point of view midway in her essay. What effect does this have?
2. Find and discuss the personification of the moth.
3. Why is Woolf so engrossed in the death of this tiny insect?

## VOCABULARY

(1) hybrid, benignant, vociferation

(2) diminutive

(3) circumspection

## WRITING PROMPTS

1. Sit someplace and write about everything within a three-foot radius.
2. Why did Woolf say that "nothing...had any chance against death"?

3. How does our culture view death? How does this compare with other cultures? Where and how do attitudes toward death develop?
4. Write your own obituary. How did writing it make you feel?

# THE FAMILY WHICH
# DWELT APART

### E. B. WHITE

On a small, remote island in the lower reaches of Barnetuck Bay there lived a family of fisherfolk by the name of Pruitt. There were seven of them, and they were the sole inhabitants of the place. They subsisted on canned corn, canned tomatoes, pressed duck, whole-wheat bread, terrapin, Rice Krispies, crabs, cheese, queen olives, and homemade wild-grape preserve. Once in a while Pa Pruitt made some whiskey and they all had a drink.

They liked the island and lived there from choice. In winter, when there wasn't much doing, they slept the clock around, like so many bears. In summer they dug clams and set off a few pinwheels and salutes on July 4th. No case of acute appendicitis had ever been known in the Pruitt household, and when a Pruitt had a pain in his side he never even noticed whether it was the right side or the left side, but just hoped it would go away, and it did.

One very severe winter Barnetuck Bay froze over and the Pruitt family was marooned. They couldn't get to the mainland by boat because the ice was too thick, and they couldn't walk ashore because the ice was too treacherous. But inasmuch as no Pruitt had anything to go ashore for, except mail (which was entirely second class), the freeze-up didn't make any difference. They stayed indoors, kept warm, and ate well, and when there was nothing better to do, they played crokinole. The winter would have passed quietly enough had not someone on the mainland remembered that the Pruitts were out there in the frozen bay. The word got passed around the county and finally reached the Superintendent of State Police, who immediately notified Pathé News and the United States Army. The Army got there first, with three bombing planes from Langley Field, which flew low over the island and dropped packages of dried apricots and bouillon cubes, which the Pruitts didn't like much. The newsreel plane, smaller than the bombers and equipped with skis, arrived next and landed on a snow-covered field on the north end of the island. Meanwhile, Major Bulk, head of the state troopers, acting on a tip that one of the Pruitt children had appendicitis, arranged for a dog team to be sent by plane from Laconia, New Hampshire, and also dispatched a squad of troopers to attempt a crossing of the bay. Snow began falling at sundown, and during the night three of the rescuers lost their lives about half a mile from shore, trying to jump from one ice cake to another.

The plane carrying the sled dogs was over southern New England when ice began forming on its wings. As the pilot circled for a forced landing, a large meat bone which one of the dogs had brought along got wedged in the socket of the main control stick, and the plane went into a steep dive and crashed against the side of a powerhouse, instantly killing the pilot and all the dogs, and fatally injuring Walter Ringstead, 7, of 3452 Garden View Avenue, Stamford, Conn.

Shortly before midnight, the news of the appendicitis reached the Pruitt house itself, when a chartered autogiro from Hearst's International News Service made a landing in the storm and reporters informed Mr. Pruitt that his oldest boy, Charles, was ill and would have to be taken to Baltimore for an emergency operation. Mrs. Pruitt remonstrated, but Charles said his side did hurt a little, and it ended by his leaving in the giro. Twenty minutes later another plane came in, bearing a surgeon, two trained nurses, and a man from the National Broadcasting Company, and the second Pruitt boy, Chester, underwent an exclusive appendectomy in the kitchen of the Pruitt home, over the Blue Network. This lad died, later, from eating dried apricots too soon after his illness, but Charles, the other boy, recovered after a long convalescence and returned to the island in the first warm days of spring.

He found things much changed. The house was gone, having caught fire on the third and last night of the rescue when a flare dropped by one of the departing planes lodged in a bucket of trash on the piazza. After the fire, Mr. Pruitt had apparently moved his family into the emergency shed which the radio announcers had thrown up, and there they had dwelt under rather difficult conditions until the night the entire family was wiped out by drinking a ten-per-cent solution of carbolic acid which the surgeon had left behind and which Pa had mistaken for grain alcohol.

Barnetuck Bay seemed a different place to Charles. After giving his kin decent burial, he left the island of his nativity and went to dwell on the mainland.

## QUESTIONS ON CONTENT

1. Where do the Pruitts live?
2. What brings them to the public's attention?
3. Who is the first to attempt a rescue of the Pruitts?
4. What ailment did the Pruitt children allegedly have that prompted rescue efforts?

## QUESTIONS ON RHETORIC

1. White's tone suggest he is telling a tale. What devices does he use to accomplish this?
2. White's essay could be called a modern allegory. How does the essay fit the definition?
3. What role does setting play in this piece?
4. Consider the details White uses. How does this description affect your attitude toward the Pruitts? Toward those who want to supposedly help?

## VOCABULARY

(1) subsisted

(3) marooned, treacherous

(5) remonstrated

(6) piazza

## WRITING PROMPTS

1. Write an allegory about homeless people, or any other group who seem to drop out of society.
2. Write about government aide and its impact on the recipients.
3. Write about the individual versus society.

# THE REWARDS OF LIVING
## A SOLITARY LIFE

### MAY SARTON

The other day an acquaintance of mine, a gregarious and charming man, told me he had found himself unexpectedly alone in New York for an hour or two between appointments. He went to the Whitney and spent the "empty" time looking at things in solitary bliss. For him it proved to be a shock nearly as great as falling in love to discover that he could enjoy himself so much alone.

What had he been afraid of, I asked myself? That, suddenly alone, he would discover that he bored himself, or that there was, quite simply, no self there to meet? But having taken the plunge, he is now on the brink of adventure; he is about to be launched into his own inner space, space as immense, unexplored and sometimes frightening as outer space to the astronaut. His every perception will come to him with a new freshness and, for a time, seem startlingly original. For anyone who can see things for himself with a naked eye becomes, for a moment or two, something of a genius. With another human being present vision becomes double vision, inevitably. We are busy wondering, what does my companion see or think of this, and what do I think of it? The original impact gets lost, or diffused.

"Music I heard with you was more than music." Exactly. And therefore music *itself* can only be heard alone. Solitude is the salt of personhood. It brings out the authentic flavor of every experience.

"Alone one is never lonely: The spirit adventures, walking / In a quiet garden, in a cool house, abiding single there."

Loneliness is most acutely felt with other people, for with others, even with a lover sometimes, we suffer from our differences of taste, temperament, mood. Human intercourse often demands that we soften the edge of perception, or withdraw at the very instant of personal truth for fear of hurting, or of being inappropriately present, which is to say naked, in a social situation. Alone we can afford to be wholly whatever we are, and to feel whatever we feel absolutely. That is a great luxury!

For me the most interesting thing about a solitary life, and mine has been that for the last twenty years, is that it becomes increasingly rewarding. When I can wake up and watch the sun rise over the ocean, as I do most days, and know that I have an entire day ahead, uninterrupted, in which to write a few pages, take a walk with my dog, lie down in the afternoon for a long think (why does one think better in a horizontal position?), read and listen to music, I am flooded with happiness.

I am lonely only when I am overtired, when I have worked too long without a break, when for the time being I feel empty and need filling up. And I am lonely sometimes when I come back home after a lecture trip, when I have seen a lot of people and talked a lot, and am full to the brim with experience that needs to be sorted out.

Then for a little while the house feels huge and empty, and I wonder where my self is hiding. It has to be recaptured slowly by watering the plants, perhaps, and looking again at each one as though it were a person, by feeding the two cats, by cooking a meal.

It takes a while, as I watch the surf blowing up in fountains at the end of the field, but the moment comes when the world falls away, and the self emerges again from the deep unconscious, bringing back all I have recently experienced to be explored and slowly understood, when I can converse again with my hidden powers, and so grow, and so be renewed, till death do us part.

## QUESTIONS ON CONTENT

1. What surprised Sarton's acquaintance?
2. How does Sarton view the solitary life?
3. When does Sarton admit she sometimes feels lonely?

## QUESTIONS ON RHETORIC

1. Why is the title fitting for this essay?
2. How does Sarton present the pros and cons of solitude?
3. Sarton supports her thesis with examples. Find them. How effective are they?

## VOCABULARY

(1) gregarious

(2) diffused

(5) intercourse

## WRITING PROMPTS

1. Do you agree or disagree with Sarton's statement: "Solitude is the salt of personhood."
2. When are you lonely?
3. Write about feeling alone while you are with people.
4. Describe your "solitary bliss."

# I Have a Dream

## Martin Luther King, Jr.

Five score years ago, a great American, in whose symbolic shadow we stand, signed the Emancipation Proclamation. This momentous decree came as a great beacon light of hope to millions of Negro slaves who had been seared in the flames of withering injustice. It came as a joyous daybreak to end the long night of captivity.

But one hundred years later, we must face the tragic fact that the Negro is still not free. One hundred years later, the life of the Negro is still sadly crippled by the manacles of segregation and the chains of discrimination. One hundred years later, the Negro lives on a lonely island of poverty in the midst of a vast ocean of material prosperity. One hundred years later, the Negro is still languishing in the corners of American society and finds himself an exile in his own land. So we have come here today to dramatize an appalling condition.

In a sense we have come to our nation's capital to cash a check. When the architects of our republic wrote the magnificent words of the Constitution and the Declaration of Independence, they were signing a promissory note to which every American was to fall heir. This note was a promise that all men would be guaranteed the unalienable rights of life, liberty, and the pursuit of happiness.

It is obvious today that America has defaulted on this promissory note insofar as her citizens of color are concerned. Instead of honoring this sacred obligation, America has given the Negro people a bad check; a check which has come back marked "insufficient funds." But we refuse to believe that the bank of justice is bankrupt. We refuse to believe that there are insufficient funds in the great vaults of opportunity of this nation. So we have come to cash this check—a check that will give us upon demand the riches of freedom and the security of justice. We have also come to this hallowed spot to remind America of the fierce urgency of *now.* This is no time to engage in the luxury of cooling off or to take the tranquilizing drugs of gradualism. *Now* is the time to make real the promises of Democracy. *Now* is the time to rise from the dark and desolate valley of segregation to the sunlit path of racial justice. *Now* is the time to open the doors of opportunity to all of God's children. *Now* is the time to lift our nation from the quicksands of racial injustice to the solid rock of brotherhood.

It would be fatal for the nation to overlook the urgency of the moment and to underestimate the determination of the Negro. This sweltering summer of the Negro's legitimate discontent will not pass until there is an invigorating autumn of freedom and equality. 1963 is not an end, but a beginning. Those who hope that the Negro needed to blow off steam and will now be content will have a rude awakening if the nation returns to business as usual. There will be neither rest nor tranquillity in America until the Negro is granted his citizenship rights. The whirlwinds of revolt will continue to shake the foundations of our nation until the bright day of justice emerges.

But there is something that I must say to my people who stand on the warm threshold which leads into the palace of justice. In the process of gaining our rightful place we must not be guilty of wrongful deeds. Let us not seek to satisfy our thirst for freedom by drinking from the cup of bitterness and hatred. We must forever conduct our struggle on the high plane of dignity and discipline. We must not allow our creative protest to degenerate into physical violence. Again and again we must rise to the majestic heights of meeting physical force with soul force. The marvelous new militancy which has engulfed the Negro community must not lead us to a distrust of all white people, for many of our white brothers, as evidenced by their presence here today, have come to realize that their destiny is tied up with our destiny and their freedom is inextricably bound to our freedom. We cannot walk alone.

And as we walk, we must make the pledge that we shall march ahead. We cannot turn back. There are those who are asking the devotees of civil rights, "When will you be satisfied?" We can never be satisfied as long as the Negro is the victim of the unspeakable horrors of police brutality. We can never be satisfied as long as our bodies, heavy with the fatigue of travel, cannot gain lodging in the motels of the highways and the hotels of the cities. We cannot be satisfied as long as the Negro's basic mobility is from a smaller ghetto to a larger one. We can never be satisfied as long as a Negro in Mississippi cannot vote and a Negro in New York believes he has nothing for which to vote. No, no, we are not satisfied, and we will not be satisfied until justice rolls down like waters and righteousness like a mighty stream.

I am not unmindful that some of you have come here out of great trials and tribulations. Some of you have come fresh from narrow jail cells. Some of you have come from areas where your quest for freedom left you battered by the storms of persecution and staggered by the winds of police brutality. You have been the veterans of creative suffering. Continue to work with the faith that unearned suffering is redemptive.

Go back to Mississippi, go back to Alabama, go back to South Carolina, go back to Georgia, go back to Louisiana, go back to the slums and ghettos of our northern cities, knowing that somehow this situation can and will be changed. Let us not wallow in the valley of despair.

I say to you today, my friends, that in spite of the difficulties and frustrations of the moment I still have a dream. It is a dream deeply rooted in the American dream.

I have a dream that one day this nation will rise up and live out the true meaning of its creed: "We hold these truths to be self-evident; that all men are created equal."

I have a dream that one day on the red hills of Georgia the sons of former slaves and the sons of former slaveowners will be able to sit down together at the table of brotherhood.

I have a dream that one day even the state of Mississippi, a desert state sweltering with the heat of injustice and oppression, will be transformed into an oasis of freedom and justice.

I have a dream that my four little children will one day live in a nation where they will not be judged by the color of their skin but by the content of their character.

I have a dream today.

I have a dream that one day the state of Alabama, whose governor's lips are presently dripping with the words of interposition and nullification, will be transformed into a situation where little black boys and black girls will be able to join hands with little white boys and white girls and walk together as sisters and brothers.

I have a dream today.

I have a dream that one day every valley shall be exalted, every hill and mountain shall be made low, the rough places will be made plain, and the crooked places will be made straight, and the glory of the Lord shall be revealed, and all flesh shall see it together.

This is our hope. This is the faith with which I return to the South. With this faith we will be able to hew out of the mountain of despair a stone of hope. With this faith we will be able to transform the jangling discords of our nation into a beautiful symphony of brotherhood. With this faith we will be able to work together, to pray together, to struggle together, to go to jail together, to stand up freedom together, knowing that we will be free one day.

This will be the day when all of God's children will be able to sing with new meaning

> My country, 'tis of thee,
> Sweet land of liberty,
> Of thee I sing:
> Land where my fathers died,
> Land of the pilgrims' pride,
> From every mountain-side
> Let freedom ring.

And if America is to be a great nation this must become true. So let freedom ring from the prodigious hilltops of New Hampshire.

Let freedom ring from the mighty mountains of New York. Let freedom ring from the heightening Alleghenies of Pennsylvania!

Let freedom ring from the snowcapped Rockies of Colorado!

Let freedom ring from the curvaceous peaks of California!

But not only that; let freedom ring from Stone Mountain of
Georgia!

Let freedom ring from Lookout Mountain of Tennessee!

Let freedom ring from every hill and molehill of Mississippi.
From every mountainside, let freedom ring.

When we let freedom ring, when we let it ring from every village and every hamlet, from every state and every city, we will be
able to speed up that day when all of God's children, black men and
white men, Jews and Gentiles, Protestants and Catholics, will be able
to join hands and sing in the words of the old Negro spiritual, "Free
at last! free at last! thank God almighty, we are free at last!"

## QUESTIONS ON CONTENT

1. Where does King deliver this speech?
2. What political documents does King mention? Why?
3. What metaphor does King use to discuss America's treatment of
   African Americans?
4. What two songs does King quote? Why would he use these songs?

## QUESTIONS ON RHETORIC

1. Find examples of repetition King uses. Why do you think he uses
   so many?
2. King talks of unity and equality, yet at the same time talks of "my
   people." Is this a contradiction? Why or why not?
3. Paragraph 18 is a biblical reference, yet King does not attribute
   it as he did with political documents. Why do you think he chose
   not to?
4. What tone does the piece evoke? How does King create it?
5. What voice do you hear in this essay?

## VOCABULARY

(1) Emancipation Proclamation

(2) languishing

(3) unalienable

(4) gradualism

(16) interposition, nullification

## WRITING PROMPTS

1. Write about your dream for a better world.
2. Have you ever been in a minority (race, gender, ethnic)? Write about your feelings in that experience.
3. Have we come a long way in achieving equality for the races? The sexes?
4. Write about oppression. Have you ever felt oppressed?
5. Write about cultural oppression in other parts of the world. What role should we play in those oppressions?

# THE ANGRY WINTER

## LOREN EISELEY

A time comes when creatures whose destinies have crossed somewhere in the remote past are forced to appraise each other as though
they were total strangers. I had been huddled beside the fire one winter night, with the wind prowling outside and shaking the windows.
The big shepherd dog on the hearth before me occasionally glanced
up affectionately, sighed, and slept. I was working, actually, amidst
the debris of a far greater winter. On my desk lay the lance point of
ice age hunters and the heavy leg bone of a fossil bison. No rem-
nants of flesh attached to these relics. The deed lay more than ten
thousand years remote. It was represented here by naked flint and
by bone so mineralized it rang when struck. As I worked in my little circle of light, I absently laid the bone beside me on the floor. The
hour had crept toward midnight. A grating noise, a heavy rasping
of big teeth diverted me. I looked down.

The dog had risen. That rock-hard fragment of a vanished beast
was in his jaws and he was mouthing it with a fierce intensity I had
never seen exhibited by him before.

"Wolf," I exclaimed, and stretched out my hand. The dog
backed up but did not yield. A low and steady rumbling began to
rise in his chest, something out of a long-gone midnight. There was
nothing in that bone to taste, but ancient shapes were moving in his

mind and determining his utterance. Only fools gave up bones. He was warning me.

"Wolf," I chided again.

As I advanced, his teeth showed and his mouth wrinkled to strike. The rumbling rose to a direct snarl. His flat head swayed low and wickedly as a reptile's above the floor. I was the most loved object in his universe, but the past was fully alive in him now. Its shadows were whispering in his mind. I knew he was not bluffing. If I made another step he would strike.

Yet his eyes were strained and desperate. "Do not," something pleaded in the back of them, some affectionate thing that had followed at my heel all the days of his mortal life, "do not force me. I am what I am and cannot be otherwise because of the shadows. Do not reach out. You are a man, and my very god. I love you, but do not put out your hand. It is midnight. We are in another time, in the snow."

"The other time," the steady rumbling continued while I paused, "the other time in the snow, the big, the final, the terrible snow, when the shape of this thing I hold spelled life. I will not give it up. I cannot. The shadows will not permit me. Do not put out your hand."

I stood silent, looking into his eyes, and heard his whisper through. Slowly I drew back in understanding. The snarl diminished, ceased. As I retreated, the bone slumped to the floor. He placed a paw upon it, warningly.

And were there no shadows in my own mind, I wondered. Had I not for a moment, in the grip of that savage utterance, been about to respond, to hurl myself upon him over an invisible haunch ten thousand years removed? Even to me the shadows had whispered— to me, the scholar in his study.

"Wolf," I said, but this time, holding a familiar leash, I spoke from the door indifferently "A walk in the snow." Instantly from his eyes that other visitant receded. The bone was left lying. He came eagerly to my side, accepting the leash and taking it in his mouth as always.

A blizzard was raging when we went out, but he paid no heed. On his thick fur the driving snow was soon clinging heavily. He frolicked a little—though usually he was a grave dog—making up to me for something still receding in his mind. I felt the snowflakes fall upon my face, and stood thinking of another time, and another time still, until I was moving from midnight to midnight under ever more remote and vaster snows. Wolf came to my side with a little whimper. It was he who was civilized now. "Come back to the fire," he nudged gently, "or you will be lost." Automatically I took the leash he offered. He led me safely home and into the house.

"We have been very far away," I told him solemnly. "I think there is something in us that we had both better try to forget." Sprawled on the rug, Wolf made no response except to thump his tail feebly out of courtesy. Already he was mostly asleep and dreaming. By the movement of his feet I could see he was running far upon some errand in which I played no part.

Softly I picked up his bone—our bone, rather—and replaced it high on a shelf in my cabinet. As I snapped off the light the white glow from the window seemed to augment itself and shine with a deep, glacial blue. As far as I could see, nothing moved in the long aisles of my neighbor's woods. There was no visible track, and certainly no sound from the living. The snow continued to fall steadily, but the wind, and the shadows it had brought, had vanished.

## QUESTIONS ON CONTENT

1. What time of day is it? Why is that significant?
2. What does Wolf do?
3. How does Eiseley change the situation?

## QUESTIONS ON RHETORIC

1. What effect does the use of dialogue have in this essay?
2. What does Wolf's part of the conversation reveal about the author?
3. Eiseley writes this piece chronologically. Would it have been as effective written in another style?
4. Personal narratives usually reveal something about the nature of the author. What does this narrative tell say about Eiseley?

## VOCABULARY

(13) augment

## WRITING PROMPTS

1. Is domestication of animals a good idea?
2. What is the source of the anger in the title?
3. Write about a time when you realized that someone else was thinking something that surprised you.

# THE DEER AT PROVIDENCIA

## ANNIE DILLARD

There were four of us North Americans in the jungle, in the Ecuadoran jungle on the banks of the Napo River in the Amazon watershed. The other three North Americans were metropolitan men. We stayed in tents in one riverside village, and visited others. At the village called Providencia we saw a sight which moved us, and which shocked the men.

The first thing we saw when we climbed the riverbank to the village of Providencia was the deer. It was roped to a tree on the grass clearing near the thatch shelter where we would eat lunch.

The deer was small, about the size of a whitetail fawn, but apparently full-grown. It had a rope around its neck and three feet caught in the rope. Someone said that the dogs had caught it that morning and the villagers were going to cook and eat it that night.

This clearing lay at the edge of the little thatched-hut village. We could see the villagers going about their business, scattering feed corn for hens about their houses, and wandering down paths to the river to bathe. The village headman was our host; he stood beside us as we watched the deer struggle. Several village boys were interested in the deer; they formed part of the circle we made around it in the clearing. So also did four businessmen from Quito who were attempting to guide us around the jungle. Few of the very different people standing in this circle had a common language. We watched the deer, and no one said much.

The deer lay on its side at the rope's very end, so the rope lacked slack to let it rest its head in the dust. It was "pretty," delicate of bone like all deer, and thin-skinned for the tropics. Its skin looked virtually hairless, in fact, and almost translucent, like a membrane. Its neck was no thicker than my wrist; it was rubbed open on the rope, and gashed. Trying to paw itself free of the rope, the deer had scratched its own neck with its hooves. The raw underside of its neck showed red stripes and some bruises bleeding inside the muscles. Now three of its feet were hooked in the rope under its jaw. It could not stand, of course, on one leg, so it could not move to slacken the rope and ease the pull on its throat and enable it to rest its head.

Repeatedly the deer paused, motionless, its eyes veiled, with only its rib cage in motion, and its breaths the only sound. Then, after I would think, "It has given up; now it will die," it would heave. The rope twanged; the tree leaves clattered; the deer's free foot beat the ground. We stepped back and held our breaths. It thrashed, kicking, but only one leg moved; the other three legs tightened inside the rope's loop. Its hip jerked; its spine shook. Its eyes rolled; its tongue, thick with spittle, pushed in and out. Then it would rest again. We watched this for fifteen minutes.

Once three young native boys charged in, released its trapped legs, and jumped back to the circle of people. But instantly the deer scratched up its neck with its hooves and snared its forelegs in the rope again. It was easy to imagine a third and then a fourth leg soon stuck, like Brer Rabbit and the Tar Baby.

We watched the deer from the circle, and then we drifted on to lunch. Our palm-roofed shelter stood on a grassy promontory from which we could see the deer tied to the tree, pigs and hens walking under village houses, and black-and-white cattle standing in the river. There was even a breeze.

Lunch, which was the second and better lunch we had that day, was hot and fried. There was a big fish called *doncella*, a kind of catfish, dipped whole in corn flour and beaten egg, then deep fried. With our fingers we pulled soft fragments of it from its sides to our plates, and ate; it was delicate fish-flesh, fresh and mild. Someone found the roe, and I ate of that too—it was fat and stronger, like egg yolk, naturally enough, and warm.

There was also a stew of meat in shreds with rice and pale brown gravy. I had asked what kind of deer it was tied to the tree; Pepe had answered in Spanish, "*Gama.*" Now they told us this was *gama* too, stewed. I suspect the word means merely game or venison. At any rate, I heard that the village dogs had cornered another deer just yesterday, and it was this deer which we were now eating in full sight of the whole article. It was good. I was surprised at its tenderness. But it is a fact that high levels of lactic acid, which builds up in muscle tissues during exertion, tenderizes.

After the fish and meat we ate bananas fried in chunks and served on a tray; they were sweet and full of flavor. I felt terrific. My shirt was wet and cool from swimming; I had had a night's sleep, two decent walks, three meals, and a swim—everything tasted good. From time to time each one of us, separately, would look beyond our shaded roof to the sunny spot where the deer was still convulsing in the dust. Our meal completed, we walked around the deer and back to the boats.

That night I learned that while we were watching the deer, the others were watching me.

We four North Americans grew close in the jungle in a way that was not the usual artificial intimacy of travelers. We liked each other. We stayed up all that night talking, murmuring, as though we rocked on hammocks slung above time. The others were from big cities: New York, Washington, Boston. They all said that I had no expression on my face when I was watching the deer—or at any rate, not the expression they expected.

They had looked to see how I, the only woman, and the youngest, was taking the sight of the deer's struggles. I looked detached, apparently, or hard, or calm, or focused, still. I don't know. I was thinking I remember feeling very old and energetic. I could say like Thoreau that I have traveled widely in Roanoke, Virginia. I have thought a great deal about carnivorousness; I eat meat. These things are not issues; they are mysteries.

Gentlemen of the city, what surprises you? That there is suffering here, or that I know it?

We lay in the tent and talked, "If it had been my wife," one man said with special vigor, amazed, "she wouldn't have cared *what* was going on; she would have dropped *everything* right at that moment and gone in the village from here to there to there, she would not have *stopped* until that animal was out of its suffering one way or another. She couldn't *bear* to see a creature in agony like that."

I nodded.

Now I am home. When I wake I comb my hair before the mirror above my dresser. Every morning for the past two years I have seen in that mirror, beside my sleep-softened face, the blackened face of a burnt man. It is a wire-service photograph clipped from a newspaper and taped to my mirror. The caption reads: "Alan McDonald in Miami hospital bed." All you can see in the photograph is a smudged triangle of face from his eyelids to his lower lip; the rest is bandages. You cannot see the expression in his eyes; the bandages shade them.

The story, headed MAN BURNED FOR SECOND TIME, begins:

"Why does God hate me?" Alan McDonald asked from his hospital bed.

"When the gunpowder went off, I couldn't believe it," he said. "I just couldn't believe it. I said, 'No, God couldn't do this to me again.'"

He was in a burn ward in Miami, in serious condition. I do not even know if he lived. I wrote him a letter at the time, cringing.

He had been burned before, thirteen years previously, by flaming gasoline. For years he had been having his body restored and his face remade in dozens of operations. He had been a boy, and then a burnt boy. He had already been stunned by what could happen, by how life could veer.

Once I read that people who survive bad burns tend to go crazy; they have a very high suicide rate. Medicine cannot ease their pain; drugs just leak away, soaking the sheets, because there is no skin to hold them in. The people just lie there and weep. Later they kill themselves. They had not known, before they were burned, that the world included such suffering, that life could permit them personally such pain.

This time a bowl of gunpowder had exploded on McDonald. "I didn't realize what had happened at first," he recounted. "And then I heard that sound from 13 years ago. I was burning. I rolled to put the fire out and I thought, 'Oh God, not again.'

"If my friend hadn't been there, I would have jumped into a canal with a rock around my neck."

His wife concludes the piece, "Man, it just isn't fair."

I read the whole clipping again every morning. This is the Big Time here, every minute of it. Will someone please explain to Alan McDonald in his dignity, to the deer at Providencia in his dignity, what is going on? And mail me the carbon.

When we walked by the deer at Providencia for the last time, I said to Pepe, with a pitying glance at the deer, "*Pobrecito*" — "poor little thing." But I was trying out Spanish. I knew at the time it was a ridiculous thing to say.

## QUESTIONS ON CONTENT

1. Where was Dillard traveling?
2. With whom was she traveling?
3. Describe the deer she saw.
4. What did she eat for lunch that day?
5. What picture did she have on her bathroom mirror?

## QUESTIONS ON RHETORIC

1. Look at the organization of Dillard's essay. What functions do paragraphs 12 and 17 serve?
2. Dillard uses two very different examples. Are they too different? Why or why not?
3. How does Dillard's gender affect the effect of this essay?
4. Dillard has a very critically observant eye. Why do you think Dillard goes to such length to describe the deer?

## VOCABULARY

(5) translucent

(8) promontory

(14) detached

## WRITING PROMPTS

1. Write about animal rights.
2. Write about the paradoxical nature of suffering.
3. Write about the difference between the way men and women view things.
4. Do you feel your gender affects the way you see the world?

# LEARNING TO LISTEN

## EUDORA WELTY

Learning stamps you with its moments. Childhood's learning is made up of moments. It isn't steady. It's a pulse.

In a children's art class, we sat in a ring on kindergarten chairs and drew three daffodils that had just been picked out of the yard; and while I was drawing, my sharpened yellow pencil and the cup of the yellow daffodils gave off whiffs just alike. That the pencil doing the drawing should give off the same smell as the flower it drew seemed part of the art lesson—as shouldn't it be? Children, like animals, use all their senses to discover the world. Then artists come along and discover it the same way, all over again. Here and there, it's the same world. Or now and then we'll hear from an artist who's never lost it.

In my sensory education I include my physical awareness of the *word*. Of a certain word, that is; the connection it has with what it stands for. At around age six, perhaps, I was standing by myself in our front yard waiting for supper, just at that hour in a late summer day when the sun is already below the horizon and the risen full moon in the visible sky stops being chalky and begins to take on light. There comes the moment, and I saw it then, when the moon goes from flat to round. For the first time it met my eyes as a globe. The word "moon" came into my mouth as though fed to me out of a silver spoon. Held in my mouth the moon became a word. It had the roundness of a Concord grape Grandpa took off his vine and gave me to suck out of its skin and swallow whole, in Ohio.

This love did not prevent me from living for years in foolish error about the moon. The new moon just appearing in the west was the rising moon to me. The new should be rising. And in early childhood the sun and moon, those opposite reigning powers, I just as easily assumed rose in east and west respectively in their opposite sides of the sky, and like partners in a reel they advanced, sun from the east, moon from the west, crossed over (when I wasn't looking) and went down on the other side. My father couldn't have known I believed that when, bending behind me and guiding my shoulder, he positioned me at our telescope in the front yard and, with careful adjustment of the focus, brought the moon close to me.

The night sky over my childhood Jackson was velvety black. I could see the full constellations in it and call their names; when I could read, I knew their myths. Though I was always waked for eclipses, and indeed carried to the window as an infant in arms and shown Halley's Comet in my sleep, and though I'd been taught at our diningroom table about the solar system and knew the earth revolved around the sun, and our moon around us, I never found out the moon didn't come up in the west until I was a writer and Herschel Brickell, the literary critic, told me after I misplaced it in a story. He said valuable words to me about my new profession: "Always be sure you get your moon in the right part of the sky."

My mother always sang to her children. Her voice came out just a little bit in the minor key. "Wee Willie Winkie's" song was wonderfully sad when she sang the lullabies.

"Oh, but now there's a record. She could have her own record to listen to," my father would have said. For there came a Victrola record of "Bobby Shafftoe" and "Rock-a-Bye Baby," all of Mother's lullabies, which could be played to take her place. Soon I was able to play her my own lullabies all day long.

Our Victrola stood in the diningroom. I was allowed to climb onto the seat of a diningroom chair to wind it, start the record turning, and set the needle playing. In a second I'd jumped to the floor, to spin or march around the table as the music called for—now there were all the other records I could play too. I skinned back onto the chair just in time to lift the needle at the end, stop the record and turn it over, then change the needle. That brass receptacle with a hole in the lid gave off a metallic smell like human sweat, from all the hot needles that were fed it. Winding up, dancing, being cocked to start and stop the record, was of course all in one the act of *listening*— to "Overture to *Daughter of the Regiment*," "Selections from *The Fortune Teller*," "Kiss Me Again," "Gypsy Dance from *Carmen*," "Stars and Stripes Forever," "When the Midnight Choo-Choo Leaves for Alabam," or whatever came next. Movement must be at the very heart of listening.

Ever since I was first read to, then started reading to myself, there has never been a line read that I didn't *hear*. As my eyes followed the sentence, a voice was saying it silently to me. It isn't my mother's voice, or the voice of any person I can identify, certainly not my own. It is human, but inward, and it is inwardly that I listen to it. It is to me the voice of the story or the poem itself. The cadence, whatever it is that asks you to believe, the feeling that resides in the printed word, reaches me through the reader-voice. I have supposed, but never found out, that this is the case with all readers—to read as listeners—and with all writers, to write as listeners. It may be part of the desire to write. The sound of what falls on the page begins the process of testing it for truth, for me. Whether I am right to trust so far I don't know. By now I don't know whether I could do either one, reading or writing, without the other.

My own words, when I am at work on a story, I hear too as they go, in the same voice that I hear when I read in books. When I write and the sound of it comes back to my ears, then I act to make my changes. I have always trusted this voice.

In that vanished time in small-town Jackson, most of the ladies I was familiar with, the mothers of my friends in the neighborhood, were busiest when they were sociable. In the afternoons there was regular visiting up and down the little grid of residential streets. Everybody had calling cards, even certain children; and newborn babies themselves were properly announced by sending out their tiny engraved calling cards attached with a pink or blue bow to those of their parents. Graduation presents to high-school pupils were often "card cases." On the hall table in every house the first thing you saw was a silver tray waiting to receive more calling cards on top of the stack already piled up like jackstraws; they were never thrown away.

My mother let none of this idling, as she saw it, pertain to her; she went her own way with or without her calling cards, and though she was fond of her friends and they were fond of her, she had little time for small talk. At first, I hadn't known what I'd missed.

When we at length bought our first automobile, one of our neighbors was often invited to go with us on the family Sunday afternoon ride. In Jackson it was counted an affront to the neighbors to start out for anywhere with an empty seat in the car. My mother sat in the back with her friend, and I'm told that as a small child I would ask to sit in the middle, and say as we started off, "Now *talk*."

There was dialogue throughout the lady's accounts to my mother. "I said" ... "He said" ... "And I'm told she very plainly said" ... "It was midnight before they finally heard, and what do you think it *was?*"

What I loved about her stories was that everything happened in *scenes*. I might not catch on to what the root of the trouble was in all that happened, but my ear told me it was dramatic. Often she said, "The crisis had come!"

This same lady was one of Mother's callers on the telephone who always talked a long time. I knew who it was when my mother would only reply, now and then, "Well, I declare," or "You don't say so," or "Surely not." She'd be standing at the wall telephone, listening against her will, and I'd sit on the stairs close by her. Our telephone had a little bar set into the handle which had to be pressed and held down to keep the connection open, and when her friend had said goodbye, my mother needed me to prize her fingers loose from the little bar; her grip had become paralyzed. "What did she say?" I asked.

"She wasn't *saying* a thing in this world," sighed my mother. "She was just ready to talk, that's all."

My mother was right. Years later, beginning with my story "Why I Live at the P.O.," I wrote reasonably often in the form of a monologue that takes possession of the speaker. How much more gets told besides!

This lady told everything in her sweet, marveling voice, and meant every word of it kindly. She enjoyed my company perhaps even more than my mother's. She invited me to catch her doodle-bugs; under the trees in her backyard were dozens of their holes. When you stuck a broom straw down one and called, "Doodlebug, doodlebug, your house is on fire and all your children are burning up," she believed this is why the doodlebug came running out of the hole. This was why I loved to call up her doodlebugs instead of ours.

My mother could never have told me her stories, and I think I knew why even then: my mother didn't believe them. But I could listen to this murmuring lady all day. She believed everything she heard, like the doodlebug. And so did I.

This was a day when ladies' and children's clothes were very often made at home. My mother cut out all the dresses and her little boys' rompers, and a sewing woman would come and spend the day upstairs in the sewing room fitting and stitching them all. This was Fannie. This old black sewing woman, along with her speed and dexterity, brought along a great provision of up-to-the-minute news. She spent her life going from family to family in town and worked right in its bosom, and nothing could stop her. My mother would try, while I stood being pinned up. "Fannie, I'd rather Eudora didn't hear that." That would be just what I was longing to hear, whatever it was. "I don't want her exposed to gossip" — as if gossip were measles and I could catch it. I did catch some of it but not enough. "Mrs. O'Neil's oldest daughter she had her wedding dress *tried on*, and all her fine underclothes feather-stitched and ribbon run in and then — " "I think that will do, Fannie," said my mother. It was tantalizing never to be exposed long enough to hear the end.

Fannie was the worldliest old woman to be imagined. She could do whatever her hands were doing without having to stop talking; and she could speak in a wonderfully derogatory way with any number of pins stuck in her mouth. Her hands steadied me like claws as she stumped on her knees around me, tacking me together. The gist of her tale would be lost on me, but Fannie didn't bother about the ear she was telling it to; she just liked telling. She was like an author. In fact, for a good deal of what she said, I daresay she *was* the author.

Long before I wrote stories, I listened for stories. Listening *for* them is something more acute than listening *to* them. I suppose it's an early form of participation in what goes on. Listening children know stories are *there*. When their elders sit and begin, children are just waiting and hoping for one to come out, like a mouse from its hole.

It was taken entirely for granted that there wasn't any lying in our family, and I was advanced in adolescence before I realized that in plenty of homes where I played with schoolmates and went to their parties, children lied to their parents and parents lied to their children and to each other. It took me a long time to realize that these very same every-day lies, and the stratagems and jokes and tricks and dares that went with them, were in fact the basis of the *scenes* I so well loved to hear about and hoped for and treasured in the conversation of adults.

My instinct—the dramatic instinct—was to lead me, eventually, on the right track for a storyteller; the *scene* was full of hints, pointers, suggestions, and promises of things to find out and know about human beings. I had to grow up and learn to listen for the unspoken as well as the spoken—and to know a truth, I also had to recognize a lie.

## QUESTIONS ON CONTENT

1. According to Welty, how do children discover the world?
2. How does Welty feel about music?
3. Why did Welty like to listen to Fannie, the "old black sewing lady"?

## QUESTIONS ON RHETORIC

1. Welty states that "Learning stamps you with moments." Find the moments she describes to support this thesis.
2. Paragraphs 6 and 10 are transitions. How do these transitions aid the reader? How do they enhance Welty's point?

3. Welty writes about "hearing a voice" in all writing. What voice do you hear in this piece?
4. What examples does Welty give to support "learning to listen for stories"?

## VOCABULARY

(22) derogatory

(24) stratagems

## WRITING PROMPTS

1. Recall a moment from your childhood when "learning stamped you."
2. Truman Capote once said that one good story was worth three dead grandmothers. Would Welty agree with him? Why or why not?
3. Where in your life could you listen for stories?
4. Write about literary license. Do writers have a right to take it to make their point?
5. Write about a difficult experience you've had with a family member and what you learned from it.

# A Miserable
# Merry Christmas

## Lincoln Steffens

What interested me in our new neighborhood was not the school, nor the room I was to have in the house all to myself, but the stable which was built back of the house. My father let me direct the making of a stall, a little smaller than the other stalls, for my pony, and I prayed and hoped and my sister Lou believed that that meant that I would get the pony, perhaps for Christmas. I pointed out to her that there were three other stalls and no horses at all. This I said in order that she should answer it. She could not. My father, sounded, said that some day we might have horses and a cow; meanwhile a stable added to the value of a house. "Some day" is a pain to a boy who lives in and knows only "now." My good little sisters, to comfort me, remarked that Christmas was coming, but Christmas was always coming and grown-ups were always talking about it, asking you what you wanted and then giving you what they wanted you to have. Though everybody knew what I wanted, I told them all again. My mother knew that I told God, too, every night. I wanted a pony, and to make sure that they understood, I declared that I wanted nothing else.

"Nothing but a pony?" my father asked.

"Nothing," I said.

"Not even a pair of high boots?"

That was hard. I did want boots, but I stuck to the pony. "No, not even boots."

"Nor candy? There ought to be something to fill your stocking with, and Santa Claus can't put a pony into a stocking."

That was true, and he couldn't lead a pony down the chimney either. But no. "All I want is a pony," I said. "If I can't have a pony, give me nothing, nothing."

Now I had been looking myself for the pony I wanted, going to sales stables, inquiring of horsemen, and I had seen several that would do. My father let me "try" them. I tried so many ponies that I was learning fast to sit a horse. I chose several, but my father always found some fault with them. I was in despair. When Christmas was at hand I had given up all hope of a pony, and on Christmas Eve I hung up my stocking along with my sisters', of whom, by the way, I now had three. I haven't mentioned them or their coming because, you understand, they were girls, and girls, young girls, counted for nothing in my manly life. They did not mind me either; they were so happy that Christmas Eve that I caught some of their merriment. I speculated on what I'd get; I hung up the biggest stocking I had, and we all went reluctantly to bed to wait till morning. Not to sleep; not right away. We were told that we must not only sleep promptly, we must not wake up till seven-thirty the next morning—or if we did, we must not go to the fireplace for our Christmas. Impossible.

We did sleep that night, but we woke up at six A.M. We lay in our beds and debated through the open doors whether to obey till, say, half-past six. Then we bolted. I don't know who started it, but there was a rush. We all disobeyed; we raced to disobey and get first to the fireplace in the front room downstairs. And there they were, the gifts, all sorts of wonderful things, mixed-up piles of presents; only, as I disentangled the mess, I saw that my stocking was empty; it hung limp; not a thing in it; and under and around it—nothing. My sisters had knelt down, each by her pile of gifts; they were squealing with delight, till they looked up and saw me standing there in my nightgown with nothing. They left their piles to come to me and look with me at my empty place. Nothing. They felt my stocking: nothing.

I don't remember whether I cried at that moment, but my sisters did. They ran with me back to my bed, and there we all cried till I became indignant. That helped some. I got up, dressed, and driving my sisters away, I went alone out into the yard, down to the stable, and there, all by myself, I wept. My mother came out to me by and by; she found me in my pony stall, sobbing on the floor, and she tried to comfort me. But I heard my father outside; he had come part way with her, and she was having some sort of angry quarrel with him. She tried to comfort me; besought me to come to breakfast. I could not; I wanted no comfort and no breakfast. She left me and went on into the house with sharp words for my father.

I don't know what kind of a breakfast the family had. My sisters said it was "awful." They were ashamed to enjoy their own toys. They came to me, and I was rude. I ran away from them. I went around to the front of the house, sat down on the steps, and, the crying over, I ached. I was wronged, I was hurt—I can feel now what I felt then, and I am sure that if one could see the wounds upon our hearts, there would be found still upon mine a scar from that terrible Christmas morning. And my father, the practical joker, he must have been hurt, too, a little. I saw him looking out of the window. He was watching me or something for an hour or two, drawing back the curtain never so little lest I catch him, but I saw his face, and I think I can see now the anxiety upon it, the worried impatience.

After—I don't know how long—surely an hour or two—I was brought to the climax of my agony by the sight of a man riding a pony down the street, a pony and a brand-new saddle; the most beautiful saddle I ever saw, and it was a boy's saddle; the man's feet were not in the stirrups; his legs were too long. The outfit was perfect; it was the realization of all my dreams, the answer to all my prayers. A fine new bridle, with a light curb bit. And the pony! As he drew near, I saw that the pony was really a small horse, what we called an Indian pony, a bay, with black mane and tail, and one white foot and a white star on his forehead. For such a horse as that I would have given, I could have forgiven, anything.

But the man, a disheveled fellow with a blackened eye and a fresh-cut face, came along, reading the numbers on the houses, and, as my hopes—my impossible hopes—rose, he looked at our door and passed by, he and the pony, and the saddle and the bridle. Too much. I fell upon the steps, and having wept before, I broke now into such a flood of tears that I was a floating wreck when I heard a voice.

"Say, kid," it said, "do you know a boy named Lennie Steffens?"

I looked up. It was the man on the pony, back again, at our horse block.

"Yes," I spluttered through my tears. "That's me."

"Well," he said, "then this is your horse. I've been looking all over for you and your house. Why don't you put your number where it can be seen?"

"Get down," I said, running out to him.

He went on saying something about "ought to have got here at seven o'clock; told me to bring the nag here and tie him to your post and leave him for you. But, hell, I got into a drunk—and a fight—and a hospital, and—"

"Get down," I said.

He got down, and he boosted me up to the saddle. He offered to fit the stirrups to me, but I didn't want him to. I wanted to ride.

"What's the matter with you?" he said, angrily. "What you crying for? Don't you like the horse? He's a dandy, this horse. I know him of old. He's fine at cattle; he'll drive 'em alone."

I hardly heard, I could scarcely wait, but he persisted. He adjusted the stirrups, and then, finally, off I rode, slowly, at a walk, so happy, so thrilled, that I did not know what I was doing. I did not look back at the house or the man, I rode off up the street, taking note of everything—of the reins, of the pony's long mane, of the carved leather saddle. I had never seen anything so beautiful. And mine! I was going to ride up past Miss Kay's house. But I noticed on the horn of the saddle some stains like rain-drops, so I turned and trotted home, and to the house but to the stable. There was the family, father, mother, sisters, all working for me, all happy. They had been putting in place the tools of my new business: blankets, curry-comb, brush, pitchfork—everything, and there was hay in the loft.

"What did you come back so soon for?" somebody asked. "Why didn't you go on riding?"

I pointed to the stains. "I wasn't going to get my new saddle rained on," I said. And my father laughed. "It isn't raining," he said. "Those are not rain-drops."

"They are tears," my mother gasped, and she gave my father a look which sent him off to the house. Worse still, my mother offered to wipe away the tears still running out of my eyes. I gave her such a look as she had given him, and she went off after my father, drying her own tears. My sisters remained and we all unsaddled the pony, put on his halter, led him to his stall, tied and fed him. It began really to rain; so all the rest of that memorable day we curried and combed that pony. The girls plaited his mane, forelock, and tail, while I pitchforked hay to him and curried and brushed, curried and brushed. For a change we brought him out to drink; we led him up and down, blanketed like a race-horse; we took turns at that. But the best, the most inexhaustible fun, was to clean him. When we went reluctantly to our midday Christmas dinner, we all smelt of horse, and my sisters had to wash their faces and hands. I was asked to, but I wouldn't, till my mother bade me look in the mirror. Then I washed up—quick. My face was caked with the muddy lines of tears that had coursed over my cheeks to my mouth. Having washed away that shame, I ate my dinner, and as I ate I grew hungrier and hungrier. It was my first meal that day, and as I filled up on the turkey and the stuffing, the cranberries and the pies, the fruit and the nuts—as I swelled. I could laugh. My mother said I still choked and sobbed now and then, but I laughed, too; I saw and enjoyed my sisters presents till—I had to go out and attend to my pony, who was there, really and truly there, the promise, the beginning, of a happy double life. And—I went and looked to make sure—there was the saddle, too, and the bridle.

But that Christmas, which my father had planned so carefully, was it the best or the worst I ever knew? He often asked me that: I never could answer as a boy. I think now that it was both. It covered the whole distance from broken-hearted misery to bursting happiness—too fast. A grown-up could hardly have stood it.

## QUESTIONS ON CONTENT

1. What did Steffens want for Christmas?
2. If he couldn't get what he wanted for Christmas, what did Steffens say he wanted?
3. How were girls viewed in the Steffens household?
4. Why was his present late getting to him that Christmas morning?
5. What "sign of shame" did Steffens describe?

## QUESTIONS ON RHETORIC

1. How does Steffens paint his family? What details does he use?
2. Early in the essay, Steffens writes that "girls counted for nothing in my manly life." Why is this attitude significant and how does it come into play later in the essay?
3. Why does Steffens mention the quarrel between his mother and father twice and yet not describe it fully? How does this affect your attitude toward his parents?
4. Why do you think Steffens's father often asked him about this particular Christmas?

## VOCABULARY

(10) indignant

## WRITING PROMPTS

1. Write about someday.
2. Think back to your best and worst holidays. Write about one of them.
3. Does society allow men today the freedom to cry? Why or why not?
4. Is there an object you got that marked a beginning for you? Write about the change it brought in your life.

# A KIOWA GRANDMOTHER

## N. SCOTT MOMADAY

A single knoll rises out of the plain in Oklahoma, north and west of the Wichita Range. For my people, the Kiowas, it is an old landmark, and they gave it the name Rainy Mountain. The hardest weather in the world is there. Winter brings blizzards, hot tornadic winds arise in the spring, and in summer the prairie is an anvil's edge. The grass turns brittle and brown, and it cracks beneath your feet. There are green belts along the rivers and creeks, linear groves of hickory and pecan, willow and witch hazel. At a distance in July or August the steaming foliage seems almost to writhe in fire. Great green and yellow grasshoppers are everywhere in the tall grass, popping up like corn to sting the flesh, and tortoises crawl about on the red earth, going nowhere in the plenty of time. Loneliness is an aspect of the land. All things in the plain are isolate; there is no confusion of objects in the eye, but *one* hill or *one* tree or *one* man. To look upon that landscape in the early morning, with the sun at your back, is to lose the sense of proportion. Your imagination comes to life, and this, you think, is where Creation was begun.

I returned to Rainy Mountain in July. My grandmother had died in the spring, and I wanted to be at her grave. She had lived to be very old and at last infirm. Her only living daughter was with her when she died, and I was told that in death her face was that of a child.

I like to think of her as a child. When she was born, the Kiowas were living the last great moment of their history. For more than a hundred years they had controlled the open range from the Smoky Hill River to the Red, from the headwaters of the Canadian to the fork of the Arkansas and Cimarron. In alliance with the Comanches, they had ruled the whole of the southern Plains. War was their sacred business, and they were among the finest horsemen the world has ever known. But warfare for the Kiowas was preeminently a matter of disposition rather than of survival, and they never understood the grim, unrelenting advance of the U.S. Cavalry. When at last, divided and ill-provisioned, they were driven onto the Staked Plains in the cold rains of autumn, they fell into panic. In Palo Duro Canyon they abandoned their crucial stores to pillage and had nothing then but their lives. In order to save themselves, they surrendered to the soldiers at Fort Sill and were imprisoned in the old stone corral that now stands as a military museum. My grandmother was spared the humiliation of those high gray walls by eight or ten years, but she must have known from birth the affliction of defeat, the dark brooding of old warriors.

Her name was Aho, and she belonged to the last culture to evolve in North America. Her forebears came down from the high country in western Montana nearly three centuries ago. They were a mountain people, a mysterious tribe of hunters whose language has never been positively classified in any major group. In the late seventeenth century they began a long migration to the south and east. It was a journey toward the dawn, and it led to a golden age. Along the way the Kiowas were befriended by the Crows, who gave them the culture and religion of the Plains. They acquired horses, and their ancient nomadic spirit was suddenly free of the ground. They acquired Tai-me, the sacred Sun Dance doll, from that moment the object and symbol of their worship, and so shared in the divinity of the sun. Not least, they acquired the sense of destiny, therefore courage and pride. When they entered upon the southern Plains they had been transformed. No longer were they slaves to the simple necessity of survival; they were a lordly and dangerous society of fighters and thieves, hunters and priests of the sun. According to their origin myth, they entered the world through a hollow log. From one point of view, their migration was the fruit of an old prophecy, for indeed they emerged from a sunless world.

Although my grandmother lived out her long life in the shadow of Rainy Mountain, the immense landscape of the continental interior lay like memory in her blood. She could tell of the Crows, whom she had never seen, and of the Black Hills, where she had never been. I wanted to see in reality what she had seen more perfectly in the mind's eye, and traveled fifteen hundred miles to begin my pilgrimage.

Yellowstone, it seemed to me, was the top of the world, a region of deep lakes and dark timber, canyons and waterfalls. But, beautiful as it is, one might have the sense of confinement there. The skyline in all directions is close at hand, the high wall of the woods and deep cleavages of shade. There is a perfect freedom in the mountains, but it belongs to the eagle and the elk, the badger and the bear. The Kiowas reckoned their stature by the distance they could see, and they were bent and blind in the wilderness.

Descending eastward, the highland meadows are a stairway to the plain. In July the inland slope of the Rockies is luxuriant with flax and buckwheat, stonecrop and larkspur. The earth unfolds and the limit of the land recedes. Clusters of trees, and animals grazing far in the distance, cause the vision to reach away and wonder to build upon the mind. The sun follows a longer course in the day, and the sky is immense beyond all comparison. The great billowing clouds that sail upon it are shadows that move upon the grain like water, dividing light. Farther down, in the land of the Crows and Blackfeet, the plain is yellow. Sweet clover takes hold of the hills and bends upon itself to cover and seal the soil. There the Kiowas paused on their way; they had come to the place where they must change their lives. The sun is at home on the plains. Precisely there does it have the certain character of a god. When the Kiowas came to the land of the Crows, they could see the dark lees of the hills at dawn across the Bighorn River, the profusion of light on the grain shelves, the oldest deity ranging after the solstices. Not yet would they veer southward to the caldron of the land that lay below; they must wean their blood from the northern winter and hold the mountains a while longer in their view. They bore Tai-me in procession to the east.

A dark mist lay over the Black Hills, and the land was like iron. At the top of a ridge I caught sight of Devil's Tower upthrust against the gray sky as if in the birth of time the core of the earth had broken through its crust and the motion of the world was begun. There are things in nature that engender an awful quiet in the heart of man; Devil's Tower is one of them. Two centuries ago, because they could not do otherwise, the Kiowas made a legend at the base of the rock. My grandmother said:

> Eight children were there at play, seven sisters and their brother. Suddenly the boy was struck dumb; he trembled and began to run upon his hands and feet. His fingers became claws, and his body was covered with fur. Directly there was a bear where the boy had been. The sisters were terrified; they ran, and the bear after them. They came to the stump of a great tree, and the tree spoke to them. It bade them climb upon it, and as they did so it began to rise into the air. The bear came to kill them, but they were just beyond its reach. It reared against the tree and scored the bark all around with its claws. The seven sisters were borne into the sky, and they became the stars of the Big Dipper.

From that moment, and so long as the legend lives, the Kiowas have kinsmen in the night sky. Whatever they were in the mountains, they could be no more. However tenuous their well-being, however much they had suffered and would suffer again, they had found a way out of the wilderness.

My grandmother had a reverence for the sun, a holy regard that now is all but gone out of mankind. There was a wariness in her, and an ancient awe. She was a Christian in her later years, but she had come a long way about, and she never forgot her birthright. As a child she had been to the Sun Dances; she had taken part in those annual rites, and by then she had learned the restoration of her people in the presence of Tai-me. She was about seven when the last Kiowa Sun Dance was held in 1887 on the Washita River above Rainy Mountain Creek. The buffalo were gone. In order to consummate the ancient sacrifice—to impale the head of a buffalo bull upon the medicine tree—a delegation of old men journeyed into Texas, there to beg and barter for an animal from the Goodnight herd. She was ten when the Kiowas came together for the last time as a living Sun Dance culture. They could find no buffalo; they had to hang an old hide from the sacred tree. Before the dance could begin, a company of soldiers rode out from Fort Sill under orders to disperse the tribe. Forbidden without cause the essential act of their faith, having seen the wild herds slaughtered and left to rot upon the ground, the Kiowas backed away forever from the medicine tree. That was July 20, 1890, at the great bend of the Washita. My grandmother was there. Without bitterness, and for as long as she lived, she bore a vision of deicide.

Now that I can have her only in memory, I see my grandmother in the several postures that were peculiar to her: standing at the wood stove on a winter morning and turning meat in a great iron skillet; sitting at the south window, bent above her beadwork, and afterwards, when her vision failed, looking down for a long time into the fold of her hands; going out upon a cane, very slowly as she did when the weight of age came upon her; praying. I remember her most often at prayer. She made long, rambling prayers out of suffering and hope, having seen many things. I was never sure that I had the right to hear, so exclusive were they of all mere custom and company. The last time I saw her she prayed standing by the side of her bed at night, naked to the waist, the light of a kerosene lamp moving upon her dark skin. Her long, black hair, always drawn and braided in the day, lay upon her shoulders and against her breasts like a shawl. I do not speak Kiowa, and I never understood her prayers, but there was something inherently sad in the sound, some merest hesitation upon the syllables of sorrow. She began in a high and descending pitch, exhausting her breath to silence; then again and again—and always the same intensity of effort, of something that is, and is not, like urgency in the human voice. Transported so in the dancing light among the shadows of her room, she seemed beyond the reach of time. But that was illusion; I think I knew then that I should not see her again.

Houses are like sentinels in the plain, old keepers of the weather watch. There, in a very little while, wood takes on the appearance of great age. All colors wear soon away in the wind and rain, and then the wood is burned gray and the grain appears and the nails turn red with rust. The window-panes are black and opaque; you imagine there is nothing within, and indeed there are many ghosts, bones given up to the land. They stand here and there against the sky, and you approach them for a longer time than you expect. They belong in the distance; it is their domain.

Once there was a lot of sound in my grandmother's house, a lot of coming and going, feasting and talk. The summers there were full of excitement and reunion. The Kiowas are a summer people; they abide the cold and keep to themselves, but when the season turns and the land becomes warm and vital they cannot hold still; an old love of going returns upon them. The aged visitors who came to my grandmother's house when I was a child were made of lean and leather, and they bore themselves upright. They wore great black hats and bright ample shirts that shook in the wind. They rubbed fat upon their hair and wound their braids with strips of colored cloth. Some of them painted their faces and carried the scars of old and cherished enmities. They were an old council of war-lords, come to remind and be reminded of who they were. Their wives and daughters served them well. The women might indulge themselves; gossip was at once the mark and compensation of their servitude. They made loud and elaborate talk among themselves, full of jest and gesture, fright and false alarm. They went abroad in fringed and flowered shawls, bright beadwork and German silver. They were at home in the kitchen, and they prepared meals that were banquets.

There were frequent prayer meetings, and great nocturnal feasts. When I was a child I played with my cousins outside, where the lamplight fell upon the ground and the singing of the old people rose up around us and carried away into the darkness. There were a lot of good things to eat, a lot of laughter and surprise. And afterwards, when the quiet returned, I lay down with my grandmother and could hear the frogs away by the river and feel the motion of the air.

Now there is a funeral silence in the rooms, the endless wake of some final word. The walls have closed in upon my grandmother's house. When I returned to it in mourning, I saw for the first time in my life how small it was. It was late at night, and there was a white moon, nearly full. I sat for a long time on the stone steps by the kitchen door. From there I could see out across the land; I could see the long row of trees by the creek, the low light upon the rolling plains, and the stars of the Big Dipper. Once I looked at the moon and caught sight of a strange thing. A cricket had perched upon the handrail, only a few inches away from me. My line of vision was such that the creature filled the moon like a fossil. It had gone there, I thought, to live and die, for there, of all places, was its small definition made whole and eternal. A warm wind rose up and purled like the longing within me.

The next morning I awoke at dawn and went out on the dirt road to Rainy Mountain. It was already hot, and the grasshoppers began to fill the air. Still, it was early in the morning, and the birds sang out of the shadows. The long yellow grass on the mountain shone in the bright light, and a scissortail hied above the land. There, where it ought to be, at the end of a long and legendary way, was my grandmother's grave. Here and there on the dark stones were ancestral names. Looking back once, I saw the mountain and came away.

## QUESTIONS ON CONTENT

1. Why does the author return to Rainy Mountain?
2. Who was Tai-me?
3. What legend did the Kiowa have about Devil's Tower?
4. Describe the prayer ritual of Momaday's grandmother.

## QUESTIONS ON RHETORIC

1. Why does Momaday begin with the description he does?
2. Mark passages that are not directly about his grandmother. Why does Momaday include those in his essay? Are they distracting or enhancing?
3. What role does color have in the essay? Why do you think this is?

4. The essay is an introduction to a book about Indian legends and stories of the Kiowa. Is it an appropriate introduction? Why?

## VOCABULARY

(2) infirm

(3) disposition, pillage

(9) deicide

(12) enmities

(14) purled

## WRITING PROMPTS

1. Write about "origin myths."
2. What memories do you have "in your blood"?
3. Write your personal history. What lessons for humankind are there?
4. If you've ever gone back to a place you lived as a child, you probably thought that it seemed smaller. Why is that? Write about going back.
5. Do you feel connected to any place? Write about that connection and how it developed and why.

# THE RIGHT TO DIE

## NORMAN COUSINS

The world of religion and philosophy was shocked recently when
Henry P. Van Dusen and his wife ended their lives by their own
hands. Dr. Van Dusen had been president of Union Theological Sem-
inary; for more than a quarter-century he had been one of the lumi-
nous names in Protestant theology. He enjoyed world status as a spiritual leader. News of the self-inflicted death of the Van Dusens,
therefore, was profoundly disturbing to all those who attach a moral
stigma to suicide and regard it as a violation of God's laws.

Dr. Van Dusen had anticipated this reaction. He and his wife left
behind a letter that may have historic significance. It was very brief,
but the essential point it made is now being widely discussed by the-
ologians and could represent the beginning of a reconsideration of
traditional religious attitudes toward self-inflicted death. The letter
raised a moral issue: does an individual have the obligation to go on
living even when the beauty and meaning and power of life are gone?

Henry and Elizabeth Van Dusen had lived full lives. In recent
years, they had become increasingly ill, requiring almost continual
medical care. Their infirmities were worsening, and they realized
they would soon become completely dependent for even the most
elementary needs and functions. Under these circumstances, little
dignity would have been left in life. They didn't like the idea of taking up space in a world with too many mouths and too little food.

They believed it was a misuse of medical science to keep them technically alive.

They therefore believed they had the right to decide when to die. In making that decision, they weren't turning against life as the highest value; what they were turning against was the notion that there were no circumstances under which life should be discontinued.

An important aspect of human uniqueness is the power of free will. In his books and lectures, Dr. Van Dusen frequently spoke about the exercise of this uniqueness. The fact that he used his free will to prevent life from becoming a caricature of itself was completely in character. In their letter, the Van Dusens sought to convince family and friends that they were not acting solely out of despair or pain.

The use of free will to put an end to one's life finds no sanction in the theology to which Pitney Van Dusen was committed. Suicide symbolizes discontinuity; religion symbolizes continuity, represented at its quintessence by the concept of the immortal soul. Human logic finds it almost impossible to come to terms with the concept of nonexistence. In religion, the human mind finds a larger dimension and is relieved of the ordeal of a confrontation with non-existence.

Even without respect to religion, the idea of suicide has been abhorrent throughout history. Some societies have imposed severe penalties on the families of suicides in the hope that the individual who sees no reason to continue his existence may be deterred by the stigma his self-destruction would inflict on loved ones. Other societies have enacted laws prohibiting suicide on the grounds that it is murder. The enforcement of such laws, of course, has been an exercise in futility.

Customs and attitudes, like individuals themselves, are largely shaped by the surrounding environment. In today's world, life can be prolonged by science far beyond meaning or sensibility. Under these circumstances, individuals who feel they have nothing more to give to life, or to receive from it, need not be applauded, but they can be spared our condemnation.

The general reaction to suicide is bound to change as people come to understand that it may be a denial, not an assertion, of moral or religious ethics to allow life to be extended without regard to decency or pride. What moral or religious purpose is celebrated by the annihilation of the human spirit in the triumphant act of keeping the body alive? Why are so many people more readily appalled by an unnatural form of dying than by an unnatural form of living?

"Nowadays," the Van Dusens wrote in their last letter, "it is difficult to die. We feel that this way we are taking will become more usual and acceptable as the years pass.

"Of course, the thought of our children and our grandchildren makes us sad, but we still feel that this is the best way and the right way to go. We are both increasingly weak and unwell and who would want to die in a nursing home?

"We are not afraid to die. . . ."

Pitney Van Dusen was admired and respected in life. He can be admired and respected in death. "Suicide," said Goethe, "is an incident in human life which, however much disputed and discussed, demands the sympathy of every man, and in every age must be dealt with anew."

Death is not the greatest loss in life. The greatest loss is what dies inside us while we live. The unbearable tragedy is to live without dignity or sensitivity.

## QUESTIONS ON CONTENT

1. What position did Dr. Van Dusen hold?
2. Why was Van Dusen's death controversial?
3. Why did the Van Dusens decide to take their own lives?

## QUESTIONS ON RHETORIC

1. Cousins uses an extended example to make his point. Is the example effective if you don't know the people involved? Why or why not?
2. Cousins said the letter the Van Dusens left "may have historic significance." How does he support this statement?

3. How does Cousins feel about suicide? Find evidence to support your answer.

## VOCABULARY

(5) caricature

(6) sanction, quintessence

## WRITING PROMPTS

1. Agree or disagree with Cousins's statement, "Death is not the greatest loss in life." (14)
2. Why do you think the American society and/or churches view suicide as sinful?
3. Write about gradual suicides—the smoker, the alcoholic, the risk taker.

# CLUTTER

## WILLIAM ZINSSER

Fighting clutter is like fighting weeds—the writer is always slightly behind. New varieties sprout overnight, and by noon they are part of American speech. It only takes a John Dean testifying on TV to have everyone in the country saying "at this point in time" instead of "now."

Consider all the prepositions that are routinely draped onto verbs that don't need any help. Head up. Free up. Face up to. We no longer head committees. We head them up. We don't face problems anymore. We face up to them when we can free up a few minutes. A small detail, you may say—not worth bothering about. It *is* worth bothering about. The game is won or lost on hundreds of small details. Writing improves in direct ratio to the number of things we can keep out of it that shouldn't be there. "Up" in "free up" shouldn't be there. Can we picture anything being freed *up?* The writer of clean English must examine every word that he puts on paper. He will find a surprising number that don't serve any purpose.

Take the adjective "personal," as in "a personal friend of mine," "his personal feeling" or "her personal physician." It is typical of the words that can be eliminated nine times out of ten. The personal friend has come into the language to distinguish him from the business friend, thereby debasing not only language but friendship. Someone's feeling *is* his personal feeling—that's what "his" means. As for the personal physician, he is that man so often summoned to the dressing room of a stricken actress so that she won't have to be treated by the impersonal physician assigned to the theater. Someday I'd like to see him identified as "her doctor."

Or take those curious intervals of time like the short minute. "Twenty-two short minutes later she had won the final set." Minutes are minutes, physicians are physicians, friends are friends. The rest is clutter.

Clutter is the laborious phrase which has pushed out the short word that means the same thing. These locutions are a drag on energy and momentum. Even before John Dean gave us "at this point in time," people had stopped saying "now." They were saying "at the present time," or "currently," or "presently" (which means "soon"). Yet the idea can always be expressed by "now" to mean the immediate moment ("Now I can see him"), or by "today" to mean the historical present ("Today prices are high"), or simply by the verb "to be" ("It is raining"). There is no need to say, "At the present time we are experiencing precipitation."

Speaking of which, we are experiencing considerable difficulty getting *that* word out of the language now that it has lumbered in. Even your dentist will ask if you are experiencing any pain. If he were asking one of his own children he would say, "Does it hurt?" He would, in short, be himself. By using a more pompous phrase in his professional role he not only sounds more important; he blunts the painful edge of truth. It is the language of the airline stewardess demonstrating the oxygen mask that will drop down if the plane should somehow run out of air. "In the extremely unlikely possibility that the aircraft should experience such an eventuality," she begins—a phrase so oxygen-depriving in itself that we are prepared for any disaster, and even gasping death shall lose its sting. As for those "smoking materials" that she asks us to "kindly extinguish," I often wonder what materials are smoking. Maybe she thinks my coat and tie are on fire.

Clutter is the ponderous euphemism that turns a slum into a depressed socioeconomic area, a salesman into a marketing representative, a dumb kid into an underachiever and garbage collectors into waste disposal personnel. In New Canaan, Conn., the incinerator is now the "volume reduction plant." I hate to think what they call the town dump.

Clutter is the official language used by the American corporation—in the news release and the annual report—to hide its mistakes. When a big company recently announced that it was "decentralizing its organizational structure into major profit-centered businesses" and that "corporate staff services will be aligned under two senior vice-presidents" it meant that it had had a lousy year.

Clutter is the language of the interoffice memo ("The trend to mosaic communication is reducing the meaningfulness of concern about whether or not demographic segments differ in their tolerance of periodicity") and the language of computers ("We are offering functional digital programming options that have built-in parallel reciprocal capabilities with compatible third-generation contingencies and hardware").

Clutter is the language of the Pentagon throwing dust in the eyes of the populace by calling an invasion a "reinforced protective reaction strike" and by justifying its vast budgets on the need for "credible second-strike capability" and "counterforce deterrence." How can we grasp such vaporous double-talk? As George Orwell pointed out in "Politics and the English Language," an essay written in 1946 but cited frequently during the Vietnam years of Johnson and Nixon, "In our time, political speech and writing are largely the defense of the indefensible. . . . Thus political language has to consist largely of euphemism, question-begging and sheer cloudy vagueness." Orwell's warning that clutter is not just a nuisance but a deadly tool did not turn out to be inoperative. By the 1960s his words had come true in America.

I could go on quoting examples from various fields—every profession has its growing arsenal of jargon to fire at the layman and hurl him back from its walls. But the list would be depressing and the lesson tedious. The point of raising it now is to serve notice that clutter is the enemy, whatever form it takes. It slows the reader and robs the writer of his personality, making him seem pretentious.

Beware, then, of the long word that is no better than the short word: "numerous" (many), "facilitate" (ease), "individual" (man or woman), "remainder" (rest), "initial" (first), "implement" (do), "sufficient" (enough), "attempt" (try), "referred to as" (called), and hundreds more. Beware, too, of all the slippery new fad words for which the language already has equivalents: overview and quantify, paradigm and parameter, input and throughput, peer group and interface, private sector and public sector, optimize and maximize, prioritize and potentialize. They are all weeds that will smother what you write.

Nor are all the weeds so obvious. Just as insidious are the little growths of perfectly ordinary words with which we explain how we propose to go about our explaining, or which inflate a simple preposition or conjunction into a whole windy phrase.

"I might add," "It should be pointed out," "It is interesting to note that"—how many sentences begin with these dreary clauses announcing what the writer is going to do next? If you might add, add it. If it should be pointed out, point it out. If it is interesting to note, *make* it interesting. Being told that something is interesting is the surest way of tempting the reader to find it dull; are we not all stupefied by what follows when someone says, "This will interest you"? As for the inflated prepositions and conjunctions, they are the innumerable phrases like "with the possible exception of" (except), "for the reason that" (because), "he totally lacked the ability to" (he couldn't), "until such time as" (until), "for the purpose of" (for).

Clutter takes more forms than you can shake twenty sticks at. Prune it ruthlessly. Be grateful for everything that you can throw away. Re-examine each sentence that you put on paper. Is every word doing new and useful work? Can any thought be expressed with more economy? Is anything pompous or pretentious or faddish? Are you hanging on to something useless just because you think it's beautiful?

Simplify, simplify.

## QUESTIONS ON CONTENT

1. What kind of clutter is the writer speaking of?
2. Why does Zinsser oppose the use of "the short minute"?
3. Give three examples of groups that use verbal clutter on a regular basis.

## QUESTIONS ON RHETORIC

1. How does Zinsser organize this essay?
2. Look at the examples Zinsser uses to define clutter. Are they relevant to most readers?
3. Notice the repetition Zinsser uses. Is this effective? Why?
4. Look at Zinsser's last sentence. Does it emphasize his point or negate it?

## VOCABULARY

(5) locutions

(6) pompous

(7) euphemism

(11) jargon

(13) insidious

## WRITING PROMPTS

1. Write about hiding meaning in words.
2. Write about a time you hid behind words.
3. Think of a simple directive. Rewrite it with the most verbose, ambiguous language you can.
4. Write about what could happen if all writing became totally uncluttered.

# I Want a Wife

## Judy Brady

I belong to that classification of people known as wives. I am A Wife. And, not altogether incidentally, I am a mother.

Not too long ago a male friend of mine appeared on the scene fresh from a recent divorce. He had one child, who is, of course, with his ex-wife. He is looking for another wife. As I thought about him while I was ironing one evening, it suddenly occurred to me that I, too, would like to have a wife. Why do I want a wife?

I would like to go back to school so that I can become economically independent, support myself, and, if need be, support those dependent upon me. I want a wife who will work and send me to school. And while I am going to school I want a wife to take care of my children. I want a wife to keep track of the children's doctor and dentist appointments. And to keep track of mine, too. I want a wife to make sure my children eat properly and are kept clean. I want a wife who will wash the children's clothes and keep them mended. I want a wife who is a good nurturant attendant to my children, who arranges for their schooling, makes sure that they have an adequate social life with their peers, takes them to the park, the zoo, etc. I want a wife who takes care of the children when they are sick, a wife who arranges to be around when the children need special care, because, of course, I cannot miss classes at school. My wife must arrange to lose time at work and not lose the job. It may mean a small cut in my wife's income from time to time, but I guess I can tolerate that. Needless to say, my wife will arrange and pay for the care of the children while my wife is working.

I want a wife who will take care of *my* physical needs. I want a wife who will keep my house clean. A wife who will pick up after my children, a wife who will pick up after me. I want a wife who will keep my clothes clean, ironed, mended, replaced when need be, and who will see to it that my personal things are kept in their proper place so that I can find what I need the minute I need it. I want a wife who cooks the meals, a wife who is a *good* cook. I want a wife who will plan the menus, do the necessary grocery shopping, prepare the meals, serve them pleasantly, and then do the cleaning up while I do my studying. I want a wife who will care for me when I am sick and sympathize with my pain and loss of time from school. I want a wife to go along when our family takes vacation so that someone can continue to care for me and my children when I need a rest and change of scene.

I want a wife who will not bother me with rambling complaints about a wife's duties. But I want a wife who will listen to me when I feel the need to explain a rather difficult point I have come across in my course of studies. And I want a wife who will type my papers for me when I have written them.

I want a wife who will take care of the details of my social life. When my wife and I are invited out by my friends, I want a wife who will take care of the babysitting arrangements. When I meet people at school that I like and want to entertain, I want a wife who will have the house clean, will prepare a special meal, serve it to me and my friends, and not interrupt when I talk about things that interest me and my friends. I want a wife who will have arranged that the children are fed and ready for bed before my guests arrive so that the children do not bother us. I want a wife who takes care of the needs of my guests so that they feel comfortable, who makes sure that they have an ashtray, that they are passed the hors d'oeuvres, that they are offered a second helping of the food, that their wine glasses are replenished when necessary, that their coffee is served to them as they like it. And I want a wife who knows that sometimes I need a night out by myself.

I want a wife who is sensitive to my sexual needs, a wife who makes love passionately and eagerly when I feel like it, a wife who makes sure that I am satisfied. And, of course, I want a wife who will not demand sexual attention when I am not in the mood for it. I want a wife who assumes the complete responsibility for birth control, because I do not want more children. I want a wife who will remain sexually faithful to me so that I do not have to clutter up my intellectual life with jealousies. And I want a wife who understands that *my* sexual needs may entail more than strict adherence to monogamy. I must, after all, be able to relate to people as fully as possible.

If, by chance, I find another person more suitable as a wife than the wife I already have, I want the liberty to replace my present wife with another one. Naturally, I will expect a fresh, new life; my wife will take the children and be solely responsible for them so that I am left free.

When I am through with school and have a job, I want my wife to quit working and remain at home so that my wife can more fully and completely take care of a wife's duties.

My God, who *wouldn't* want a wife?

## QUESTIONS ON CONTENT

1. What prompted the author to write this essay?
2. List several duties of wives, as the author sees them.
3. How does the author end the essay?
4. What classification of duties does the author use?

## QUESTIONS ON RHETORIC

1. How many times does the phrase "I want a wife..." appear? What effect does this repetition have?
2. Does the author give only one side of the issue? Cite examples.

3. Six paragraphs begin with the words "I want…" What impact does this have on the essay?
4. Is this essay nothing but "male bashing"?
5. Is the last paragraph an appropriate ending?
6. How does paragraph 2 establish the author's credibility?

## VOCABULARY

(3) nurturant

(6) replenished

(7) adherence, monogamy

## WRITING PROMPTS

1. Write this essay from the male perspective: "I want a husband who…"
2. The essay was written almost 30 years ago. Is it still relevant? If so, how?
3. Are there things you can or cannot do because of your gender?
4. Write about gender as an asset.

# THE BOYFRIEND

## SUSAN ALLEN TOTH

Just when I was approaching sixteen, I found Peter Stone. Or did he find me? Perhaps I magicked him into existence out of sheer need. I was spooked by the boys who teased us nice girls about being sweet-sixteen-and-never-been-kissed. I felt that next to being an old maid forever, it probably was most demeaning to reach sixteen and not to have experienced the kind of ardent embrace Gordon MacRae periodically bestowed on Kathryn Grayson between choruses of "Desert Song." I was afraid I would never have a real boyfriend, never go parking, never know true love. So when Peter Stone asked his friend Ted to ask Ted's girlfriend Emily who asked me if I would ever neck with anyone, I held my breath until Emily told me she had said to Ted to tell Peter that maybe I would.

Not that Peter Stone had ever necked with anyone either. But I didn't realize that for a long time. High-school courtship usually was meticulously slow, progressing through inquiry, phone calls, planned encounters in public places, double or triple dates, single dates hand-holding, and finally a good-night kiss. I assumed it probably stopped there, but I didn't know. I had never gotten that far. I had lots of time to learn about Peter Stone. What I knew at the beginning already attracted me: he was a year ahead of me, vice-president of Hi-Y, a shot-putter who had just managed to earn a letter sweater. An older man, *and* an athlete. Tall, heavy, and broad-shouldered, Peter had a sweet slow smile. Even at a distance there was something endearing about the way he would blink nearsightedly through his glasses and light up with pleased recognition when he saw me coming toward him down the hall.

For a long while I didn't come too close. Whenever I saw Peter he was in the midst of his gang, a group of five boys as close and as self protective as any clique we girls had. They were an odd mixture: Jim, an introspective son of a lawyer; Brad, a sullen hot-rodder; Ted, an unambitious and gentle boy from a poor family; Andy, a chubby comedian; and Peter. I was a little afraid of all of them, and they scrutinized me carefully before opening their circle to admit me, tentatively, as I held tight to Peter's hand. The lawyer's son had a steady girl, a fast number who was only in eighth grade but looked eighteen; the hot-rodder was reputed to have "gone all the way" with his adoring girl, a coarse brunette with plucked eyebrows; gentle Ted pursued my friend Emily with hangdog tenacity; but Peter had never shown real interest in a girlfriend before.

Although I had decided to go after Peter, I was hesitant about how to plot my way into the interior of his world. It was a thicket of strange shrubs and tangled branches. Perhaps I see it that way because I remember the day Peter took me to a wild ravine to shoot his gun. Girls who went with one of "the guys" commiserated with each other that their boyfriends all preferred two other things to them: their cars and their guns. Although Peter didn't hunt and seldom went to practice at the target range, still he valued his gun. Without permits, "the guys" drove outside of town to fire their guns illegally. I had read enough in my *Seventeen* about how to attract boys to know I needed to show enthusiasm about Peter's hobbies, so I asked him if some day he would take me someplace and teach me how to shoot.

One sunny fall afternoon he did. I remember rattling over gravel roads into a rambling countryside that had surprising valleys and woods around cultivated farmland. Eventually we stopped before a barred gate that led to an abandoned bridge, once a railroad trestle, now a splintering wreck. We had to push our way through knee-high weeds to get past the gate. I was afraid of snakes. Peter took my hand; it was the first time he had ever held it, and my knees weakened a little. I was also scared of walking onto the bridge, which had broken boards and sudden gaps that let you look some fifty feet down into the golden and rust-colored brush below. But I didn't mind being a little scared as long as Peter was there to take care of me.

I don't think I had ever held a gun until Peter handed me his pistol, a heavy metal weapon that looked something like the ones movie sheriffs carried in their holsters. I was impressed by its weight and power. Peter fired it twice to show me how and then stood close to me, watching carefully, while I aimed at an empty beer can he tossed into the air. I didn't hit it. The noise of the gun going off was terrifying. I hoped nobody was walking in the woods where I had aimed. Peter said nobody was, nobody ever came here. When I put the gun down, he put his arm around me, very carefully. He had never done that before, either. We both just stood there, looking off into the distance, staring at the glowing maples and elms, dark red patches of sumac, brown heaps of leaves. The late afternoon sun beat down on us. It was hot, and after a few minutes Peter shifted uncomfortably. I moved away, laughing nervously, and we walked back to the car, watching the gaping boards at our feet.

What Peter and I did with our time together is a mystery. I try to picture us at movies or parties or somebody's house, but all I can see is the two of us in Peter's car. "Going for a drive!" I'd fling at my mother as I rushed out of the house; "rinking" was our high-school term for it, drawn from someone's contempt for the greasy "hoods" who hung out around the roller-skating rink and skidded around corners on two wheels of their souped-up cars. Peter's car barely made it around a corner on all four wheels. Though he had learned something about how to keep his huge square Ford running, he wasn't much of a mechanic. He could make jokes about the Ford, but he didn't like anyone else, including me, to say it looked like an old black hearse or remind him it could scarcely do forty miles an hour on an open stretch of highway. Highways were not where we drove, anyway, nor was speed a necessity unless you were trying to catch up with someone who hadn't seen you. "Rinking" meant cruising aimlessly around town, looking for friends in *their* cars, stopping for conversations shouted out of windows, maybe parking somewhere for a while, ending up at the A&W Root Beer Stand or the pizza parlor or the Rainbow Cafe.

Our parents were often puzzled about why we didn't spend time in each other's homes. "Why don't you invite Peter in?" my mother would ask a little wistfully, as I grabbed my billfold and cardigan and headed toward the door. Sometimes Peter would just pause in front of the house and honk; if I didn't come out quickly, he assumed I wasn't home and drove away. Mother finally made me tell him at least to come to the door and knock. I couldn't explain to her why we didn't want to sit in the living room, or go down to the pine-paneled basement at the Harbingers', or swing on the Harrises' front porch. We might not have been bothered at any of those places, but we really wouldn't have been alone. Cars were our private space, a rolling parlor, the only place we could relax and be ourselves. We could talk, fiddle with the radio if we didn't have much to say, look out the window, watch for friends passing by. Driving gave us a feeling of freedom.

Most of my memories of important moments with Peter center in that old black Ford. One balmy summer evening I remember particularly because my friend Emily said I would. Emily and Ted were out cruising in his rusty two-tone Chevy, the lawyer's son Jim and his girl had his father's shiny Buick, and Peter and I were out driving in the Ford. As we rumbled slowly down Main Street, quiet and dark at night, Peter saw Ted's car approaching. We stopped in the middle of the street so the boys could exchange a few laconic grunts while Emily and I smiled confidentially at each other. We were all in a holiday mood, lazy and happy in the warm breezes that swept through the open windows. One of us suggested that we all meet later at Camp Canwita, a wooded park a few miles north of town. Whoever saw Jim would tell him to join us too. We weren't sure what we would do there, but it sounded like an adventure. An hour or so later, Peter and I bumped over the potholes in the road that twisted through the woods to the parking lot. We were the first ones there. When Peter turned off the motor, we could hear grasshoppers thrumming on all sides of us and leaves rustling in the dark. It was so quiet, so remote, I was a little frightened, remembering one of my mother's unnerving warnings about the dangerous men who sometimes preyed upon couples who parked in secluded places. We didn't have long to wait, though, before Ted's car coughed and sputtered down the drive. Soon Jim arrived too, and then we all pulled our cars close together in a kind of circle so we could talk easily out the windows. Someone's radio was turned on, and Frank Sinatra's mournful voice began to sing softly of passing days and lost love. Someone suggested that we get out of the cars and dance. It wouldn't have been Peter, who was seldom romantic. Ted opened his door so the overhead light cast a dim glow over the tiny area between the cars. Solemnly, a little self-consciously, we began the shuffling steps that were all we knew of what we called "slow dancing." Peter was not a good dancer, nor was I, though I liked putting my head on his bulky shoulder. But he moved me around the small lighted area as best he could trying not to bump into Ted and Emily or Jim and his girl. I tried not to step on his toes. While Sinatra, Patti Page, and the Four Freshmen sang to us about moments to remember and Cape Cod, we all danced, one-two back, one-two back. Finally Emily, who was passing by my elbow, looked significantly at me and said: "This is something we'll be able to tell our grandchildren." Yes, I nodded, but I wasn't so sure. The mosquitoes were biting my legs and arms, my toes hurt, and I was getting a little bored. I think the others were too, because before long we all got into our cars and drove away.

Not all the time we spent in Peter's car was in motion. After several months, we did begin parking on deserted country roads, side streets, even sometimes my driveway, if my mother had heeded my fierce instructions to leave the light turned off. For a while we simply sat and talked, with Peter's arm draped casually on the back of the seat. Gradually I moved a little closer. Soon he had his arm around me, but even then it was a long time before he managed to kiss me goodnight. Boys must have been as scared as we girls were, though we always thought of them as having much more experience.

We all compared notes, shyly, about how far our boyfriends had gone; was he holding your hand yet, or taking you parking, or...? When a girl finally got kissed, telephone lines burned with the news next day. I was getting a little embarrassed about how long it was taking Peter to get around to it. My sixteenth birthday was only a few weeks away, and so far I had nothing substantial to report. I was increasingly nervous too because I still didn't know quite how I was going to behave. We girls joked about wondering where your teeth went and did glasses get in the way, but no one could give a convincing description. For many years I never told anyone about what *did* happen to me that first time. I was too ashamed. Peter and I were parked down the street from my house, talking, snuggling, listening to the radio. During a silence I turned my face toward him, and then he kissed me, tentatively and quickly. I was exhilarated but frightened. I wanted to respond in an adequate way, but my instincts did not entirely cooperate. I leaned towards Peter, but at the last moment I panicked. Instead of kissing him, I gave him a sudden lick on the cheek. He didn't know what to say. Neither did I.

Next morning I was relieved that it was all over. I dutifully reported my news to a few key girlfriends who could pass it on to others. I left out the part about the lick. That was my last bulletin. After a first kiss, we girls also respected each other's privacy. What more was there to know? We assumed that couples sat in their cars and necked, but nice girls, we also assumed, went no farther. We knew the girls who did. Their names got around. We marveled at them, uncomprehending as much as disapproving. Usually they talked about getting married to their boyfriends, and eventually some of them did. A lot of "nice" girls suffered under this distinction. One of them told me years later how she and her steady boyfriend had yearned and held back, stopped just short, petted and clutched and gritted their teeth. "When we went together to see the movie *Splendor in the Grass,* we had to leave the theatre," she said ruefully. "The part about how Natalie Wood and Warren Beatty wanted to make love so desperately and couldn't.... Well, that was just how we felt."

My mother worried about what was going on in the car during those long evenings when Peter and I went "out driving." She needn't have. Amazing as it seems now, when courting has speeded up to a freeway pace, when I wonder if a man who doesn't try to get me to bed immediately might possibly be gay, Peter and I gave each other hours of affection without ever crossing the invisible line. We sat in his car and necked, a word that was anatomically correct. We hugged and kissed, nuzzling ears and noses and hairlines. But Peter never put a hand on my breast, and I wouldn't have known whether Peter had an erection if it had risen up and thwapped me in the face. I never got that close. Although we probably should have perished from frustration in fact I reveled in all that holding and touching. Peter seemed pleased too, and he never demanded more. Later, I suppose, he learned quickly with someone else about what he had been missing. But I remember with gratitude Peter's awkward tenderness and the absolute faith I had in his inability to hurt me.

After Peter graduated and entered the university, our relationship changed. Few high-school girls I knew went out with college men; it was considered risky, like dating someone not quite in your social set or from another town. You were cut off. At the few fraternity functions Peter took me to, I didn't know anyone there. I had no idea what to talk about or how to act. So I refused to go, and I stopped asking Peter to come with me to parties or dances at the high school. I thought he didn't fit in there either. When I was honest with myself, I admitted that romance had gone. Already planning to go away to college, I could sense new vistas opening before me, glowing horizons whose light completely eclipsed a boyfriend like Peter. When I got on the Chicago & Northwestern train to go east to Smith, I felt with relief that the train trip was erasing one problem for me. I simply rode away from Peter.

On my sixteenth birthday, Peter gave me a small cross on a chain. All the guys had decided that year to give their girlfriends crosses on chains, even though none of them was especially religious. It was a perfect gift, they thought, intimate without being soppy. Everyone's cross cost ten dollars, a lot of money, because it was real sterling silver. Long after Peter and I stopped seeing each other, I kept my cross around my neck, not taking it off even when I was in the bathtub. Like my two wooden dolls from years before, I clung to that cross as a superstitious token. It meant that someone I had once cared for had cared for me in return. Once I had had a boyfriend.

## QUESTIONS ON CONTENT

1. What was one of the biggest fears for girls in Toth's time?
2. What kind of car did Toth's boyfriend have?
3. What was the main pastime for teenagers in Toth's circle?
4. What did the teens do at Camp Canwita?
5. What did her boyfriend give her for her sixteenth birthday?

## QUESTIONS ON RHETORIC

1. Look at the last sentence in the first paragraph. What tone does this sentence set up?
2. What do you learn about courting rituals in the 1950s? Look for categories and examples.
3. Toth's essay is chronological. Does she maintain your interest? If so, how? If not, why?
4. Where does Toth add social commentary? Does this interfere with her story?

## VOCABULARY

(1) ardent
(2) meticulously
(3) scrutinized
(4) commiserated
(9) laconic
(13) vistas

## WRITING PROMPTS

1. How do dating customs today compare with Toth's?
2. Write about your first kiss.
3. Write about your first love.
4. Write about your sixteenth birthday.
5. What is the greatest fear teens have today?

# THE POWER OF DETAIL

## NATALIE GOLDBERG

I am in Costa's Chocolate Shop in Owatonna, Minnesota. My friend is opposite me. We've just finished Greek salads and are writing in our notebooks for a half hour among glasses of water, a half-sipped Coke, and a cup of coffee with milk. The booths are orange, and near the front counter are lines of cream candies dipped in chocolate. Across the street is the Owatonna Bank, designed by Louis Sullivan, Frank Lloyd Wright's teacher. Inside the bank is a large cow mural and beautiful stained-glass windows.

Our lives are at once ordinary and mythical. We live and die, age beautifully or full of wrinkles. We wake in the morning, buy yellow cheese, and hope we have enough money to pay for it. At the same instant we have these magnificent hearts that pump through all sorrow and all winters we are alive on the earth. We are important and our lives are important, magnificent really, and their details are worthy to be recorded. This is how writers must think, this is how we must sit down with pen in hand. We were here; we are human beings; this is how we lived. Let it be known, the earth passed before us. Our details are important. Otherwise, if they are not, we can drop a bomb and it doesn't matter.

Yad Vashem, a memorial for the Holocaust, is in Jerusalem. It has a whole library that catalogues the names of the six million martyrs. Not only did the library have their names, it also had where they lived, were born, anything that could be found out about them. These people existed and they mattered. *Yad Vashem*, as a matter of fact, actually means "memorial to the name." It was not nameless masses that were slaughtered; they were human beings.

Likewise, in Washington, D.C., there is the Vietnam memorial. There are fifty thousand names listed—middle names, too—of American soldiers killed in Vietnam. Real human beings with names were killed and their breaths moved out of this world. There was the name of Donald Miller, my second-grade friend who drew tanks, soldiers, and ships in the margins of all his math papers. Seeing names makes us remember. A name is what we carry all our life, and we respond to its call in a classroom, to its pronunciation at a graduation, or to our name whispered in the night.

It is important to say the names of who we are, the names of the places we have lived, and to write the details of our lives. "I lived on Coal Street in Albuquerque next to a garage and carried paper bags of groceries down Lead Avenue. One person had planted beets early that spring, and I watched their red/green leaves grow."

We have lived; our moments are important. This is what it is to be a writer: to be the carrier of details that make up history, to care about the orange booths in the coffee shop in Owatonna.

Recording the details of our lives is a stance against bombs with their mass ability to kill, against too much speed and efficiency. A writer must say yes to life, to all of life: the water glasses, the Kemp's half-and-half, the ketchup on the counter. It is not a writer's task to say, "It is dumb to live in a small town or to eat in a café when you can eat macrobiotic at home." Our task is to say a holy yes to the real things of our life as they exist—the real truth of who we are: several pounds overweight, the gray, cold street outside, the Christmas tinsel in the showcase, the Jewish writer in the orange booth across from her blond friend who has black children. We must become writers who accept things as they are, come to love the details, and step forward with a yes on our lips so there can be no more noes in the world, noes that invalidate life and stop these details from continuing.

## QUESTIONS ON CONTENT

1. Where is the author sitting to write this essay?
2. What two memorials does she write about?
3. Why does the Goldberg believe it's important to capture details of daily life?

## QUESTIONS ON RHETORIC

1. List the details in the opening paragraph. Why are they important to the piece?
2. The essay is divided into three parts. What are they? Is their order of sequence important?
3. Why does the author come back to the opening scene in her final paragraph?

## VOCABULARY

(2) mythical

(7) invalidate

## WRITING PROMPTS

1. Sit in your favorite room and describe it in minute detail.
2. Write about the contents of your pocket, purse, or bookbag. What do these contents say about you?
3. Write about what archeologists would think of the country America or the locale we are in if they uncovered remains 300 years from now. What would they surmise about us as a civilization?
4. Write fully about one day in your life.

# I Get Born

## Zora Neale Hurston

This is all hear-say. Maybe some of the details of my birth as told me might be a little inaccurate, but it is pretty well established that I really did get born.

The saying goes like this. My mother's time had come and my father was not there. Being a carpenter, successful enough to have other helpers on some jobs, he was away often on building business, as well as preaching. It seems that my father was away from home for months this time. I have never been told why. But I did hear that he threatened to cut his throat when he got the news. It seems that one daughter was all that he figured he could stand. My sister, Sarah, was his favorite child, but that one girl was enough. Plenty more sons, but no more girl babies to wear out shoes and bring in nothing. I don't think he ever got over the trick he felt that I played on him by getting born a girl, and while he was off from home at that. A little of my sugar used to sweeten his coffee right now. That is a Negro way of saying his patience was short with me. Let me change a few words with him—and I am of the word changing kind—and he was ready to change ends. Still and all, I looked more like him than any child in the house. Of course, by the time I got born, it was too late to make any suggestions, so the old man had to put up with me. He was nice about it in a way. He didn't tie me in a sack and drop me in the lake, as he probably felt like doing.

People were digging sweet potatoes, and then it was hog-killing time. Not at our house, but it was going on in general over the country like, being January and a bit cool. Most people were either butchering for themselves, or off helping other folks do their butchering, which was almost just as good. It is a gay time. A big pot of hasslits cooking with plenty of seasoning, lean slabs of fresh-killed pork frying for the helpers to refresh themselves after the work is done. Over and above being neighborly and giving aid, there is the food, the drinks and the fun of getting together.

So there was no grown folks close around when Mama's water broke. She sent one of the smaller children to fetch Aunt Judy, the midwife, but she was gone to Woodbridge, a mile and a half away, to eat at a hog-killing. The child was told to go over there and tell Aunt Judy to come. But nature, being indifferent to human arrangements, was impatient. My mother had to make it alone. She was too weak after I rushed out to do anything for herself, so she just was lying there, sick in the body, and worried in mind, wondering what would become of her, as well as me. She was so weak, she couldn't even reach down to where I was. She had one consolation. She knew I wasn't dead, because I was crying strong.

Help came from where she never would have thought to look for it. A white man of many acres and things, who knew the family well, had butchered the day before. Knowing that Papa was not at home, and that consequently there would be no fresh meat in our house, he decided to drive the five miles and bring a half of a shoat, sweet potatoes, and other garden stuff along. He was there a few minutes after I was born. Seeing the front door standing open, he came on in, and hollered, "Hello, there! Call your dogs!" That is the regular way to call in the country because nearly everybody who has anything to watch has biting dogs.

Nobody answered, but he claimed later that he heard me spreading my lungs all over Orange County, so he shoved the door open and bolted on into the house.

He followed the noise and then he saw how things were, and being the kind of a man he was, he took out his Barlow Knife and cut the navel cord, then he did the best he could about other things.

When the midwife, locally known as a granny, arrived about an hour later, there was a fire in the stove and plenty of hot water on. I had been sponged off in some sort of a way, and Mama was holding me in her arms.

As soon as the old woman got there, the white man unloaded what he had brought, and drove off cussing about some blankety-blank people never being where you could put your hands on them when they were needed. He got no thanks from Aunt Judy. She grumbled for years about it. She complained that the cord had not been cut just right, and the bellyband had not been put on tight enough. She was mighty scared I was going to have a weak back, and that I would have trouble holding my water until I reached puberty. I did.

The next day or so a Mrs. Neale, a friend of Mama's, came in and reminded her that she had promised to let her name the baby in case it was a girl. She had picked up a name somewhere which she thought was very pretty. Perhaps she had read it somewhere, or somebody back in those woods was smoking Turkish cigarettes. So I became Zora Neale Hurston.

There is nothing to make you like other human beings so much as doing things for them. Therefore, the man who grannied me was back next day to see how I was coming along. Maybe it was a pride in his own handiwork, and his resourcefulness in a pinch, that made him want to see it through. He remarked that I was a God-damned fine baby, fat and plenty of lung-power. As time went on, he came infrequently, but somehow kept a pinch of interests in my welfare. It seemed that I was spying noble, growing like a gourd vine, and yelling bass like a gator. He was the kind of man that had no use for puny things, so I was all to the good with him. He thought my mother was justified in keeping me.

But nine months rolled around, and I just would not get on with the walking business. I was strong, crawling well, but showed no inclination to use my feet. I might remark in passing, that I still don't like to walk. Then I was over a year old, but still I would not walk. They made allowances for my weight, but yet, that was no real reason for my not trying.

They tell me that an old sow-hog taught me how to walk. That is, she didn't instruct me in detail, but she convinced me that I really ought to try. It was like this. My mother was going to have collard greens for dinner, so she took the dishpan and went down to the spring to wash the greens. She left me sitting on the floor, and gave me a hunk of cornbread to keep me quiet. Everything was going along all right, until the sow with her litter of pigs in convoy came abreast of the door. She must have smelled the cornbread I was messing with and scattering crumbs about the floor. So, she came right on in, and began to nuzzle around.

My mother heard my screams and came running. Her heart must have stood still when she saw the sow in there, because hogs have been known to eat human flesh.

But I was not taking this thing sitting down. I had been placed by a chair, and when my mother got inside the door, I had pulled myself up by that chair and was getting around it right smart.

As for the sow, poor misunderstood lady, she had no interest in me except my bread. I lost that in scrambling to my feet and she was eating it. She had much less intention of eating Mama's baby, than Mama had of eating hers. With no more suggestions from the sow or anybody else, it seems that I just took to walking and kept the thing a-going. The strangest thing about it was that once I found the use of my feet, they took to wandering. I always wanted to go. I would wander off in the woods all alone, following some inside urge to go places. This alarmed my mother a great deal. She used to say that she believed a woman who was an enemy of hers had sprinkled "travel dust" around the doorstep the day I was born. That was the only explanation she could find. I don't know why it never occurred to her to connect my tendency with my father, who didn't have a thing on his mind but this town and the next one. That should have given her a sort of hint. Some children are just bound to take after their fathers in spite of women's prayers.

## QUESTIONS ON CONTENT

1. Why did Hurston's father not want another daughter?
2. Where was Hurston's father when she was born?

3. Who attended the birth?
4. How did Hurston learn to walk?

## QUESTIONS ON RHETORIC

1. Look at Hurston's first sentence. What effect does it have on readers?
2. The second paragraph is not really about Hurston's birth. Why do you think she included it?
3. What bits of folklore and local color do you find? How does this add to Hurston's story?
4. Hurston's story actually has two parts. What would be some good titles for the second half?
5. How could Hurston write with such detail about a time that she probably does not remember?

## VOCABULARY

(3) hasslits
(5) shoat
(10) grannied
(12) convoy

## WRITING PROMPTS

1. Write your birth story. If need be, ask relatives or friends for details.
2. Write about something significant that happened in the early years of your life.
3. Write about your parents when you were young. How does that compare to your parents now?
4. Write about any "inside urge" you have.
5. Where do you come from?
6. What life messages did you get from your father? From your mother? How do they compare? How do they differ?

# 2
---
# POPULAR PRESS
## ESSAYS

# SENIOR-TEENER.
# A NEW HYBRID

## DOROTHY NOYES

Come next May, there's no denying the fact that I'll have racked up 89 years as an inhabitant of planet earth. One glance and you'd know I'm a Senior. The hair on my head is white, and although my face is not overly lined, it's obvious that I'm past 50 or 60 or even 70. While I work at standing erect, my shoulders slouch a bit. And, despite regular swim sessions and frequent brisk walks, I have difficulty hiding my protruding belly. But the *inner* me, the *emotional* me, is so frequently a Teener. I feel much as I did 75 years ago: alone, tremulous and fearful about my future.

Were Charles Darwin to arise from the dead, I'd say to him, "There's a new subspecies abroad today, sir." And I'd tell him about its evolution during the latter part of the 20th century when humankind—particularly womankind—was living longer and longer in an amazing state of physical health. But I'd have to come clean as to the emotional downside: the sense of queasiness that from time to time overtakes an otherwise reasonably fit body. For today I'm often jittery and "out of it" as in long-ago days—no special boyfriend or agemates. Three husbands have predeceased me, and my longtime female intimates have also made their final exits.

At the start of my adolescence, my self-confidence was on the low side. Because I was born a southpaw, conventional wisdom forced me to learn to write with the "right" hand. Even now, my friends' exhortations to "type, don't write" can be amusing but far from uplifting. That I was clumsy was dinned into me time and again. Well, I still feel clumsy.

Transplant shock also took its toll. When I was 12, and for the next several years, we lived in cities in three different states. This meant four high schools. I've never succeeded in blocking out the memory of that sense of desolation when I was 13 ½ and a sophomore in Montclair High School in New Jersey—far from the kids I knew as a freshman in Evanston, Ill. That unforgettable moment when I saw the spot on my white skirt: I was a child no longer. How to blot it out? Where to go?

This is somewhat comparable to one of Seniors' embarrassing problems: the need for protective garments to cope with the unexpected lack of control over failing body parts. While Senior and Teener are not *look*-alikes, they're so often *act*-alikes.

Obviously, the female bodily changes of Teener and Senior are not the same. Teener's route is onward and upward, though it doesn't always seem so to her as she deplores some of the external blemishes. For Senior it's mostly downhill, obliged as she is to spend more and more time in body-repair shops to compensate for eyes and ears and other organs that malfunction. Our commonality lies in our need to face up to the inevitable biologic changes with equanimity—to learn the art of self-mastery, of peaceful acceptance of the inevitable and of our own self-worth as life cycle spirals on. Living comfortably with one's own body with its limitations and defects is no easy assignment.

One of our most difficult challenges comes from the outside world. It's another factor that makes our struggle to mature so alike: coping with those numerous unsympathetic, contemptuous and sometimes outright hostile others. Like those folk who accuse Teeners of being too self-absorbed, irresponsible, sex-driven, booze-drinking, "no good"; and for those who look upon Seniors with much disdain, not as national treasures.

Virtually from the first moment last spring when I was introduced to the about-to-be-15-year-old stepdaughter of my godson, I remembered how, long ago, I cherished the companionship of an elderly spinster who paid special attention to insecure young me. This probably prompted me to issue a spur-of-the-moment invitation to Christine. She seemed ecstatic at the thought of spending part of a holiday weekend with me. All during the first day as we meandered through Central Park and again at dinner and at the dance theater, I was struck by her apparent maturity—fascinated as she was in studying people's faces. "What do you suppose they're thinking about, Dorothy?" But this confidence—this absorption with others—was not to last. Christine was pondering her trip home the next day: alone in a taxi and the crowd at Penn Station! She hated to bother me, but would I mind coming along as a pal, just in case...? Of course I went. Her scary moment of panic came when she couldn't find the platform for the train's departure. (I experience comparable panicky self-doubt when I'm under pressure.)

In the early '60s, when Doubleday was about to publish my first book, there was great discussion as to the title of this parental "how to" guide. It was understandable that it should be called "Your Child," based as it was in part on my syndicated newspaper column with that title. The big question was: should we add "from birth to maturity"? Not *to* maturity, I insisted, but rather *toward* maturity. For who knows when maturity has been reached? And, besides, what kind of maturity are we thinking about?

For Teener, maturity means graduation from kid-dom—the search for personhood in her own right, the freedom to find her own worth and her own place. For Senior, maturity means greater acceptance of waning physical powers and the ability to continue to grow in understanding and, yes, in wisdom—to accept death as part of life. Neither Teener nor Senior can control biological maturity, but each can have much effect over psychological and philosophical maturity.

Many times, the Teener part of this hybrid is thrown by what she feels must be grasped to gain self-mastery and to appreciate what life is all about. So, too, the Senior is frequently nonplussed by how much more there is to discover about our universe. And time is running short—gotta crowd in as much as possible as fast as possible! Each of us must deal with continuing bodily changes and our reactions to them as well as with our changing relationships with our fellow earthlings. Both of us long for many of those Others to appreciate what seems to be the professional consensus that Teeners and Seniors both are almost *over*endowed with heartfelt compassion for all humankind.

## Questions on Content

1. How old is the author? How old does she feel?
2. What two groups does the author compare?
3. How does Noyes define maturity?

## Questions on Rhetoric

1. What is the new subspecies Noyes would tell Darwin about?
2. What comparisons between senior and teenagers does Noyes use? Do you feel they are apt? How does she develop her comparisons?
3. Noyes talks of the "outright hostile others." Who are they? Why do they have such an impact?
4. Do you find it interesting that a 15-year-old girl would ask an 89-year-old woman to come along to the train station?

## Vocabulary

(3) exhortations, dinned
(4) desolation
(6) equanimity
(8) spinster
(11) hybrid, consensus

## Writing Prompts

1. Have you ever had a friendship with someone of a vastly different age? Write about that relationship and why it existed.
2. How does our culture view the elderly? How does that equate with other cultures?
3. Write about the "graying of America."
4. When did you decide you were mature? Write about that realization.

# THE TRIUMPH OF THE YELL

## DEBORAH TANNEN

I put the question to a journalist who had written a vitriolic attack on a leading feminist researcher: "Why do you need to make others wrong for you to be right?" Her response: "It's an argument!"

That's the problem. More and more these days, journalists, politicians and academics treat public discourse as an argument— not in the sense of *making* an argument, but in the sense of *having* one, of having a fight.

When people have arguments in private life, they're not trying to understand what the other person is saying. They're listening for weaknesses in logic to leap on, points they can distort to make the other look bad. We all do this when we're angry, but is it the best model for public intellectual interchange? This breakdown of the boundary between public and private is contributing to what I have come to think of as a culture of critique.

Fights have winners and losers. If you're fighting to win, the temptation is great to deny facts that support your opponent's views and present only those facts that support your own.

At worst, there's a temptation to lie. We accept this style of arguing because we believe we can tell when someone is lying. But we can't. Paul Ekman, a psychologist at the University of California at San Francisco, has found that even when people are very sure they can tell whether or not someone is dissembling, their judgments are as likely as not to be wrong.

If public discourse is a fight, every issue must have two sides— no more, no less. And it's crucial to show "the other side," even if one has to scour the margins of science or the fringes of lunacy to find it. The culture of critique is based on the belief that opposition leads to truth: when both sides argue, the truth will emerge. And because people are presumed to enjoy watching a fight, the most extreme views are presented, since they make the best show. But it is a myth that opposition leads to truth when truth does not reside on one side or the other but is rather a crystal of many sides. Truth is more likely to be found in the complex middle than in the simplified extremes, but the spectacles that result when extremes clash are thought to get higher ratings or larger readership.

Because the culture of critique encourages people to attack and often misrepresent others, those others must waste their creativity and time correcting the misrepresentations and defending themselves. Serious scholars have had to spend years of their lives writing books proving that the Holocaust happened, because a few fanatics who claim it didn't have been given a public forum. Those who provide the platform know that what these people say is, simply put, not true, but rationalize the dissemination of lies as showing "the other side." The determination to find another side can spread disinformation rather than lead to truth.

The culture of critique has given rise to the journalistic practice of confronting prominent people with criticism couched as others' views. Meanwhile, the interviewer has planted an accusation in readers' or viewers' minds. The theory seems to be that when provoked, people are spurred to eloquence and self-revelation. Perhaps some are. But others are unable to say what they know because they are hurt, and begin to sputter when their sense of fairness is outraged. In those cases, opposition is not the path to truth.

When people in power know that what they say will be scrutinized for weaknesses and probably distorted, they become more guarded. As an acquaintance recently explained about himself, public figures who once gave long, free-wheeling press conferences now limit themselves to reading brief statements. When less information gets communicated, opposition does not lead to truth.

Opposition also limits information when only those who are adept at verbal sparring take part in public discourse, and those who cannot handle it, or do not like it, decline to participate. This winnowing process is evident in graduate schools, where many talented students drop out because what they expected to be a community of intellectual inquiry turned out to be a ritual game of attack and counterattack.

One such casualty graduated from a small liberal arts college, where she "luxuriated in the endless discussions." At the urging of her professors, she decided to make academia her profession. But she changed her mind after a year in an art history program at a major university. She felt she had fallen into a "den of wolves." "I wasn't cut out for academia," she concluded. But does academia have to be so combative that it cuts people like her out?

In many university classrooms, "critical thinking" means reading someone's life work, then ripping it to shreds. Though critique is surely one form of critical thinking, so are integrating ideas from disparate fields and examining the context out of which they grew. Opposition does not lead to truth when we ask only "What's wrong with this argument?" and never "What can we use from this in building a new theory, and a new understanding?"

Several years ago I was on a television talk show with a representative of the men's movement. I didn't foresee any problem, since there is nothing in my work that is anti-male. But in the room where guests gather before the show I found a man wearing a shirt and tie and a floor-length skirt, with waist-length red hair. He politely introduced himself and told me he liked my book. Then he added: "When I get out there, I'm going to attack you. But don't take it personally. That's why they invite me on, so that's what I'm going to do."

When the show began, I spoke only a sentence or two before this man nearly jumped out of his chair, threw his arms before him in gestures of anger and began shrieking—first attacking me, but soon moving on to rail against women. The most disturbing thing about his hysterical ranting was what it sparked in the studio audience: they too became vicious, attacking not me (I hadn't had a chance to say anything) and not him (who wants to tangle with someone who will scream at you?) but the other guests: unsuspecting women who had agreed to come on the show to talk about their problems communicating with their spouses.

This is the most dangerous aspect of modeling intellectual interchange as a fight: it contributes to an atmosphere of animosity that spreads like a fever. In a society where people express their anger by shooting, the result of demonizing those with whom we disagree can be truly demonic.

I am not suggesting that journalists stop asking tough questions necessary to get at the facts, even if those questions may appear challenging. And of course it is the responsibility of the media to represent serious opposition when it exists, and of intellectuals everywhere to explore potential weaknesses in others' arguments. But when opposition becomes the overwhelming avenue of inquiry, when the lust for opposition exalts extreme views and obscures complexity, when our eagerness to find weaknesses blinds us to strengths, when the atmosphere of animosity precludes respect and poisons our relations with one another, then the culture of critique is stifling us. If we could move beyond it, we would move closer to the truth.

## QUESTIONS ON CONTENT

1. Define *argument* as Tannen sees it.
2. Who does Tannen blame for the disintegration of discourse?
3. According to Tannen, where is truth found?

## QUESTIONS ON RHETORIC

1. What is the purpose of the first paragraph?
2. What's the difference in making an argument and having an argument?

3. Do you agree with Tannen that the media has perpetuated the degeneration of public discourse?
4. What purpose does the example of the talk show guest (paragraphs 14–15) serve?

## VOCABULARY

(1) vitriolic

(5) dissembling

(7) critique

(8) dissemination

(11) sparring, winnowing

(13) disparate

(16) animosity

## WRITING PROMPTS

1. Write about talk shows that become yelling matches and their effect on the public.
2. Write about Tannen's title to this piece.
3. Do you feel you communicate differently than the other gender? How so?
4. Are you involved in a "culture of critique" at work or school? Describe its effects on you.

# Women in the Wild Blue Yonder

## Elaine Tyler May

Now that Congress has opened the door for women to enter the ranks of combat pilots, many Americans find themselves uncomfortable with the idea. Why do so many people cringe at the thought of women in combat? Full access to the military is a logical next step on the road to equal opportunity for women. Perhaps the real question is why it has taken so long for women to enter battle.

The combat barrier somehow seems different, more ominous than other rights gained by women. Not because it marks the invasion of women into one of the few remaining bastions of masculinity, but because it threatens what is perhaps the sole surviving gender myth of the twentieth century: that women are the world's nurturers. Can a nurturer also be a destroyer?

Those opposed to sending women into combat sidestep the issue. Some claim that women are not physically strong enough to serve as fighter pilots. That argument collapses at a time when strength and endurance are as readily developed in women as in men. Besides, these women would be flying planes, not lifting them. And with sophisticated weaponry, women can push the buttons to drop the bombs as easily as men can.

Others argue that men should protect women, not the other way around. That chivalry might make some sense if it operated anywhere else in our society. But women are at risk in other occupations, where hazards to their safety abound. It is disingenuous to hear calls for their protection in battle when they are not even protected at home, where domestic abuse and violence against women are widespread.

Still, maybe war is different. Since our War of Independence, women have participated in warfare. They have provided supplies and medical care, even on the front lines. During World War I, men were urged to fight for mothers, wives and sweethearts back home.

In World War II, sentimental views of women were replaced by other images. Rosie the Riveter became a national icon, doing "men's work" in war industries. These female workers were glorified, though they were expected to relinquish their well-paying, physically demanding jobs after the war. At the same time, symbols of female sexuality entered the iconography of war. Pinups appeared in military barracks; the noses of thousands of bombers were decorated with erotic portraits.

If the U.S. hires women as professional killers, allowing them into the cockpit, what remains of the sentimental ideal of women as pure and gentle creatures might vanish. It is not so much that women might get killed; it is that they might kill.

The ability to kill is the ultimate equalizer. Indeed, the integration of combat units after World War II signaled a major change in the nation's racial relations. The symbolic impact of women fighting in combat cannot be overlooked.

Power, of course, is intimately connected to sex. It is no accident that another policy under discussion bans homosexuals from the armed forces. In World War II and the cold war, women and gays were barred from combat, in part because they were believed to be security risks.

We now know that in spite of the ban, many gay men and women served heroically in World War II. Still, military policies are based on the theory that the only good fighting force is one in which heterosexual men pursue their mission free from sexual temptation. Since no such force has ever existed, it is difficult to know if there is any truth to the myth.

There are those on the other side of the debate who argue that women are really less warlike than men and that bringing them fully into the military would humanize the armed services. Perhaps. But we won't know, at least not until women fill the leadership ranks of the military establishment—from running major defense industries and the Pentagon to serving as the Commander in Chief herself.

## QUESTIONS ON CONTENT

1. What is the "combat barrier"?
2. What happened to the image of women in World War II?
3. The idea of sentimental women is being replaced with what idea?

## QUESTIONS ON RHETORIC

1. What arguments does May offer in support of the combat barrier? In opposition?
2. Does she present both sides objectively?
3. Is the issue of gays in the military a red herring, or a diversion, or does it have relevance to the argument?
4. What it the gender myth? Is it alive in the twenty-first century?
5. Who is May's audience? Why do you think so?

## VOCABULARY

(2) ominous, bastions
(4) chivalry, disingenuous
(6) icon
(8) symbolic

## WRITING PROMPTS

1. Write about May's question, "Can a nurturer also be a destroyer?"
2. Are you a victim of the gender myth?
3. Write about women in the military and include both sides of the issue.
4. Write about a man in our society who chooses to be a nurturer rather than a destroyer.

# Just Walk On By

## Brent Staples

My first victim was a woman—white, well dressed, probably in her early twenties. I came upon her late one evening on a deserted street in Hyde Park, a relatively affluent neighborhood in an otherwise mean, impoverished section of Chicago. As I swung onto the avenue behind her, there seemed to be a discreet, uninflammatory distance between us. Not so. She cast back a worried glance. To her, the youngish black man—a broad six feet two inches with a beard and billowing hair, both hands shoved into the pockets of a bulky military jacket—seemed menacingly close. After a few more quick glimpses, she picked up her pace and was soon running in earnest. Within seconds she disappeared into a cross street.

That was more than a decade ago. I was 22 years old, a graduate student newly arrived at the University of Chicago. It was in the echo of that terrified woman's footfalls that I first began to know the unwieldy inheritance I'd come into—the ability to alter public space in ugly ways. It was clear that she thought herself the quarry of a mugger, a rapist, or worse. Suffering a bout of insomnia, however, I was stalking sleep, not defenseless wayfarers. As a softy who is scarcely able to take a knife to a raw chicken—let alone hold it to a person's throat—I was surprised, embarrassed, and dismayed all at once. Her flight made me feel like an accomplice in tyranny. It also made it clear that I was indistinguishable from the muggers who occasionally seeped into the area from the surrounding ghetto. That first encounter, and those that followed, signified that a vast, unnerving gulf lay between nighttime pedestrians—particularly women—and me. And I soon gathered that being perceived as dangerous is a hazard in itself. I only needed to turn a corner into a dicey situation, or crowd some frightened, armed person in a foyer somewhere, or make an errant move after being pulled over by a policeman. Where fear and weapons meet—and they often do in urban America—there is always the possibility of death.

In that first year, my first away from my hometown, I was to become thoroughly familiar with the language of fear. At dark, shadowy intersections in Chicago, I could cross in front of a car stopped at a traffic light and elicit the *thunk, thunk, thunk, thunk* of the driver—black white, male, or female—hammering down the door locks. On less traveled streets after dark, I grew accustomed to but never comfortable with people who crossed to the other side of the street rather than pass me. Then there were the standard unpleasantries with police, doormen, bouncers, cab drivers, and others whose business it is to screen out troublesome individuals *before* there is any nastiness.

I moved to New York nearly two years ago and I have remained an avid night walker. In central Manhattan, the near-constant crowd cover minimizes tense one-on-one street encounters. Elsewhere—visiting friends in SoHo, where sidewalks are narrow and tightly spaced buildings shut out the sky—things can get very taut indeed.

Black men have a firm place in New York mugging literature. Norman Podhoretz in his famed (or infamous) 1963 essay, "My Negro Problem—And Ours," recalls growing up in terror of black males; they "were tougher than we were, more ruthless," he writes—and as an adult on the Upper West Side of Manhattan, he continues, he cannot constrain his nervousness when he meets black men on certain streets. Similarly, a decade later, the essayist and novelist Edward Hoagland extols a New York where once "Negro bitterness bore down mainly on other Negroes." Where some see mere panhandlers, Hoagland sees "a mugger who is clearly screwing up his nerve to do more than just *ask* for money." But Hoagland has "the New Yorker's quickhunch posture for broken-field maneuvering," and the bad guy swerves away.

I often witness that "hunch posture," from women after dark on the warrenlike streets of Brooklyn where I live. They seem to set their faces on neutral and, with their purse straps strung across their chests bandolier style, they forge ahead as though bracing themselves against being tackled. I understand, of course, that the danger they perceive is not a hallucination. Women are particularly vulnerable to street violence, and young black males are drastically overrepresented among the perpetrators of that violence. Yet these truths are no solace against the kind of alienation that comes of being ever the suspect, against being set apart, a fearsome entity with whom pedestrians avoid making eye contact.

It is not altogether clear to me how I reached the ripe old age of 22 without being conscious of the lethality nighttime pedestrians attributed to me. Perhaps it was because in Chester, Pennsylvania, the small, angry industrial town where I came of age in the 1960s, I was scarcely noticeable against a backdrop of gang warfare, street knifings, and murders. I grew up one of the good boys, had perhaps a half-dozen fist fights. In retrospect, my shyness of combat has clear sources.

Many things go into the making of a young thug. One of those things is the consummation of the male romance with the power to intimidate. An infant discovers that random flailings send the baby bottle flying out of the crib and crashing to the floor. Delighted, the joyful babe repeats those motions again and again, seeking to duplicate the feat. Just so, I recall the points at which some of my boyhood friends were finally seduced by the perception of themselves as tough guys. When a mark cowered and surrendered his money without resistance, myth and reality merged — and paid off. It is, after all, only manly to embrace the power to frighten and intimidate. We, as men, are not supposed to give an inch of our lane on the highway; we are to seize the fighter's edge in work and in play and even in love; we are to be valiant in the face of hostile forces.

Unfortunately, poor and powerless young men seem to take all this nonsense literally. As a boy, I saw countless tough guys locked away. I have since buried several, too. They were babies, really—a teenage cousin, a brother of 22, a childhood friend in his mid-twenties—all gone down in episodes of bravado played out in the streets. I came to doubt the virtues of intimidation early on. I chose, perhaps even unconsciously, to remain a shadow—timid, but a survivor.

The fearsomeness mistakenly attributed to me in public places often has a perilous flavor. The most frightening of these confusions occurred in the late 1970s and early 1980s when I worked as a journalist in Chicago. One day, rushing into the office of a magazine I was writing for with a deadline story in hand, I was mistaken for a burglar. The office manager called security and, with an ad hoc posse, pursued me through the labyrinthine halls, nearly to my editor's door. I had no way of proving who I was. I could only move briskly toward the company of someone who knew me.

Another time I was on assignment for a local paper and killing time before an interview. I entered a jewelry store on the city's affluent Near North Side. The proprietor excused herself and returned with an enormous red Doberman pinscher straining at the end of a leash. She stood, the dog extended toward me, silent to my questions, her eyes bulging nearly out of her head. I took a cursory look around, nodded, and bade her good night. Relatively speaking, however, I never fared as badly as another black male journalist. He went to nearby Waukegan, Illinois, a couple of summers ago to work on a story about a murderer who was born there. Mistaking the reporter for the killer, police hauled him from his car at gunpoint and but for his press credentials would probably have tried to book him. Such episodes are not uncommon. Black men trade tales like this all the time.

In "My Negro Problem—And Ours," Podhoretz writes that the hatred he feels for blacks makes itself known to him through a variety of avenues—one being his discomfort with that "special brand of paranoid touchiness" to which he says blacks are prone. No doubt he is speaking here of black men. In time, I learned to smother the rage I felt at so often being taken for a criminal. Not to do so would surely have led to madness—via that special "paranoid touchiness" that so annoyed Podhoretz at the time he wrote the essay.

I began to take precautions to make myself less threatening. I move about with care, particularly late in the evening. I give a wide berth to nervous people on subway platforms during the wee hours, particularly when I have exchanged business clothes for jeans. If I happen to be entering a building behind some people who appear skittish, I may walk by, letting them clear the lobby before I return, so as not to seem to be following them. I have been calm and extremely congenial on those rare occasions when I've been pulled over by the police.

And on late-evening constitutionals along streets less traveled by, I employ what has proved to be an excellent tension-reducing measure. I whistle melodies from Beethoven and Vivaldi and the more popular classical composers. Even steely New Yorkers hunching toward nighttime destinations seem to relax, and occasionally they even join in the tune. Virtually everybody seems to sense that a mugger wouldn't be warbling bright, sunny selections from Vivaldi's *Four Seasons*. It is my equivalent of the cowbell that hikers wear when they know they are in bear country.

## RESPONDING TO READING

1. Staples speaks quite matter-of-factly of the fear he inspires. Does your experience support his assumption that black men have the "ability to alter public space"? Why or why not? Do you believe white men also have this ability? Explain.
2. In paragraph 13, Staples suggests some strategies that he believes make him "less threatening." What else, if anything, do you think he could do? Do you believe he should adopt such strategies? Explain your position.
3. Although Staples says he arouses fear in others, he also admits that he himself feels fearful. Why? Do you think he has reason to be fearful?

## Questions on Content

1. Staples states, "My first victim was a woman." Victim of what?
2. Why does Staples feel black men have the "ability to alter public space"?
3. What does Staples do now when he walks alone at night to reduce tension?

## Questions on Rhetoric

1. Why does Staples call his first encounter with this situation "a victim"?
2. What examples does the author give to build his case that the phenomenon is real?
3. Why does Staples include quotes form Podhoretz and Hoagland? Who are they? Does it matter?
4. Paragraph 8 states, "Many things go into the making of a young thug." Does this statement refer only to black males?
5. Do you believe that the "ability to alter public space" is based on race? Why?

## Vocabulary

(1) uninflammatory, menacingly

(2) unwieldy, quarry, tyranny, errant

(4) taut

(6) warrenlike, bandolier, solace, entity

(8) valiant

(10) perilous, ad hoc

(12) paranoid

## WRITING PROMPTS

1. Have you ever been judged solely on your appearance?
2. Have you ever been in a minority? How did it affect your behavior?
3. Write about stereotypes.
4. Write about a time when no one would listen to you.

# WHAT, ME? SHOWING OFF?

## JUDITH VIORST

We're at the Biedermans' annual blast, and over at the far end of the living room an intense young woman with blazing eyes and a throbbing voice is decrying poverty, war, injustice and human suffering. Indeed, she expresses such anguish at the anguish of mankind that attention quickly shifts from the moral issues she is expounding to how very, very, very deeply she cares about them.

She's showing off.

Down at the other end of the room an insistently scholarly fellow has just used *angst, hubris,* Kierkegaard and *epistemology* in the same sentence. Meanwhile our resident expert in wine meditatively sips, then pushes away, a glass of unacceptable Beaujolais.

They're showing off.

And then there's us, complaining about how tired we are today because we went to work, rushed back to see our son's school play, shopped at the market and hurried home in order to cook gourmet, and then needlepointed another dining-room chair.

And what we also are doing is showing off.

Indeed everyone, I would like to propose, has some sort of need to show off. No one's completely immune. Not you. And not I. And although we've been taught that it's bad to boast, that it's trashy to toot our own horn, that nice people don't strut their stuff, seek attention or name-drop, there are times when showing off may be forgivable and maybe even acceptable.

But first let's take a look at showing off that *is* obnoxious, that's *not* acceptable, that's never nice. Like showoffs motivated by a fierce, I'm-gonna-blow-you-away competitiveness. And like narcissistic showoffs who are willing to do anything to be—and stay—the center of attention.

Competitive showoffs want to be the best of every bunch. Competitive showoffs must outshine all others. Whatever is being discussed, they have more—expertise or money or even aggravation—and better—periodontists or children or marriages or recipes for pesto—and deeper—love of animals or concern for human suffering or orgasms. Competitive showoffs are people who reside in a permanent state of sibling rivalry, insisting on playing Hertz to everyone else's Avis.

(You're finishing a story, for instance, about the sweet little card that your five-year-old recently made for your birthday when the CSO interrupts to relate how her daughter not only made her a sweet little card, but also brought her breakfast in bed and saved her allowance for months and months in order to buy her—obviously much more beloved—mother a beautiful scarf for her birthday. *Grrr.*)

Narcissistic showoffs, however, don't bother to compete because they don't even notice there's anyone there to compete with. They talk nonstop, they brag, they dance, they sometimes quote Homer in Greek, and they'll even go stand on their head if attention should flag. Narcissistic showoffs want to be the star while everyone else is the audience. And yes, they are often adorable and charming and amusing—but only until around the age of six.

(I've actually seen an NSO get up and leave the room when the conversation shifted from his accomplishments. "What's the matter?" I asked when I found him standing on the terrace, brooding darkly. "Oh, I don't know," he replied, "but all of a sudden the talk started getting so superficial." *Aagh!*)

Another group of showoffs—much more sympathetic types—are showoffs who are basically insecure. And while there is no easy way to distinguish the insecure from the narcissists and competitors, you may figure out which are which by whether you have the urge to reassure or to strangle them.

Insecure showoffs show off because, as one close friend explained, "How will they know that I'm good unless I tell them about it?" And whatever the message—I'm smart, I'm a fine human being, I'm this incredibly passionate lover—showoffs have many different techniques for telling about it.

Take smart, for example.

A person can show off explicitly by using flashy words, like the hubris-Kierkegaard fellow I mentioned before.

Or a person can show off implicitly, by saying not a word and just wearing a low-cut dress with her Phi Beta Kappa key gleaming softly in the cleavage.

A person can show off satirically, by mocking showing off: "My name is Bill Sawyer," one young man announces to every new acquaintance, "and I'm bright bright bright bright bright."

Or a person can show off complainingly: "I'm sorry my daughter takes after me. Men are just so frightened of smart women."

Another way showoffs show off about smart is to drop a Very Smart Name—if this brain is my friend, goes the message, I must be a brain too. And indeed, a popular showing-off ploy—whether you're showing off smartness or anything else—is to name-drop a glittery name in the hope of acquiring some gilt by association.

The theory seems to be that Presidents, movie stars, Walter Cronkite and Princess Di could be friends, if they chose, with anyone in the world, and that if these luminaries have selected plain old Stanley Stone to be friends with, Stanley Stone must be one hell of a guy. (Needless to say, old Stanley Stone might also be a very dreary fellow, but if Walt and Di don't mind him, why should I?)

Though no one that I know hangs out with Presidents and movie stars, they do (I too!) sometimes drop famous names.

As in: "I go to John Travolta's dermatologist."

Or: "I own the exact same sweater that Jackie Onassis wore in a newspaper photograph last week."

Or: "My uncle once repaired a roof for Sandra Day O'Connor."

Or: "My cousin's neighbor's sister-in-law has a child who is Robert Redford's son's best friend."

We're claiming we've got gilt—though by a very indirect association. And I think that when we do, we're showing off.

Sometimes showoffs ask for cheers to which they're not entitled. Sometimes showoffs earn the praise they seek. And sometimes folks achieve great things and nonetheless do not show off about it.

Now *that's* impressive.

Indeed, when we discover that the quiet mother of four with whom we've been talking intimately all evening has recently been elected to the state senate—*and she never even mentioned it!*—we are filled with admiration, with astonishment, with awe.

What self-restraint!

For we know damn well—*I* certainly know—that if we'd been that lucky lady, we'd have worked our triumph into the conversation. As a matter of fact, I'll lay my cards right on the table and confess that the first time some poems of mine were published, I not only worked my triumph into every conversation for months and months, but I also called almost every human being I'd ever known to proclaim the glad tidings both local and long distance. Furthermore—let me really confess—if a stranger happened to stop me on the street and all he wanted to know was the time or directions, I tried to detain him long enough to enlighten him with the news that the person to whom he was speaking was a Real Live Genuine Honest-to-God Published Poet.

Fortunately for everyone, I eventually—it took me awhile—calmed down.

Now, I don't intend to defend myself—I was showing off, I was bragging and I wasn't the slightest bit shy or self-restrained, but a golden, glowing, glorious thing had happened in my life and I had an overwhelming need to exult. Exulting, however (as I intend to argue farther on), may be a permissible form of showing off.

Exulting is what my child does when he comes home with an *A* on his history paper ("Julius Caesar was 50," it began, "and his good looks was pretty much demolished") and wants to read me the entire masterpiece while I murmur appreciative comments at frequent intervals.

Exulting is what my husband does when he cooks me one of his cheese-and-scallion omelets and practically does a tap dance as he carries it from the kitchen stove to the table, setting it before me with the purely objective assessment that this may be the greatest omelet ever created.

Exulting is what my mother did when she took her first grandson to visit all her friends, and announced as she walked into the room, "Is he gorgeous? Is that a gorgeous baby? Is that the most gorgeous baby you ever saw?"

And exulting is what that mother of four would have done if she'd smiled and said, "Don't call me 'Marge' any more. Call me 'Senator.'"

Exulting is shamelessly shouting our talents or triumphs to the world. It's saying: I'm taking a bow and I'd like to hear clapping. And I think if we don't overdo it (stopping strangers to say you've been published is overdoing it), and I think if we know when to quit ("Enough about me. Let's talk about you. So what do you think about me?" does not count as quitting), and I think if we don't get addicted (i.e., crave a praise-fix for every poem or *A* or omelet), and I think if we're able to walk off the stage (and clap and cheer while others take their bows), then I think we're allowed, from time to time, to exult.

Though showing off can range from very gross to very subtle, and though the point of showing off is sometimes nasty, sometimes needy, sometimes nice, showoffs always run the risk of being thought immodest, of being harshly viewed as...well...showoffs. And so for folks who want applause without relinquishing their sense of modesty, the trick is keeping quiet and allowing someone else to show off *for* you.

And I've seen a lot of marriages where wives show off for husbands and where husbands, in return, show off for wives. Where Joan, for instance, mentions Dick's promotion and his running time in the marathon. And where Dick, for instance, mentions all the paintings Joanie sold at her last art show. And where both of them lean back with self-effacing shrugs and smiles and never once show off about themselves.

Friends also may show off for friends, and parents for their children, though letting parents toot our horns is risky. Consider, for example, this sad tale of Elliott, who was a fearless and feisty public-interest lawyer:

"My son," his proud mother explained to his friends, "has always been independent." (Her son blushed modestly.)

"My son," his proud mother continued, "was the kind of person who always knew his own mind." (Her son blushed modestly.)

"My son," his proud mother went on, "was never afraid. He never kowtowed to those in authority." (Her son blushed modestly.)

"My son," his proud mother concluded, "was so independent and stubborn and unafraid of authority that we couldn't get him toilet-trained—he wet his pants till he was well past four." (Her son...)

But showing off is always a risk, whether we do it ourselves or whether somebody else is doing it for us. And perhaps we ought to consider the words Lord Chesterfield wrote to his sons: "Modesty is the only sure bait when you angle for praise."

And yes, of course he's right, we know he's right, he must be right. But sometimes it's so hard to be restrained. For no matter what we do, we always have a lapse or two. So let's try to forgive each other for showing off.

## QUESTIONS ON CONTENT

1. According to Viorst, who is immune to showing off?
2. What are three categories of show-offs?
3. What was Viorst's first show-off?

## QUESTIONS ON RHETORIC

1. Look at Viorst's organization pattern. What effect does it have?
2. Do the categories Viorst use overlap? Have subcategories? Get confusing?

3. Do the narratives interspersed add to Viorst's point or distract from it? Would her essay be as effective without them?
4. Do you agree with Viorst that some show-offs are acceptable?
5. Look at the vocalizations at the end of paragraphs 10 and 12. How do these affect the tone of the essay?

## VOCABULARY

(1) intense

(8) narcissistic

(16) explicitly

(17) implicitly

(18) satirically

(21) luminaries

(34) exult

(41) self-effacing

## WRITING PROMPTS

1. Write about a show-off you know.
2. Write about the time you showed off.
3. Who and what are you likely to notice?
4. Write a coping guide for dealing with show-offs.

# RECALLING A FATHER
# WHO DIED

## ELLEN GOODMAN

My father died when I was 24. It was much too soon. For both of us. In the last months, this most articulate man who loved humor and debate was literally at a loss for words. In some final cruelty, cancer took his language before it took his life.

On my last visit, we didn't say much to each other. He couldn't locate the right words in the vast, jumbled dictionary of his remaining consciousness. It was if he typed RED on a piece of paper and it came out a DOG or SHE. He was cursed with knowing that.

I couldn't find the right words either. Goodbye was too simple and too terrible. I busied both of us with the comfort of daily bulletins of family life.

In the year that followed his death, on the long flat Michigan highway between home and work, I held conversations with him in the car. The car was always a good place to talk.

I was a grown-up by every formal measure, but I often felt like a fatherless child. On those commutes, I was trying to talk with him as one adult to another. We'd never quite crossed that bridge.

This dialogue went on for a long time. In the late '60s, I imagined how this veteran and I might have argued about Vietnam. In the early 1970s. I wondered how this patriarch and I would have sparred over women's liberation.

In three decades of fatherless Father's Days there have been dozens of moments when I felt the presence and absence of this family man.

Sometimes, when my daughter was a toddler, restless and affectionate, I watched her wiggle off my mother's lap and wished that she had also had this grandfather. Again and again, I felt the loss for a child who didn't know what my sister and I had known—the man whose smile graced our childhoods.

Through my adulthood, he was there, at the outer edge of my vision. As the parent of a schoolchild, I would ask myself, how did he do this parenting thing? How did he get us to meet his high standards without making us fear his disapproval if we fell short? As the parent of an adolescent I wondered: How did he teach us—relentlessly at times—without sowing a rebellion?

Parents remain our touchstones—fellow travelers—even after death. They are both missing and present. So when I succeeded, I would glance sideways and see a snapshot of how my father handled success: with wry pleasure and a strong sense of the capriciousness of life.

When I failed, I would glance sideways and remember how he handled failure: with grit and perspective. He got up, put on his tie and went back to work. "Well, it isn't cancer," he would say, until of course, it was.

I always think of him when Father's Day comes with its offerings of greeting cards and gifts. But for me, this Father's Day is different. This year I have officially, numerically, outlived my father. I am just now older than he ever became.

I am older than my own father. I cannot tell you how oddly that rings in my middle-aged ear.

You know the questions that precocious children ask about heaven? "What happens if an old widower meets his young wife in heaven—will they both be 30 or 70?"

For me the fantasy is much more earthly. If my father and I met here and now, I would be older. If he and my husband finally met—

a long harbored wish—my husband too would be the older of these two men. We are the elders of the man who is my elder.

This is a passage of no small proportion. In the past year or so, when I tried to think about my future—what happens next at midlife?—I kept hitting a blank wall. It was only when my birthday came and went that I understood the nature of that dead-end. What my father did at my age—to put it as bluntly as I experienced it— was die.

To outlive a parent—especially a father—is by no means my unique experience. To live beyond our parents' age is the norm. But that moment carries an unexpected echo of the original loss. The father-in-my-memory, the man who was once out there ahead of me or beside me—this is how you do 30, 40, 50—is no longer available as a guide.

Age is an accumulation of life and loss. Adulthood is a series of lines crossed. So I pass a father threshold in middle age, just as I did at 24. From here on out, I'm on my own.

## QUESTIONS ON CONTENT

1. How old was the author when her father died?
2. What were some of the things she wished she could have talked with her dad about?
3. What did Goodman do on rides home from work?
4. What was ironic about Goodman's last birthday?

## QUESTIONS ON RHETORIC

1. How can writing about an intensely personal event like the loss of a father be a successful newspaper column?
2. What time span does the article cover? Why is that significant?
3. What does Goodman mean when she writes, "I am now older than he ever became"?
4. Consider the question Goodman poses about meetings in heaven and ages.

## VOCABULARY

(10) capriciousness

## WRITING PROMPTS

1. Write about the death of your parent or someone close to you.
2. Write about those who will be forever young.
3. Write about an older adult who is in your life now and the impact they have on your life.
4. Consider Goodman's statement: "Adulthood is a series of lines crossed."

# THE EMBRACE OF OLD AGE

## DONALD HALL

When I spent my summers here [Wilmot, New Hampshire] as a boy, my grandparents took me everywhere they went. We had no car. We didn't hitch up the horse to go to a drive-in movie, but we rode behind Riley to church on Sunday morning, and on Sunday night returned in the buggy for Christian Endeavor. We attended annual social events, in July the Church Fair and in August Old Home Day. Although my grandparents lived without anything that passes for entertainment in the 1990s—no car, no television, no VCR, no restaurants, no cocktail parties—they were remarkably cheerful. My grandfather especially had a fortunate temperament. He liked his work, and a little amusement went a long way. Occasionally we hitched up Riley for a special occasion: a family reunion, an auction, an eightieth birthday party, a funeral, a long-delayed visit to a dying cousin. When I was fourteen years old we went to Willard and Alice Buzzle's diamond wedding anniversary.

In preparation, my grandmother made three blueberry pies and a bagful of ginger snaps; my grandfather dusted the horse carriage, wiped off the harness, and curried Riley. Because the buggy's iron rims rattled on its wooden wheels—a dry August—we drove it across the railroad tracks to Eagle Pond and urged Riley against his better judgment to wade, pulling the carriage into shallow water. We sat there for a few minutes as I delighted in the strangeness, sitting still in the buggy in the pond's shallows while the wood swelled tight inside the rims. Then we drove back to the farm to dress and set out.

Willard and Alice were older than my grandparents, who were in their sixties. I remembered the Buzzles from Old Home Day: They were *old*. Alice had been seventeen when she was married, which made her ninety-two on her seventy-fifth wedding anniversary. Willard was exactly one hundred, married the day he turned twenty-five, which of course made today's celebration double. Diamond wedding anniversaries were rare enough; today we added a simultaneous one hundredth birthday party. Three weekly newspapers sent photographer-reporters to the Danbury Grange.

Horses and buggies were uncommon on the roads, though horse farmers were not unknown in 1943. The war kept traffic down, but a few dark square cars passed us on Route 4. My grandfather kept the buggy's right wheels on the shoulder, and I watched sand spin off the wheels like Fourth of July nightworks fountains. When we arrived at the Grange Hall, it was decorated red, white, and blue. As we alighted my grandfather spoke in Riley's ear and tied him loosely to a young maple, so that he could bend his neck to eat grass. Inside, the Grange walls were covered with photographs of past Grange presidents, and there was an American flag beside the stage in the front, the drawn curtain showing a view of Mount Kearsage painted by a local artist in 1906. We were early, of course, and so was everyone else. My grandmother cut her pies and set the pieces out on a long table covered with pies and cookies. Willard and Alice's sons Clarence and Frank scurried about, old men who moved with the sprightly energy of children anxious to please. Then a shout from the door told us that the bridal couple had arrived. I looked out to see Willard's Model A parked at the front door, driven by their surviving daughter Ada. Bride and bridegroom tottered up the steps, walking with canes held in outside hands so that they could join inside arms. They gripped each other fiercely, as if each were convinced that the other needed help. Willard looked the frailer as he climbed the Grange steps on his hundredth birthday and his seventy-fifth wedding anniversary, wavering over the worn wood stairs.

At the opened double doors Clarence and Frank took charge, each grasping one parent, and led them into the hall, where my grandmother at the organ belted out the Wedding March. Now the ancient small parents, on the arms of ancient small sons, with ancient daughter in the rear, walked slowly the length of the hall between the folding chairs set up for the ceremony, waving and acknowledging our waves like conquerors returned from the war that was not over. When Alice and Willard reached the end of the hall, my grandmother's fingers switched to "Happy Birthday." Everyone sang while a huge cake, big enough for everyone present, was wheeled into the crowd, topped with a hundred candles and the figurines of a bride and groom. Willard and Alice conspired with Ada, Clarence, and Frank to blow out the candles, taking many breaths, after a pause for a wish.

And I thought, What could they wish for? Not for a long life! Maybe for an easy winter? I studied Willard's infirmity. The skin of his hands was brown with liver spots, flesh hung like turkey wattles from his neck, and everything about him shook: his arms, his head on its frail stem, and his bony knees visibly trembling against his trouser legs. I felt horror—as if it were indecent to be alive with no future, each day merely a task for accomplishment. My vision of old age shook me as Willard shook.

Our minister, Kate's brother my uncle Luther, was host and master of ceremonies for half an hour of reminiscences and songs: "The Old Oaken Bucket," "When You and I Were Young, Maggie," "Down by the Old Mill Stream." Luther read two telegrams, one for the wedding and one for the birthday, from President Franklin Delano Roosevelt. When we broke to eat I heaped my paper plate with hermits and brownies and cherry pie, not forgetting a piece of wedding cake. Returning for seconds, I gathered the last piece of my grandmother's blueberry.

Then I was bored. I was rarely bored in my grandparents' company but today they paid me no mind. They had done introducing me and I had done with comments on how tall I was. Now they stood with other old people recollecting together. And I felt separate, separated especially because I understood that I was the *only one* in this crowd able to see clearly the futility and ugliness of old age.

So I prowled around the building, exploring the stage behind the painted curtain, finding a closet full of ancient costumes, trying on a top hat and derby. Then I opened a door I had not entered before, a green room to the side of the stage, and walked into the dimness without sensing the presence of others. In low light from a shaded window I saw two bodies embracing as they leaned against a wardrobe. I was embarrassed, I suppose because notions of embracing had begun to occupy me day and night. I started to back out, then saw that it was Willard and Alice who clung to each other, having crept from their thronged relatives and neighbors to this privacy. Their twin canes leaned on a box while their arms engaged each other. For a quick moment it was as if I saw, beyond the ancients in the green room, a young couple, seventy-five years back, who found a secret place to kiss and hug in.

Then I heard what she said: "Alice, Alice, Alice." She spoke urgently, "Alice, Alice," as if she were warning herself of something. At that moment I felt my grandfather's hand on my shoulder—it was time to go home; he had sought me out—and when I looked up I saw that he had heard. It was not until we were driving home that he mentioned it. I listened as he spoke—his voice controlled, as if he made a neutral observation, about the weather perhaps, that although the day was bright he wouldn't be surprised if it rained—saying, "Kate, Willard didn't know who Alice was."

## QUESTIONS ON CONTENT

1. What celebration did Hall go to with his grandparents?
2. Why was the celebration significant?
3. How does Hall establish the time period?
4. What did young Hall find when he went exploring in the old building?

## QUESTIONS ON RHETORIC

1. Look at the details Hall uses to establish a time period. Why are these important to the essay?

2. In paragraph 4, Hall writes of the "surviving daughter" without further reference to other children. Why do you suppose he did that?
3. What kind of shift does the first sentence in paragraph 8 accomplish?
4. What tone does Hall establish in the first part of the essay? What effect does the last paragraph have on the tone of the essay? The last sentence?

## VOCABULARY

(2) curried

(6) infirmity

(7) reminiscences

(8) recollecting

## WRITING PROMPTS

1. How old do you want to get? Why?
2. Write about our society's view of old age.
3. Why do you think people try to avoid aging? Consider the products designed to prevent aging.
4. What is your vision of old age?
5. Write about the irony of Hall's title.

# THE PERFECT FAMILY

## ALICE HOFFMAN

When I was growing up in the 50s, there was only one sort of family, the one we watched on television every day. Right in front of us, in black and white, was everything we needed to know about family values: the neat patch of lawn, the apple tree, the mother who never once raised her voice, the three lovely children: a Princess, a Kitten, a Bud and, always, the father who knew best.

People stayed married forever back then, and roses grew by the front door. We had glass bottles filled with lightning bugs and brand-new swing sets in the backyard, and softball games at dusk. We had summer nights that lasted forever and well-balanced meals, three times a day, in our identical houses, on our identical streets. There was only one small bargain we had to make to exist in this world: we were never to ask questions, never to think about people who didn't have as much or who were different in any way. We ignored desperate marriages and piercing loneliness. And we were never, ever, to wonder what might be hidden from view, behind the unlocked doors, in the privacy of our neighbors' bedrooms and knotty-pine-paneled dens.

This was a bargain my own mother could not make. Having once believed that her life would sort itself out to be like the television shows we watched, only real and in color, she'd been left to care for her children on her own, at a time when divorce was so uncommon I did not meet another child of divorced parents until 10 years later when I went off to college.

Back then, it almost made sense when one of my best friends was not allowed to come to my house; her parents did not approve of divorce or my mother's life style. My mother, after all, had a job and boyfriend and, perhaps even more incriminating, she was the one who took the silver-colored trash cans out to the curb on Monday nights. She did so faithfully, on evenings when she had already balanced the checkbook and paid the bills and ministered to sore throats and made certain we'd had dinner; but all up and down the street everybody knew the truth: taking out the trash was clearly a job for fathers.

When I was 10, my mother began to work for the Department of Social Services, a world in which the simple rules of the suburbs did not apply. She counseled young unwed mothers, girls and women who were not allowed to make their own choices, most of whom had not been allowed to finish high school or stay in their own homes, none of whom had been allowed to decide not to continue their pregnancies. Later, my mother placed most of these babies in foster care, and still later, she moved to the protective-services department, investigating charges of abuse and neglect, often having to search a child's back and legs for bruises or welts.

She would have found some on my friend, left there by her righteous father, the one who wouldn't allow her to visit our home but blackened her eye when, a few years later, he discovered that she was dating a boy he didn't approve of. But none of his neighbors had dared to report him. They would never have imagined that someone like my friend's father, whose trash cans were always tidily placed at the curb, whose lawn was always well cared for, might need watching.

To my mother, abuse was a clear-cut issue, if reported and found, but neglect was more of a judgment call. It was, in effect, passing judgment on the nature of love. If my father had not sent the child support checks on time, if my mother hadn't been white and college-educated, it could have easily been us in one of those apartments she visited, where the heat didn't work on the coldest days, and the dirt was so encrusted you could mop all day and still be called a poor housekeeper, and there was often nothing more for dinner than Frosted Flakes and milk, or, if it was toward the end of the month, the cereal might be served with tap water. Would that have meant my mother loved her children any less, that we were less of a family?

My mother never once judged who was a fit mother on the basis of a clean floor, or an unbalanced meal, or a boyfriend who sometimes spent the night. But back then, there were good citizens who were only too ready to set their standards for women and children, factoring out poverty or exhaustion or simply a different set of beliefs.

There are always those who are ready to deal out judgment with the ready fist of the righteous. I know this because before the age of 10 I was one of the righteous, too. I believed that mothers were meant to stay home and fathers should carry out the trash on Monday nights. I believed that parents could create a domestic life that was the next best thing to heaven, if they just tried. That is what I'd been told, that in the best of all worlds we would live identical lives in identical houses.

It's a simple view of the world, too simple even for childhood. Certainly, it's a vision that is much too limited for the lives we live now, when only one in 19 families is made up of a wage-earner father, a mother who doesn't work outside the home and two or more children. And even long ago, when I was growing up, we paid too high a price when we cut ourselves off from the rest of the world. We ourselves did not dare to be different. In the safety we created, we became trapped.

There are still places where softball games are played at dusk and roses grow by the front door. There are families with sons named Bud, with kind and generous fathers, and mothers who put up strawberry preserves every June and always have time to sing lullabies. But do these families love their children any more than the single mother who works all day? Are their lullabies any sweeter? If I felt deprived as a child, it was only when our family was measured against some notion of what we were supposed to be. The truth of it was, we lacked for little.

And now that I have children of my own, and am exhausted at the end of the day in which I've probably failed in a hundred different ways, I am amazed that women alone can manage. That they do, in spite of everything, is a simple fact. They rise from sleep in the middle of the night when their children call out to them. They rush for the cough syrup and cold washcloths and keep watch till dawn. These are real family values, the same ones we knew when we were children. As far as we were concerned our mother could cure a fever with a kiss. This may be the only thing we ever need to know about love. The rest, no one can judge.

## QUESTIONS ON CONTENT

1. What determined the concept of family when Hoffman was growing up?
2. What made Hoffman's family different?
3. Why couldn't her best friend come over to her house?
4. What was important about the ritual of taking the trash can to the curb?

## QUESTIONS ON RHETORIC

1. Find the cultural mores in Hoffman's essay for the 1950s. Why is it important to include those in this essay?
2. How do families today differ?
3. How does society's view of the family differ? Or does it?
4. How does Hoffman make the point that abuse and neglect cross socioeconomic lines?
5. What does Hoffman mean when she writes, "In the safety we created, we became trapped." (10)

## Vocabulary

(4) incriminating

(11) deprived

## Writing Prompts

1. Describe your view of the perfect family.
2. Compare and contrast the 1950s family with the current family.
3. Write about stereotypical standards that define elements of our society.

# MARY CASSATT

## MARY GORDON

When Mary Cassatt's father was told of her decision to become a painter, he said: "I would rather see you dead." When Edgar Degas saw a show of Cassatt's etchings, his response was: "I am not willing to admit that a woman can draw that well." When she returned to Philadelphia after twenty-eight years abroad, having achieved renown as an Impressionist painter and the esteem of Degas, Huysmans, Pissarro, and Berthe Morisot, the *Philadelphia Ledger* reported: "Mary Cassatt, sister of Mr. Cassatt, president of the Pennsylvania Railroad, returned from Europe yesterday. She has been studying painting in France and owns the smallest Pekingese dog in the world."

Mary Cassatt exemplified the paradoxes of the woman artist. Cut off from the experiences that are considered the entitlement of her male counterpart, she has access to a private world a man can only guess at. She has, therefore, a kind of information he is necessarily deprived of. If she has almost impossible good fortune—means, self-confidence, heroic energy and dedication, the instinct to avoid the seductions of ordinary domestic life, which so easily become a substitute for creative work—she may pull off a miracle: she will combine the skill and surety that she has stolen from the world of men with the vision she brings from the world of women.

Mary Cassatt pulled off such a miracle. But if her story is particularly female, it is also American. She typifies one kind of independent American spinster who keeps reappearing in our history in forms as various as Margaret Fuller and Katharine Hepburn. There is an astringency in such women, a fierce discipline, a fearlessness, a love of work. But they are not inhuman. At home in the world, they embrace it with a kind of aristocratic greed that knows nothing of excess. Balance, proportion, an instinct for the distant and the formal, an exuberance, a vividness, a clarity of line: the genius of Mary Cassatt includes all these elements. The details of the combination are best put down to grace; the outlines may have been her birthright.

She was one of those wealthy Americans whose parents took the children abroad for their education and medical care. The James family comes to mind and, given her father's attitude toward her career, it is remarkable that Cassatt didn't share the fate of Alice James. But she had a remarkable mother, intelligent, encouraging of her children. When her daughter wanted to study in Paris, and her husband disapproved, Mrs. Cassatt arranged to accompany Mary as her chaperone.

From her beginnings as an art student, Cassatt was determined to follow the highest standards of craftsmanship. She went first to Paris, then to Italy, where she studied in Parma with Raimondi and spent many hours climbing up scaffolding (to the surprise of the natives) to study the work of Correggio and Parmigianino. Next, she was curious to visit Spain to look at the Spanish masters and to make use of the picturesque landscape and models. Finally, she returned to Paris, where she was to make her home, and worked with Degas, her sometime friend and difficult mentor. There has always been speculation as to whether or not they were lovers; her burning their correspondence gave the rumor credence. But I believe that they were not; she was, I think, too protective of her talent to make herself so vulnerable to Degas as a lover would have to be. But I suppose I don't believe it because I cherish, instead, the notion that a man and a woman can be colleagues and friends without causing an excuse for raised eyebrows. Most important, I want to believe they were not lovers because if they were, the trustworthiness of his extreme praise grows dilute.

She lived her life until late middle age among her family. Her beloved sister, Lydia, one of her most cherished models, had always lived as a semi-invalid and died early, in Mary's flat, of Bright's disease. Mary was closely involved with her brothers and their children. Her bond with her mother was profound: when Mrs. Cassatt died, in 1895, Mary's work began to decline. At the severing of her last close familial tie, when her surviving brother died as a result of an illness he contracted when traveling with her to Egypt, she broke down entirely. "How we try for happiness, poor things, and how we don't find it. The best cure is hard work—if only one has the health for it," she said, and lived that way.

Not surprisingly, perhaps, Cassatt's reputation has suffered because of the prejudice against her subject matter. Mothers and children: what could be of lower prestige, more vulnerable to the charge of sentimentality. Yet if one looks at the work of Mary Cassatt, one sees how triumphantly she avoids the pitfalls of sentimentality because of the astringent rigor of her eye and craft. The Cassatt iconography dashes in an instant the notion of the comfortable, easily natural fit of the maternal embrace. Again and again in her work, the child's posture embodies the ambivalence of his or her dependence. In *The Family,* the mother and child exist in positions of unease; the strong diagonals created by their postures of opposition give the pictures their tense strength, a strength that renders sentimental sweetness impossible. In *Ellen Mary Cassatt in a White Coat* and *Girl in the Blue Arm Chair,* the children seem imprisoned and dwarfed by the trappings of respectable life. The lines of Ellen's coat, which create such a powerful framing device, entrap the round and living child. The sulky little girl in the armchair seems about to be swallowed up by the massive cylinders of drawing room furniture and the strong curves of emptiness that are the floor. In *The Bath,* the little girl has all the unformed charming awkwardness of a young child: the straight limbs, the loose stomach. But these are not the stuff of Gerber babies—even of the children of Millais. In this picture, the center of interest is not the relationship between the mother and the child but the strong vertical and diagonal stripes of the mother's dress, whose opposition shapes the picture with an insistence that is almost abstract.

Cassatt changed the iconography of the depiction of mothers and children. Hers do not look out into and meet the viewer's eye; neither supplicating nor seductive, they are absorbed in their own inner thoughts. Minds are at work here, a concentration unbroken by an awareness of themselves as objects to be gazed at by the world.

The brilliance of Cassatt's colors, the clarity and solidity of her forms, are the result of her love and knowledge of the masters of European painting. She had a second career as adviser to great collectors: she believed passionately that America must, for the sake of its artists, possess masterpieces, and she paid no attention to the outrage of her European friends, who felt their treasures were being sacked by barbarians. A young man visiting her in her old age noted her closed mind regarding the movement of the moderns. She thought American painters should stay home and not become "café loafers in Paris. Why should they come to Europe?" she demanded. "When I was young it was different.... Our Museums had not great paintings for the students to study. Now that has been corrected and something must be done to save our young over here."

One can hear the voice of the old, irascible, still splendid aunt in that comment and see the gesture of her stick toward the Left Bank. Cassatt was blinded by cataracts; the last years of her life were spent in a fog. She became ardent on the subjects of suffragism, socialism, and spiritualism; the horror of the First World War made her passionate in her conviction that mankind itself must change. She died at her country estate near Grasse, honored by the French, recipient of the Légion d'honneur, but unappreciated in America, rescued only recently from misunderstanding, really, by feminist art critics. They allowed us to begin to see her for what she is: a master of line and color whose great achievement was to take the "feminine" themes of mothers, children, women with their thoughts alone, to endow them with grandeur without withholding from them the tenderness that fits so easily alongside the rigor of her art.

## QUESTIONS ON CONTENT

1. What did Mary Cassatt's father say to her when he found that she wanted to be a painter?
2. Where did Cassatt study art?
3. Who were Cassatt's subjects for her paintings?
4. Why did she stop painting?
5. Why did she discourage young artists from America from going to Europe to study as she did?

## QUESTIONS ON RHETORIC

1. What impact do the quotes in the first paragraph have on the essay? What tone is established?
2. Gordon writes that Cassatt exemplifies the "paradoxes of the woman artist." Find evidence to support this point.
3. Why does Gordon include the speculation about Cassatt and Degas being lovers?
4. Cassatt was wealthy, according to Gordon. How important a factor is this in Cassatt's accomplishments?

## VOCABULARY

(1) renown, Impressionist

(2) exemplified, paradoxes

(3) astringency, aristocratic

(5) dilute

(7) iconography, ambivalence

(10) irascible, rigor

## WRITING PROMPTS

1. Virginia Woolf said to write, a woman needed two things: money and a room of her own. How does Cassatt's story support Woolf's idea?
2. Can money buy happiness?
3. Write about a determination or dream you have.
4. Have you ever been stymied in a quest? What did you do?
5. Do women have to "avoid the seductions of ordinary domestic life" to become successful?

# NEWS OF THE WILD

## SCOTT RUSSELL SANDERS

My daughter Eva and I are preparing for a trip into the Boundary Waters of northern Minnesota. This will be my first long canoe journey since the death of my father, who taught me how to paddle, and for Eva it will be the first ever. As I work through the checklist of items to pack, I find myself wondering how I let her reach the age of twenty without our having taken such a trip before. I could easily blame circumstances, the demands of work and family, the cost. But the deeper source of my delay, I realize, has been a worry that I cannot be as true a guide for Eva in wild places as my father was for me.

Although he spent his working years in factories and offices, when I think of my father I see him outdoors. Whether in a garden, pasture, or woods, on a river or lake, he was always looking around, sniffing the air, listening, and he always seemed utterly at ease. "Happy as a hog in corn," he used to say. Mosquitoes would not bite him, bees would not sting him, poison ivy would not cause him the least itch. Bucking horses gentled under his hand, barking dogs lowered their hackles when he spoke, surly bears and gluttonous raccoons padded away after exchanging stares with him, and snakes kept clear of his feet. If wildness ever frightened him—including the wildness of a quirky heart that would eventually kill him—he never let on.

His favorite excuse for leaving the house was the old and respectable one of fishing. He took me first to dangle hooks in ponds, then in reservoirs, then farther and farther afield, beyond the scruffy edges of towns, beyond roofs and roads and utility wires, until we came at last into country where the human signs were too faint for us to see. "Looks like God just now closed up the toolbox and finished work on this place," he told me once on an island in Ontario's Algonquin Park. No matter how wild or tame the place, he seemed equally at home. He never complained of being tired or sore, hot or hungry or cold. He would as soon camp beside a spillway as beside a waterfall. He inspected pebbles with the same attention he gave to mountains. If we caught fish, fine; if not, that also was fine.

These outings were never trials of endurance, with a quota of miles to cover and hazards to overcome, but always musing saunters. "Will you look at this," he would say, and time and again we paused to look. Paddling through rapids, portaging between moosey lakes, hunting for arrowheads in a plowed field, or picking beans in the yard, he moved with the same deliberation and delight. The point was to be in contact with dirt and water and wood and sky, in the presence of animals, wide awake. Whatever his indoor faults, and he certainly had them, when he was outdoors my father radiated a steady, savoring attentiveness, and that was a great gift. He was so mindful of the Creation that in his company I forgot clocks and calendars, let go of words, and became mindful as well.

Remembering him as I pack for the canoe trip, I realize that I must add tobacco to my checklist. Eva raises her eyebrows at this. I explain to her that the Ojibwa, through whose country we will paddle, sprinkled tobacco on the water before setting out in a canoe, as an offering to the spirits for a safe journey. Unless honored in this way, the Water Monster might devour you or Thunderbirds might drown you. When I first learned of this practice and told my father, he said that sounded like a mighty sensible idea, as sensible as the design for canoes, moccasins, and domed wigwam tents we borrowed from the Great Lakes tribes. After that, every time he and I traveled by water, he would hand me one of his cigarettes, and I would tear it open and scatter the brown shreds on the waves.

This awkward ceremony gave me a hint of the dignity that tobacco still possessed for a people who used it only in solemn dealings with one another and in speaking with the gods. Just as we have stripped the holiness from tobacco with our incessant smoking, so we have stripped the holiness from travel with our commuting, our tourism, our idle shuttling about. When America was all wilderness except for occasional villages and orchards and cleared fields, a journey of any distance was a serious undertaking, whatever your ancestry, for there was always a good chance you would become lost, be captured by enemies, be injured, or die. Knowing the dangers, you prepared yourself with song and sacred tales and prayers. Traveling through forest or desert, over prairies, along rivers, you could never forget that your life depended on the wild web of creatures and forces, nor could you forget how vanishingly small a knot you were in that great web.

If you belonged to the Ojibwa or some other rooted people, when you returned from a long and perilous journey, your family and neighbors would ask if you had learned a new song, met a new animal, come upon a healing herb or a source of food or a holy place. What vision had you brought back for the community? The prime reason for traveling, after all, was to enrich the life at home.

"What did you find?" my father would ask when I returned from a camping trip or an after-dinner stroll. And I would show him a fossil or feather, tell him how sun lit up the leaves of a hickory, how a skunk looked me over; I would recall for him the taste of elderberries or the rush of wind in white pines or the crunch of locust shells underfoot. Only in that sharing of what I had found was the journey completed, the circle closed.

I have put some version of my father's question to both of my children, my son Jesse as well as Eva, from the time they could toddle. What did you find? What did you see? What's out there? I ask not merely because my father did, nor in paleskin imitation of the native people, but because I want to know the answer. I want to know what is out there, for my children, for me, for all of us. I want to bring what is out there in here, inside the walls where I live most of my hours, inside my porous and temporary skin, into the tumbling river of my thoughts, into my soul. By speaking of soul, a word worn slick from rolling over too many tongues, I wish to name that within me which rises up in response to the power and beauty I meet in the world. Whether we are bound through our depths to anything eternal, I cannot say; but I am certain we are bound, through and through, to all of nature. Our dependence on the great web is easier to see in the backwoods, but it is no less true in the backyard. Bringing home news from the wild is only a way of acknowledging that the wild is always and inescapably our home.

If I can help Eva to feel that, I will have passed on to her something of my father's gift to me. Talking of what we hope to see, she and I begin our journey long before we dip our paddles in the water, before we load the canoe, before we lace our boots, and the journey will continue after we have taken our seats once more beside the kitchen table. At the beginning we will say a prayer or two, and at the end, if we keep ourselves open and if the spirits bless us, we will bring back a few good stories. We will carry a pouch of tobacco to placate the old water monsters, along with a water-treatment kit to placate the new ones, those poisons and parasites we two-leggeds have flushed into the remotest rivers and lakes. We will also take bottles of sunscreen to compensate for the tattering of the ozone screen. There is no getting beyond the human reach, even in the Boundary Waters, just as there is no getting beyond the sway of earth, nor without a spaceship.

The criterion for deciding what to load in a canoe or backpack is the same as that for deciding what to load in a spaceship: Is it worth its weight? Eva and I have winnowed down our gear and food to an amount we can carry. What we portage across land and paddle across water is only a tiny portion of what we need, of course. To provide everything we need, we would have to carry the sun and moon and stars, fruitful grass, fertile soil, nourishing sea, trees and ferns, bacteria and bears, rock and rain and air, and the countless moorings of our love. No pack smaller than the universe would hold it all.

## QUESTIONS ON CONTENT

1. Why has the author not taken his daughter canoeing before?
2. How did Sanders's father feel about the outdoors?

3. What ceremony did Sanders and his father do at the beginning of each canoe trip? Why?
4. What was the purpose of travel according to Ojibwa belief?
5. What is the deciding factor on each item packed for a canoe trip?

## Questions on Rhetoric

1. In the first paragraph, Sanders worries that he will not be as good a guide as his father. How does he relate his father's expertise? How does he relate his own?
2. Sanders says we have "stripped the holiness from travel with our commuting, our tourism, our idle strutting about." Do you agree with him?
3. How did Sanders pass to his children some of the lessons his father taught him?

## Vocabulary

(4) musing, saunters, portaging

(7) perilous

(9) porous

(10) placate, tattering

(11) criterion

## Writing Prompts

1. Write about your favorite natural setting or place.
2. Is it necessary to keep some places "beyond human reach"?
3. What lessons have you learned from your parents that you are passing on or will pass on?
4. What would you pack in a survival pack?
5. What lesson have you learned from something in nature?
6. Find a natural object. Observe it at length. Write about it.

# FIGHTING BACK

## STANTON L. WORMLEY, JR.

In the spring of 1970, I was an 18-year-old army private at Fort Jackson, S.C. I had been in the Army for less than six months and was still making the difficult transition from life as an only child in an upper-middle-class black family. One rite of passage was particularly intense: on a cool April night, a drunken white soldier whom I barely knew attacked me as I lay sleeping.

My recollection of the incident is, in some details, still hazy. Like the seven other men in the squad bay, I was asleep in my bunk. I half-remember some vigorous off-key singing, the ceiling light going on and someone roughly shaking my foot. I sat up, drowsily irritated at being disturbed. Everything happened very quickly then: a voice began shouting, an arm tightened around my neck and a fist pounded the top of my head. I was still somewhat asleep and confused. Why was this happening to me? It didn't occur to me to fight. I simply covered my head as best I could. There was a hubbub, arms reaching in to separate us and then the sight of the man above me, struggling against the others holding him back, his face red with fury. By then I was fully awake, and I saw the strained tendons in the man's neck, the wormlike vein pulsing at his temple, the spittle that sprayed as he screamed obscenities at me. I wasn't hurt, at least not physically, and all I could do was stare, bewildered. I never did discover what had provoked him.

Afterward, I was angrily confronted by a young black streetwise soldier named Morris. He eyed me with unconcealed contempt. "What the hell's wrong with you, man?" he demanded. "Why didn't you fight back? I would've killed that mother." I had no answer for him. How could I have made him understand the sheltered world of my childhood, in which violence was deplored and careful deliberation encouraged. I was brought up to *think*, not just react.

Nevertheless, that question—*Why didn't I fight back?*— haunted me long after the incident had been forgotten by everyone else. Was I less of a man for not having beaten my attacker to a bloody pulp? Morris—and undoubtedly others—certainly thought so. And so, perhaps, would the majority of American men. The ability and the will to fight back are integral parts of our society's conception of manhood. It goes beyond mere self-defense, I think, for there is a subtle but significant difference between self-defense and fighting back. Self-defense is essentially passive; it involves no rancor, pride or ego. Running away from danger is what martial-arts instructors sometimes recommend as the appropriate response, the best self-defense strategy. Fighting back, on the other hand, is active and defiant. It involves the adoption of an attitude that one's retribution is morally justified—or even, at times, morally obligatory.

And we American men buy that attitude—especially those of us who are members of minority groups. For us, largely disenfranchised and often victimized by discrimination and poverty, fighting back is a statement of individual potency and self-determination. It is the very antithesis of victimization: it is a sign of empowerment. The symbolic consequences of fighting back—or failing to do so— reflect upon the group as a whole. To Morris, I had disgraced the entire black American population.

I suppose that there are still situations in which immediate, violent retaliation is necessary. Sometimes it seems that fighting back is the only way to command respect in the world. Women are now learning that unfortunate lesson, as did blacks and other minorities in recent decades. I can't help feeling, however, that when one gains the ability to fight back one loses something as well. What that something is, I can't easily define: a degree of compassion, perhaps, or tolerance or empathy. It is a quality I hope is possessed by the men in Washington and Moscow who have the power to dispense the ultimate retribution.

Once in a great while, past events are repeated, granting people a chance either to redeem themselves or to relive their mistakes. Two years ago, in a small roadside diner in Virginia, a man—again white, again drunk—chanced to make a derogatory remark to me. I was sitting with my back to him and ignored it. Thinking I had not heard him, he drew close to repeat his taunt, grabbing my shoulder. I suppose I could have moved away, shaken his hand off or complained to the manager. But the accumulated frustrations of years of ignoring such remarks—plus the memory of the incident at Fort Jackson—dictated otherwise. Before I knew what was happening, I was up out of my chair. I hit the man hard in the stomach and he sank to one knee with a moan. Grasping his collar, I almost hit again, but it was obvious that he had had enough. He looked up at me, gasping, his face contorted with pain and fear. The man was perhaps 50, of average size, with a fleshy, florid face surmounted by close-cropped gray bristle. I noted that he had bad teeth, a fact that gave me a moment of spiteful satisfaction. Suddenly sober, he stammered something unintelligible—it might have been an apology—and I let him go.

As I walked away, I was filled with a feeling of exultation. I had not stopped to wonder why; I had not been checked by compassion or sympathy. I had retaliated and it had felt good. But later, my exhilaration passed, leaving a strange sensation of hollowness. I felt vaguely embarrassed, even ashamed. In my mind I was still confident I had acted rightly, but my heart was no longer sure. I remembered my fury, and the quiet way the people in the diner had watched me stalk angrily away. I remembered, too, the abject grimace on the man's face, partly from the pain of the blow and partly in anticipation of a second; and I realized that there was a trace of sadness in the knowledge that I, too, had learned to fight back.

## QUESTIONS ON CONTENT

1. What happened to Wormley when he first entered the army?
2. What kind of home background did Wormley come from?

3. What happened in the diner?
4. Why were Wormley's reactions to the attacks different?

## QUESTIONS ON RHETORIC

1. Look at the facts in paragraph 1. How do those facts establish Wormley's credibility for telling this story?
2. What purpose does paragraph 2 serve?
3. Twice Wormley talks of "American men" with no distinction for race. What point does that make?
4. Wormley states, "...when one gains the ability to fight back one loses something as well." How does Wormley illustrate this point?

## VOCABULARY

(3) deplored

(4) obligatory

(5) disenfranchised, antitheses

(6) retribution

(7) derogatory, taunt

(8) exultation, abject

## WRITING PROMPTS

1. Write about a time you had to deal with a jerk.
2. Is it better to "turn the other cheek"?
3. Is there a comparable story from the female perspective? Write about it.
4. Why do you think women seldom have physical fights with each other?
5. Write about preconceptions.

# LIMITED SEATING
# ON BROADWAY

## JOHN HOCKENBERRY

The show at the Virginia Theater, "Jelly's Last Jam," is in previews, and even though tickets are $60 for orchestra seats (the only option for patrons in wheelchairs), the price was a minor impediment to the prospect of an evening of Jelly Roll Morton's jazz.

The art community in New York City has a reputation for being progressive. It is the forum and agent for challenging America's hard-ened perceptions about race, politics, class, gender, religion and, more recently, AIDS and homophobia. In particular, the theater world likes to think of itself as a seeker of such challenges and is proudest when a play or musical becomes a vehicle for change.

I thought of this two Saturdays ago as I sat at the top of some stairs in the Virginia Theater waiting to be helped into my seat. Because the Virginia, like virtually all Broadway theaters, refuses to take orders for wheelchair tickets over the phone, except for pur-chases well in advance, I had to make a special trip to the box office the day before to buy my ticket.

At the box office, I was told that a ticket was available but that I would have to sit far from my friend. I was told the house man-ager would seat me when I arrived. Here again, minor hassles well worth bearing on the way to an evening of good theater.

But that didn't happen. Two minutes before curtain time the house manager emerged from a white door with a copy of the theater's "Policy for Disabled Patrons." He abruptly told me to leave the theater. I was shocked and asked why. He asked if I could walk, something I thought was fairly clear when I had bought the ticket the day before. He mentioned stairs for the first time and noted that since I could not walk and had not brought my own crew with me that it was impossible to seat me. I said that there was no problem and that I would show him how to get me up the stairs with the help of the usher standing next to him.

He said in a loud voice audible to everyone around us: "Sir, we are not allowed to touch you. Our staff is not allowed to do that." I reminded him that my friend had already taken her seat at the suggestion of the usher and would react with some alarm if she saw my seat empty after the show began. "I'm sorry, sir, you'll have to leave," was his only response.

Having had many close calls with the inaccessible infrastructure of the world, I still could not believe I would not be able to see the show. I recalled an incident some years before at the Hakawati Theater in East Jerusalem when four fellow patrons and the playwright, all strangers helped me up 12 stairs to see a puppet show. They demanded that I be carried even when I was doubtful.

The theatergoers at the Virginia eyed me with the detached, craven interest that New Yorkers reserve for the white chalk outline of a corpse at a crime scene. "You are a fire hazard, sir," the manager insisted. Only moments before I had been a component of his cash flow. I grabbed his collar and told him what he could do with his Policy for Disabled Patrons. I was easily overpowered and ushered, the only ushering would experience that night, to the 52d Street sidewalk.

I sat powerless and humiliated; all dressed up, nowhere to go. Of course, the Virginia Theater staff probably thought differently. They might recall a rude, angry man trying to get rules bent in his favor. But outside, it seemed as if I was the only one who thought that a few stairs shouldn't stand in the way of seeing a play. Certainly there was no one to complain to about the lack of ramps. There was no meaning to the incident at all.

The Virginia Theater was not my first such encounter with New York City's art community. Some months ago on 10th Avenue I tried to empty a bottle of urine I had carried for 40 blocks. In the absence of any public restroom I rolled into a dirty parking lot to pour out the jar in a discreet corner. Two attendants with all the righteousness of crusaders grabbed me and threw me out of my chair and onto the sidewalk as people walked by.

Not long after the event I learned that a proposal for handicapped-accessible public restrooms on city streets was opposed by the Public Art Commission, which had determined that the structures would be too ugly. (Uglier even than public defecation, and heaven knows the arts community knows best about that.)

Artists might shrink from taking blame for the insensitive acts of architects, producers and theater owners. But as society's voice of protest, are artists to be excused for ignoring discrimination that hasn't yet made it to Broadway?

Maybe if I was an artist who daringly confronted whole flights of stairs in front of a paying audience and who carried around bottles of urine just to make a point about society I might keep from wetting my pants and, better yet, get to see "Jelly's Last Jam." But then that wouldn't be honest. Art and theater are nothing if not honest.

## QUESTIONS ON CONTENT

1. What show was Hockenberry trying to see?
2. Why couldn't he get to his seat?
3. What three things did the house manager tell Hockenberry?
4. Why did the parking lot attendants do to Hockenberry?

## QUESTIONS ON RHETORIC

1. What is the tone of this piece? Find examples to support your answer.

2. Find the irony in the description of the art community in New York City.
3. Why does Hockenberry say, "There was no meaning to the incident at all"?

## VOCABULARY

(7) infrastructure

## WRITING PROMPTS

1. Write about turning negative experiences into something positive.
2. If you know someone who uses a wheelchair, talk with them about everyday activities and write about it.
3. If possible, use a wheelchair for a full day and record the experience.
4. Write about life being unfair.
5. Should all places be accessible to everyone?

# My World Now

## Anna Mae Halgrim Seaver

This is my world now; it's all I have left. You see, I'm old. And, I'm
not as healthy as I used to be. I'm not necessarily happy with it but
I accept it. Occasionally, a member of my family will stop in to see
me. He or she will bring me some flowers or a little present, maybe
a set of slippers—I've got 8 pair. We'll visit for awhile and then they
will return to the outside world and I'll be alone again.

Oh, there are other people here in the nursing home. Residents,
we're called. The majority are about my age. I'm 84. Many are in
wheelchairs. The lucky ones are passing through—a broken hip, a
diseased heart, something has brought them here for rehabilitation.
When they're well they'll be going home.

Most of us are aware of our plight—some are not. Varying
stages of Alzheimer's have robbed several of their mental capacities.
We listen to endlessly repeated stories and questions. We meet them
anew daily, hourly or more often. We smile and nod gracefully each
time we hear a retelling. They seldom listen to my stories, so I've
stopped trying.

The help here is basically pretty good, although there's a large
turnover. Just when I get comfortable with someone he or she
moves on to another job. I understand that. This is not the best job
to have.

I don't much like some of the physical things that happen to us. I don't care much for a diaper. I seem to have lost the control acquired so diligently as a child. The difference is that I'm aware and embarrassed but I can't do anything about it. I've had 3 children and I know it isn't pleasant to clean another's diaper. My husband used to wear a gas mask when he changed the kids. I wish I had one now.

Why do you think the staff insists on talking baby talk when speaking to me? I understand English. I have a degree in music and am a certified teacher. Now I hear a lot of words that end in "y." Is this how my kids felt? My hearing aid works fine. There is little need for anyone to position their face directly in front of mine and raise their voice with those "y" words. Sometimes it takes longer for a meaning to sink in; sometimes my mind wanders when I am bored. But there's no need to shout.

I tried once or twice to make my feelings known. I even shouted once. That gained me a reputation of being "crotchety." Imagine me, crotchety. My children never heard me raise my voice. I surprised myself. After I've asked for help more than a dozen times and received nothing more than a dozen condescending smiles and a "Yes, deary, I'm working on it," something begins to break. That time I wanted to be taken to a bathroom.

I'd love to go out for a meal, to travel again. I'd love to go to my own church, sing with my own choir. I'd love to visit my friends. Most of them are gone now or else they are in different "homes" of their children's choosing. I'd love to play a good game of bridge but no one here seems to concentrate very well.

My children put me here for my own good. They said they would be able to visit me frequently. But they have their own lives to lead. That sounds normal. I don't want to be a burden. They know that. But I would like to see them more. One of them is here in town. He visits as much as he can.

Something else I've learned to accept is loss of privacy. Quite often I'll close my door when my roommate—imagine having a roommate at my age—is in the TV room. I do appreciate some time to myself and believe that I have earned at least that courtesy. As I sit thinking or writing, one of the aides invariably opens the door unannounced and walks in as if I'm not there. Sometimes she even opens my drawers and begins rummaging around. Am I invisible? Have I lost my right to respect and dignity? What would happen if the roles were reversed? I am still a human being. I would like to be treated as one.

The meals are not what I would choose for myself. We get variety but we don't get a choice. I am one of the fortunate ones who can still handle utensils. I remember eating off such cheap utensils in the Great Depression. I worked hard so I would not have to ever use them again. But here I am.

Did you ever sit in a wheelchair over an extended period of time? It's not comfortable. The seat squeezes you into the middle and applies constant pressure on your hips. The armrests are too narrow and my arms slip off. I am luckier than some. Others are strapped into their chairs and abandoned in front of the TV. Captive prisoners of daytime television; soap operas, talk shows and commercials.

One of the residents died today. He was a loner who, at one time started a business and developed a multimillion-dollar company. His children moved him here when he could no longer control his bowels. He didn't talk to most of us. He often snapped at the aides as though they were his employees. But he just gave up; willed his own demise. The staff has made up his room and another man has moved in.

A typical day. Awakened by the woman in the next bed wheezing—a former chain smoker with asthma. Call an aide to wash me and place me in my wheelchair to wait for breakfast. Only 67 minutes until breakfast. I'll wait. Breakfast in the dining area. Most of the residents are in wheelchairs. Others use canes or walkers. Some sit and wonder what they are waiting for. First meal of the day. Only 3 hours and 26 minutes until lunch. Maybe I'll sit around and wait for it. What is today? One day blends into the next until day and date mean nothing.

Let's watch a little TV. Oprah and Phil and Geraldo and who cares if some transvestite is having trouble picking a color-coordinated wardrobe from his husband's girlfriend's mother's collection. Lunch. Can't wait. Dried something with puréed peas and coconut pudding. No wonder I'm losing weight.

Back to my semiprivate room for a little semiprivacy or a nap.
I do need my beauty rest, company may come today. What is today,
again? The afternoon drags into early evening. This used to be my
favorite time of the day. Things would wind down. I would kick off
my shoes. Put my feet up on the coffee table. Pop open a bottle of
Chablis and enjoy the fruits of my day's labor with my husband. He's
gone. So is my health. This is my world.

## Questions on Content

1. Where does Seaver live?
2. How does she spend a typical day?
3. What happens when a resident dies?
4. How does Seaver describe sitting in a wheelchair?

## Questions on Rhetoric

1. Does the tone of the essay match the life depicted? How?
2. Many sentences are short, almost choppy. What effect does this
   have on the essay?
3. Why are there so many questions in the essay? What impact do
   they have on you as the reader?

## Vocabulary

(7) crotchety
(7) condescending
(13) demise

## Writing Prompts

1. Write about a nursing home or an assisted-living home you have
   been to.
2. Write about attention paid to such places during holidays.

3. Write about getting old.
4. "I don't want to be a burden." Do people really mean this when they say it?
5. Several generations used to live in the same house and people died at home. Why have we gotten away from that practice?

# Our Animal Rites

## Anna Quindlen

The bear had the adenoidal breathing of an elderly man with a passion for cigars and a tendency toward emphysema. My first thought, when I saw him contemplating me through tiny eyes from a rise just beyond the back porch, was that he looked remarkably bearlike, like a close-up shot from a public television nature program.

I screamed. With heavy tread—pad, pad, pad, harrumph, harrumph—the bear went off into the night, perhaps to search for garbage cans inexpertly closed and apiaries badly lighted. I sat on the porch, shaking. Everyone asks, "Was he big?" My answer is, "Compared to what?"

What I leave out when I tell the story is my conviction that the bear is still watching. At night I imagine he is staring down from the hillside into the lighted porch, as though he had a mezzanine seat for a performance on which the curtain had already gone up. "A nice female, but not very furry," I imagine him thinking, "I see the cubs have gone to the den for the night."

Sometimes I suspect I think this because the peace and quiet of the country have made me go mad, and if only I could hear a car alarm, an ambulance siren, the sound of a boom box playing "The Power" and its owner arguing with his girlfriend over whether or not he was flirting with Denise at the party, all that would drive the bear clear out of my head.

Sometimes I think it is because instead of feeling that the bear is trespassing on my property, in my heart I believe that I am trespassing on his.

That feeling is not apparent to city people, although there is something about the sight of a man cleaning up after a sheepdog with a sheet of newspaper that suggests a kind of horrible atonement. The city is a place built by the people, for the people. There we say people are acting like animals when they do things with guns and bats and knives that your ordinary bear would never dream of doing. There we condescend to our animals, with grooming parlors and cat carriers, using them to salve our loneliness and prepare us for parenthood.

All you who lost interest in the dog after the baby was born, you know who you are.

But out where the darkness has depth, where there are no street lights and the stars leap out of the sky, condescension, a feeling of supremacy, what the animal-rights types call speciesism, is impossible. Oh, hunters try it, and it is pathetic to consider the firepower they require to bring down one fair-sized deer. They get three bear days in the autumn, and afterward there is at least one picture in the paper of a couple of smiling guys in hats surrounding the carcass of an animal that looks, though dead, more dignified than they do.

Each spring, after the denning and the long, cold drowse, we wait to see if the bear that lives on the hill above our house beat the bullets. We discover his triumph through signs: a pile of bear dung on the lawn, impossible to assign to any other animal unless mastodons still roam the earth. A garbage box overturned into the swamp, the coleslaw container licked clean. Symmetrical scratch marks five feet up on a tree.

They own this land. Once, long ago, someone put a house on it. That was when we were tentative interlopers, when we put a farmhouse here and a barn there. And then we went nuts, built garden condos with pools and office complexes with parking garages and developments with names that always included the words Park, Acres, or Hills. You can't stop progress, especially if it's traveling 65 miles an hour. You notice that more this time of year, when the possums stiffen by the side of the road.

Sometimes the animals fight back. I was tickled by the people who bought a house with a pond and paid a good bit of money for a little dock from which to swim. It did not take long for them to discover that the snapping turtles were opposed to the addition to their ecosystem of humans wearing sunscreen. An exterminator was sent for. The pond was dredged. A guest got bit. The turtles won.

I've read that deer use the same trails all their lives. Someone comes along and puts a neo-Colonial house in the middle of their deer paths, and the deer will use the paths anyway, with a few detours. If you watch, you can see that it is the deer that belong and the house which does not. The bats, the groundhogs, the weasels, the toads—a hundred years from now, while our family will likely be scattered, their descendants might be in this same spot. Somewhere out there the bear is watching, picking his nits and his teeth, breathing his raggedy bear breath, and if he could talk, maybe he'd say, "I wonder when they're going back where they belong."

## QUESTIONS ON CONTENT

1. What animal frightens Quindlen?
2. What bothers the author about living in the woods?
3. Why does Quindlen think people have dogs?
4. Who does Quindlen think the land belongs to?

## QUESTIONS ON RHETORIC

1. What is the tone of the essay? Find the elements of humor. How do they affect the tone?
2. Quindlen makes an interesting point about "people acting like animals." Discuss it.
3. Why do you think developers use words such as *park, acres,* and *hills* in naming subdivisions?
4. Is Quindlen giving animals more insight than they have? Is she humanizing them?

## VOCABULARY

(1) adenoidal, emphysema

(2) apiaries

(3) mezzanine

(6) atonement, condescend

(7) speciesism

(10) interlopers

## WRITING PROMPTS

1. Do humans have domain over all the earth?
2. What would happen if animals could talk to humans? What would they tell us?
3. Write about "acting like an animal."
4. Whose land is it, anyway?

# The Woods Stalker

## Constance Gray

Sounds of the highway fade as I hike deeper into one of the largest remaining dabs of Minnesota Big Woods, not far from my home. The day before, a friend had asked me if I was nervous about hiking alone here nearly every day. I'd replied with a truthful "no."

The fallen basswood, maple, and oak leaves underfoot have mellowed to the color of a fawn's back; the bark of the trees is a gray-brown that allows grown deer to blend in even after the leaves have dropped. Still, I can't miss the three deer on a high ridge. They see me, too. Their white tails lift skyward like truce flags before they leap away in flawless unison.

I head down a canyon and ford a slender creek by scrambling over a fallen maple. Gold and scarlet leaves float in a small pool of water trapped by a series of moss-covered stones. A fine green mist shimmers above the moss. After a steep uphill climb, I flop across a gray-blue boulder, and look down at the winding creek below. The water's surface, touched with filtered sunlight, glints like mercury. The sun is snuffed out by a cloud and the quicksilver fades. It is because of these fleeting and private moments that I come here. A slight wind shakes the leafless trees above me. Suddenly I know why I am not afraid to walk alone in the woods. I first encountered danger and violence inside the houses I grew up in, where I had little room to maneuver. I learned that outside was safer.

I continue along the high trail that leads downward to the lake. At the water's edge I contemplate whether or not to hike to the far shore when I notice a man 30 feet away. He's dressed neck to toe in green camouflage. Why would a hunter be in these woods? But I note that he carries no rifle. He lingers on the path ahead, so I also dawdle. He glances over his shoulder at me not once, but twice. I think about the many times I've passed men walking in these woods and always the drill is the same: They glance up to show they see me, then look down to signal that they're no threat. A second glance is out of the question. But this young man seems not to understand this ritual. He looks again. A small smile upturns the corners of his mouth. I stop dead and feign interest in a trio of mallards as they rise from the lake. The man moves on. He must now choose to go uphill along the broad trail leading back to the parking lot, or to skirt around the lake on a path snaking through the most remote part of the woods. Whichever path he chooses, I will choose the opposite.

He strikes uphill along the broad path, walking slowly and glancing down at me two more times before disappearing from view. I follow the narrow lake trail, then cut uphill on a steep path. I take a few deep breaths and think how lucky I am to be rid of the young man. Unless he knows of the deer trail connecting his path and mine, I shouldn't see him again. I'm 20 feet from the intersection of the deer trail when I spot him. He already has noticed me, and his face seems to say, "Good, you're just where I thought you'd be."

A ghostly image of my 3-year-old son's face flickers inside my brain like tattered newsreel footage. Then my mind's screen splits in half and I see two possibilities play themselves out side by side. In one, the young man and I pass by each other without incident. I do not wish to dwell on the other. The few remaining seconds before one of these possibilities unfolds into reality seem to stretch into minutes. I calculate that I will reach the union of our paths before he will. I will then have to hike through the most remote part of the forest with him a few feet at my back. Or I can turn onto the deer trail and face him. We are 15 feet apart. I turn toward him. I look him in the eye and do not look away. With only 6 feet between us, I call out.

"Hi, how ya doin'?" I'm surprised that my voice sounds friendly. He does not answer. The smile drops from his mouth. I keep my eyes on his face. He slips his left hand into a deep pocket. For a fleeting second I wonder what sort of weapon he might have concealed there. We pass. I walk with a measured pace until I'm out of view. Then I run.

When I reach the main trail I slow, then cut through a grove of sumac and down a service road to the highway. I step onto the gravel shoulder of the paved road. The split screen in my brain dissolves into just one picture again, just one unfolding reality, as the traffic rips past. I head toward my car, my heart thrashing like that of a startled doe.

## QUESTIONS ON CONTENT

1. Where does Gray go walking?
2. What time of year is it?
3. Why does Gray walk alone?
4. Whom does she meet on the trail?

## QUESTIONS ON RHETORIC

1. What sentence in the first paragraph foreshadows the event in the essay?
2. How do the verbs Gray uses add to the tone of the piece?
3. Does the last paragraph resolve the issue raised or leave it hanging?
4. Look at the short sentences in the next-to-last paragraph. What effect do they have?

## WRITING PROMPTS

1. Write about your most fearful moment or incident
2. What frightens you?
3. Write about jumping to conclusions.

# Running the Table

## Frank Conroy

When I was fifteen and living in New York City, I was supposed to be going to Stuyvesant High School and in fact I did actually show up three or four times a week, full of gloom, anger and adolescent narcissism. The world was a dark place for me in those days. I lived in a kind of tunnel of melancholy, constantly in trouble at home, in school and occasionally with the police. (Pitching pennies, sneaking into movies, jumping the turnstile in the subway, stealing paperback books—fairly serious stuff in that earlier, more innocent time.) I was haunted by a sense of chaos, chaos within and chaos without. Which is perhaps why the orderliness of pool, the Euclidean cleanness of it, so appealed to me. The formality of pool struck me as soothing and reassuring, a sort of oasis of coolness, utterly rational and yet not without its elegant little mysteries. But I'm getting ahead of myself.

One day, meandering around 14th Street, I stepped through the open doors on an impulse and mounted the long, broad stairway. Halfway up I heard the click of the balls. What a marvelous sound! Precise, sharp, crisp, and yet somehow mellow. There was an intimacy to the sound that thrilled me. At the top of the stairs I pushed through saloon-style swinging doors and entered a vast, hushed, dim hall. Rows of pool tables stretched away in every direction, almost all of them empty at this early hour, but here and there in the distance, a pool of light, figures in silhouette circling, bending, taking shots. Nearby, two old men were playing a game I would later learn to be billiards on a large table without pockets. The click of the three balls, two white, one red, was what I had heard on the stairs. The men played unhurriedly, pausing now and then with their cues held like walking sticks to stare down at the street below. Cigar smoke swirled in the air.

I had walked into Julian's, little knowing that it was one of the most important pool halls on the East Coast. I was impressed by the stark functionality of the place—the absence of decoration of any kind. It seemed almost institutional in its atmosphere, right down to the large poster hung on the cashier's cage setting out the rules and regulations. No drinking, no eating, no sitting on the edges of the tables, no spitting except in the cuspidors, no massé shots, etc. Tables were twenty-five cents an hour. Cue sticks were to be found on racks against the walls. Balls available from the cashier as he clocked you in.

"How do you play?" I asked.

The cashier was bald and overweight. He wore, for some reason, a green eyeshade. "You from Stuyvesant?"

I nodded, and he grunted, reached down to some hidden shelf and gave me a small paper pamphlet, pushing it forward across the worn wooden counter. I scanned it quickly. Basic information about straight pool, eight ball, nine ball, billiards, snooker and a few other games. "Start with straight pool," he said. "Go over there and watch those guys on twenty-two for a while. Sit still, don't talk, and don't move around."

I did as I was told, sitting on a kind of mini-bleachers against the wall, my chin in my hands. The two men playing were in their twenties, an Abbott-and-Costello duo, thin Bud wearing a vest and smoking constantly, pudgy Lou moving delicately around the table, using the bridge now and then because of his short arms. They paid no attention to me and played with concentration, silent except for calling combinations.

"Six off the thirteen," Lou said.

Bud nodded. They only called combinations. All straight shots, no matter how difficult, were presumably obvious. After a while, with a few discreet glances at my pamphlet, I began to get the hang of it. All the balls, striped and solid, were fair game. You simply kept shooting until you missed, and then it was the other guy's turn. After each run, you moved some beads on a wire overhead with the tip of your cue, marking up the number of balls you'd sunk. So much for the rules. What was amazing was the shooting.

Object balls clipped so fine they moved sideways. Bank shots off the cushion into a pocket. Long combinations. Breakout shots in which a whole cluster of balls would explode in all directions while one from the middle would limp into a nearby pocket. And it didn't take long to realize that making a given shot was only part of what was going on. Controlling the position of the cue ball after the shot was equally important, so as to have a markable next shot. I could see that strategy was involved, although how they made the cue ball behave so differently in similar situations seemed nothing short of magical. Lou completed a run of nine or ten balls and reached fifty on the wire overhead. He had won, apparently.

"Double or nothing?"

Bud shook his head. Money changed hands. Lou put the balls in a tray, turned out the light over the table, and both men checked out at the cashier's. I sat for a while, thinking over what I had seen, reading the pamphlet again. I didn't have enough money to play that day, but I knew I was coming back.

Sometime in the late sixties, as an adult, I went to the Botanic Garden in Brooklyn to visit the recently completed Zen rock garden. It was a meticulous re-creation of a particular installation from a particular Japanese monastery. No one else was there. I sat on the bench gazing at the spiral patterns in the sand, looking at the black rocks set like volcanic islands in a white sea. Peace. Tranquility. As absurd as it may sound, I was reminded of my childhood experience of Julian's on a quiet afternoon—a sense of harmony, of an entirely disinterested material world entirely unaffected by one's perception of it.

For me, at fifteen, Julian's was a sort of retreat, a withdrawal from the world. I would shoot for hours at a time, racking up, breaking, shooting, racking up, breaking, shooting, in a solitary trance.

Or I would surrender to the ritual of practice—setting up long shots over the length of the table again and again, trying to sink a shot with the same configuration ten times in a row, and then twenty, and then a more difficult configuration to a different pocket three times in a row, and then five, etc. I did not get bored with the repetition. Every time a ball went in the pocket I felt satisfaction. When I missed I simply ignored the fact, reset the shot and tried again. This went on for several weeks at a remote table in a far corner of the hall—table nineteen—which nobody else ever seemed to want. Once in a while I'd play with another kid, usually also from Stuyvesant, and split the time. After a couple of months I would sometimes play for the time—loser pays—against opponents who looked even weaker than myself. But most of the time I played alone.

Late one afternoon, racking up on table nineteen for perhaps the tenth time, I noticed a man sitting in the gloom up against the wall. He was extremely thin, with a narrow face and a protruding brow. He wore a double-breasted suit and two-tone shoes, one leg dangling languidly over the other. He gave me an almost imperceptible nod. I chalked the tip of my cue, went to the head of the table and stroked a clean break. Aware that I was being watched, I studied the lie of the balls for a moment and proceeded to sink seven in a row, everything going according to plan, until I scratched. I pulled up the cue ball and the object ball, recreated the shot and scratched again.

"Why don't you use English?" he asked quietly.

I stared at the table. "What's English?"

A moment's pause. "Set it up again," he said.

I did so.

"Aim, but don't hit. Pretend you're going to shoot."

I made a bridge with my left hand, aimed at the object ball and held the tip of my stick right behind the center of the cue ball.

"All right. All lined up?"

"Yes," I said, almost flat on the table.

"Do not change the line. Are you aiming at the center of the cue ball?"

"Yes."

"Aim a quarter of an inch higher."

"You mean I should...." For some reason what he was suggesting seemed almost sacrilegious.

"Yes, yes. Don't hit the cue ball in the center. Strike a quarter of an inch above. Now go ahead. Shoot."

I made my stroke, watched the object ball go in, and watched the cue ball take a different path after impact than it had before. It didn't scratch this time, but missed the pocket, bounced smartly off the cushion and rolled to a stop near the center of the table for an easy next shot.

"Hey. That's terrific!" I said.

"That's English." He unfolded his legs and stood up. He came over and took the pool cue from my hands. "If a person pays attention," he said, "a person can learn about ninety-five percent of what he needs to know in about ten minutes. Ten minutes for the principles, then who knows how many years for the practice." His dark, deep-set eyes gave his face a vaguely ominous cast. "You want to learn?"

"Absolutely," I said without hesitation. "Yes."

As it turned out, it took about half an hour. The man teaching me was called Smilin' Jack, after the comic-strip character and presumably because of his glum demeanor. He was a Julian's regular, and it was my good luck to have caught him when somebody had stood him up for what was to have been a money game. I could sense that he enjoyed going through the drill—articulate, methodical, explicating on cause and effect with quiet relish, moving the balls around the table with no wasted motion whatsoever, executing the demo shots with a stroke as smooth as powdered silk—it was an elegant dance, with commentary. A sort of offering to the gods of pool.

I cannot possibly recount here what I learned. Follow, draw, left and right English and how they affect the movement of the cue ball after impact. The object ball picking up opposite English from the cue ball. The effectiveness of different kinds of English as a function of distance (between cue ball and object ball) and of speed. *Sliding* the cue ball. Playing the diamond points. Shooting a ball frozen on the cushion. How to read combinations, and on and on. I paid very close attention and jotted down what notes I could. (*Over*shoot bank shots to the side pockets. *Under*shoot bank shots to the corner pockets.) At the end of the half hour my head ached. In addition to trying to grasp the principles, I'd been trying to film the whole thing, to superimpose an eidetic memory on the cells of my brain, so I could retrieve what I'd seen at will. I was exhausted.

He handed me the stick, shot his cuffs and adjusted the front of his jacket with a slight forward movement of his shoulders. "That should keep you busy for a while." Then he simply walked away.

"Thanks," I called after him.

Without looking back, he raised his hand and gave a laconic little wave.

Practice, practice. Months of practice. It was a delicate business, English, affected by things like the relative roughness of the cue tip and its ability to hold chalk, or the condition of the felt, or infinitesimal degrees of table lean. But it worked. There was no doubt about it, when you got the feel of it you greatly increased your power over the all-important position of the cue ball. There was a word for it—the "leave," as in "good shot, but a tough leave." And of course the more you could control the leave, the more deeply involved was the strategy—planning out how to sink twelve balls in a row, rather than just five or six. Progress was slow, but it was tangible, and very, very satisfying. I began to beat people. I moved off table nineteen up toward the middle of the hall and began to beat almost everybody from Stuyvesant.

The most important hurdle for a straight-pool player involves being able to run into the second rack. You have to sink fourteen balls and leave the fifteenth ball and the cue ball positioned in such a way as to be able to sink the last ball (breaking open the new rack at the same time) and have a good enough leave to start all over again. I achieved this shortly before my sixteenth birthday, with a run of twenty-three.

The owners of Julian's recognized the accomplishment as a significant rite of passage and awarded certain privileges to those who had achieved it. During my last year of high school a cue of my own selection, with my name taped to the handle, was kept in a special rack behind the cashier's cage. No one else could use that particular cue stick. It was reserved, along with thirty or forty others for young players who had distinguished themselves.

I was a nonentity at school, but I could walk up to the cage at Julian's and the cashier would reach back for my stick and say, "Hey, Frank. How's it going?"

What a splendid place it was.

There's a lot to feel in pool, a physical aspect to the game, which means you have to play all the time to stay good. I've lost most of my chops (to borrow a word from jazz), but I still drop down to my local bar, the Foxhead, every now and then to play on the undersize table. It's a challenge arrangement. Put your name on the chalkboard, slip two quarters in the slot when it's your turn, and try to win.

There's a good deal more chance in eight ball, your basic bar game, than in straight pool, but it's fun. We've got some regulars. Jerry, a middle-aged man with a gorgeous stroke (a nationally ranked player in his youth), can beat anybody who walks into the place if he isn't furious at having to play doubles, at kids slopping beer onto the felt, or some other infraction of civilized behavior. There's Doug, a graduate student who always looks as if he'd spent the previous night in a cardboard box in an alley and who hits every shot as hard as he can, leaving the question of where the cue ball is going to end up more or less to the gods, in the hope that they will thus tangibly express the favor in which they hold him. (He is a poet.) We have George, an engineer, who exhausts our patience by approaching each situation with extreme care, circling the table several times, leaning over to stare down at a cluster of balls in what appears to be a hypnotic trance, chalking up with the care of Vermeer at the easel and running through a complicated series of various facial and physical tics before committing himself. There's Henry, who programs the jukebox to play "Brown Sugar" ten times in a row before he racks up. We've got students, working people, teachers, nurses (Yes. Women! Smilin' Jack would be scandalized) and barflies. We've got everybody at the Foxhead.

There are nights when I can hold the table for a couple of hours, but not very often. My touch is mostly gone, and bifocals make things difficult. Still, a bit of Julian's is still with me and, at the very least, I talk a good game.

## QUESTIONS ON CONTENT

1. How did Conroy first learn to play pool?
2. What did the Zen rock garden at the Brooklyn Botanic Garden remind Conroy of?
3. How did Conroy learn the art of "English"?
4. What rite of passage did Conroy accomplish? What was his reward?

## QUESTIONS ON RHETORIC

1. How does Conroy organize his essay? What time frame does it cover?
2. Does the essay contain too many stories to be one, or are they all necessary to his point?
3. Conroy uses a lot of pool jargon. Does it hinder the reader? Why or why not?
4. Why does Conroy add the last three paragraphs? Would the story have the same impact without them?

## VOCABULARY

(1) narcissism, melancholy, chaos, Euclidean, oasis

(13) meticulous

(15) imperceptible

(27) sacrilegious

(31) ominous

(33) demeanor, explicating

(34) eidetic

(37) laconic

(38) infinitesimal

(41) nonentity

## WRITING PROMPTS

1. Think about something you like doing. Describe whatever it is and what you think about while doing it. Figure out what causes you to like doing this.
2. Write of a time when you tried something new.
3. Write of something you haven't done but want to.
4. Write about someone who taught you something. Why did you choose to learn this from them?
5. Write about your escape from reality.

# HOME IS A PLACE IN TIME

## PAUL GRUCHOW

What if one's life were not a commodity, not something to be bartered to the highest bidder, or made to order? What if one's life were governed by needs more fundamental than acceptance or admiration? What if one were simply to stay home and plant some manner of garden?

To plant a garden is to enter the continuum of time. Each seed carries in its genome the history that will propel it into the future, and in planting it we stretch one of the long threads of our culture into tomorrow.

A home, like a garden, exists as much in time as in space. A home is the place in the present where one's past and one's future come together, the crossroads between history and heaven. I learned this truth the day we buried my mother.

In the previous month, I had felt often like a man without an anchor. We were living in St. Paul and expecting our first child. For my wife it was a difficult and somewhat dangerous pregnancy. Christmas passed and the days turned toward the new year. The baby was overdue. In those same days, Mother was lying in a hospital bed in Montevideo, Minnesota, emaciated and in pain. She had already lost a brave battle against cancer but was unwilling, just yet, to concede defeat, for reasons, that were, to me, mysterious. She was long past delusion about her prospects. My own heart resided in both places, full of fear and hope at the same time. I did not know where my body should be.

On the penultimate day of the old year, the baby, after a stubborn resistance of her own, finally came. She was big and beautiful and healthy. She gave one lusty cry as she entered the world and then lay quietly while she was bathed and dressed, looking about the room in wide-eyed wonder.

I telephoned Mother with the news. She said with surprising energy that she hoped she might see the baby before she died. But that day a fierce cold front had settled over Minnesota. For more than a week daytime temperatures did not rise above zero. We were, as I suppose first-time parents always are, terrified of our responsibilities. The baby seemed so helpless and fragile. We did not dare risk the three-hour drive to the hospital.

One cloudy morning in mid-January the weather at last broke. We bundled up the baby and made a dash for Montevideo. In the darkened hospital room, we introduced grandmother and granddaughter. The baby slept against the rails of the bed while Mother fondled her with eyes too small for their bony sockets. They joined hands, the baby's soft, fat, and warm, Mother's cold, gaunt, and hard. With tremendous effort, Mother whispered three words barely audible above the hum of the humidifier.

"Is she healthy?" she asked. We wept, because she was.

When we arrived back home, the telephone was ringing. A nurse was on the line with the word, hardly news, that Mother had died.

The weather was still bitter and gray the day we buried her in the little cemetery at St. John's Lutheran Church. After the ceremony the three children—Kathy, Paulette, and I—who felt strangely like children again that day, vulnerable and bewildered in an impossibly big world, took refuge one last time in the farmhouse where we had laughed and cried, together and alone, so many times.

We had meant to see to the household goods. There would not be many other opportunities for it; we lived at a distance from one another and seldom found ourselves together. But almost the first items we came across were the photo albums.

We sat in the living room then, not bothering to light the lamp, looking at the pictures and talking until the day died.

"Do you remember when Mother turned toward the back seat of the car and said, 'Where's your sister?' and Paul said, 'Oh, she fell out a long time ago,' and she *had?*"

"Do you remember the day Mother told the neighbor she couldn't go to the Women's Christian Temperance Union meeting because her wine was ready for bottling?"

"Do you remember the day Kathy fell through the outhouse hole?"

"Do you remember the day you rode your bicycle down the driveway with no hands and it made me so mad I stomped the spokes out of my bicycle's wheels?"

"Do you remember the time we floated a pound of butter in Mother's hot laundry starch?"

Do you remember?

Do you remember?

The stories tumbled as if out of an overstuffed closet. Sometimes we had three of them going at once. We laughed until we ached. I remember it now as one of the happiest afternoons of my life, the metamorphosis of a friendship deepening as the years pass and we three face our own mortalities. I think that I have never been more exactly at home, more tenaciously alive, than that afternoon, when old joy and new sorrow and present love reverberated together inside me.

All history is ultimately local and personal. To tell what we remember, and to keep on telling it, is to keep the past alive in the present. Should we not do so, we could not know, in the deepest sense, how to inhabit a place. To inhabit a place means literally to have made it a habit, to have made it the custom and ordinary practice of our lives, to have learned how to wear a place like a familiar garment, like the garments of sanctity that nuns once wore. The word habit, in its now-dim original form, meant *to own*. We own places not because we possess the deeds to them, but because they have entered the continuum of our lives. What is strange to us— unfamiliar—can never be home.

It is the fashion just now to disparage nostalgia. Nostalgia, we believe, is a cheap emotion. But we forget what it means. In its Greek roots it means, literally, the return to home. It came into currency as a medical word in nineteenth-century Germany to describe the failure to thrive of the displaced persons, including my own ancestors, who had crowded into that country from the east. Nostalgia is the clinical term for homesickness, for the desire to be rooted in a place — to know clearly, that is, what time it is. This desire need not imply the impulse to turn back the clock, which of course we cannot do. It recognizes, rather, the truth — if home is a place in time — that we cannot know where we are now unless we can remember where we have come from. The real romantics are those who believe that history is the story of the triumphal march of progress, that change is indiscriminately for the better. Those who would demythologize the past seem to forget that we also construct the present as a myth, that there is nothing in the wide universe so vast as our own ignorance. Knowing that is our one real hope.

## QUESTIONS ON CONTENT

1. Gruchow felt torn between being in two places. What were they?
2. Why didn't they take the baby to meet the grandmother the week it was born?
3. What did the grandmother ask about the baby?
4. What was the first item the siblings came across after their mother's funeral?
5. How did they spend the afternoon after the funeral?

## QUESTIONS ON RHETORIC

1. What function does the last sentence of paragraph 2 serve?
2. Look at the contrast in the description of the hands in paragraph 7. What effect does this have?
3. What purpose do the stories of "Do you remember..." serve? How do they change the tone of the piece?

4. The essay begins with the impersonal "one" and ends with "our." How does Gruchow accomplish this shift?

## VOCABULARY

(1) commodity, bartered

(2) continuum, genome

(4) emaciated, delusion

(5) penultimate

(7) gaunt

(20) metamorphosis, tenaciously

(22) disparage, nostalgia, demythologize

## WRITING PROMPTS

1. Where/what is home for you?
2. Why do we need to tell stories of the past, especially at times like funerals?
3. Write about a family story.
4. Make a list of "I remember..."
5. Write about "If home is a place in time..."

# In Praise of the Humble Comma

## Pico Iyer

The gods, they say, give breath, and they take it away. But the same could be said—could it not?—of the humble comma. Add it to the present clause, and, of a sudden, the mind is, quite literally, given pause to think; take it out if you wish or forget it and the mind is deprived of a resting place. Yet still the comma gets no respect. It seems just a slip of a thing, a pedant's tick, a blip on the edge of our consciousness, a kind of printer's smudge almost. Small, we claim, is beautiful (especially in the age of the microchip). Yet what is so often used, and so rarely recalled, as the comma—unless it be breath itself?

Punctuation, one is taught, has a point: to keep up law and order. Punctuation marks are the road signs placed along the highway of our communication—to control speeds, provide directions and prevent head-on collisions. A period has the unblinking finality of a red light; the comma is a flashing yellow light that asks us only to slow down; and the semicolon is a stop sign that tells us to ease gradually to a halt, before gradually starting up again. By establishing the relations between words, punctuation establishes the relations between the people using words. That may be one reason why schoolteachers exalt it and lovers defy it ("We love each other and belong to each other let's don't ever hurt each other Nicole let's don't ever hurt each other," wrote Gary Gilmore to his girlfriend). A comma, he must have known, "separates inseparables," in the clinching words of H.W. Fowler, King of English Usage.

Punctuation, then, is a civic prop, a pillar that holds society upright. (A run-on sentence, its phrases piling up without division, is as unsightly as a sink piled high with dirty dishes.) Small wonder, then, that punctuation was one of the first proprieties of the Victorian age, the age of the corset, that the modernists threw off: the sexual revolution might be said to have begun when Joyce's Molly Bloom spilled out all her private thoughts in 36 pages of unbridled, almost unperioded and officially censored prose; and another rebellion was surely marked when E.E. Cummings first felt free to commit "God" to the lower case.

Punctuation thus becomes the signature of cultures. The hot-blooded Spaniard seems to be revealed in the passion and urgency of his doubled exclamation points and question marks (*"¡Caramba! ¿Quien sabe?"*), while the impassive Chinese traditionally added to his so-called inscrutability by omitting directions from his ideograms. The anarchy and commotion of the '60s were given voice in the exploding exclamation marks, riotous capital letters and Day-Glo italics of Tom Wolfe's spray-paint prose; and in Communist societies, where the State is absolute, the dignity—and divinity—of capital letters is reserved for Ministries, Sub-Committees and Secretariats.

Yet punctuation is something more than a culture's birthmark; it scores the music in our minds, gets our thoughts moving to the rhythm of our hearts. Punctuation is the notation in the sheet music of our words, telling us when to rest, or when to raise our voices; it acknowledges that the meaning of our discourse, as of any symphonic composition, lies not in the units but in the pauses, the pacing and the phrasing. Punctuation is the way one bats one's eyes, lowers one's voice or blushes demurely. Punctuation adjusts the tone and color and volume till the feeling comes into perfect focus: not disgust exactly, but distaste; not lust, or like, but love.

Punctuation, in short, gives us the human voice, and all the meanings that lie between the words. "You aren't young, are you?" loses its innocence when it loses the question mark. Every child knows the menace of a dropped apostrophe (the parent's "Don't do that" shifting into the more slowly enunciated "Do not do that"), and every believer, the ignominy of having his faith reduced to "faith." Add an exclamation point to "To be or not to be…" and the gloomy Dane has all the resolve he needs; add a comma, and the noble sobriety of "God save the Queen" becomes a cry of desperation bordering on double sacrilege.

Sometimes, of course, our markings may be simply a matter of aesthetics. Popping in a comma can be like slipping on the necklace that gives an outfit quiet elegance, or like catching the sound of running water that complements, as it completes, the silence of a Japanese landscape. When V.S. Naipaul, in his latest novel, writes, "He was a middle-aged man, with glasses," the first comma can seem a little precious. Yet it gives the description a spin, as well as a subtlety, that it otherwise lacks, and it shows that the glasses are not part of the middle-agedness, but something else.

Thus all these tiny scratches give us breadth and heft and depth. A world that has only periods is a world without inflections. It is a world without shade. It has a music without sharps and flats. It is a martial music. It has a jackboot rhythm. Words cannot bend and curve. A comma, by comparison, catches the gentle drift of the mind in thought, turning in on itself and back on itself, reversing, redoubling and returning along the course of its own sweet river music; while the semicolon brings clauses and thoughts together with all the silent discretion of a hostess arranging guests around her dinner table.

Punctuation, then, is a matter of care. Care for words, yes, but also, and more important, for what the words imply. Only a lover notices the small things: the way the afternoon light catches the nape of a neck, or how a strand of hair slips out from behind an ear, or the way a finger curls around a cup. And no one scans a letter so closely as a lover, searching for its small print, straining to hear its nuances, its gasps, its sighs and hesitations, poring over the secret messages that lie in every cadence. The difference between "Jane (whom I adore)" and "Jane, whom I adore," and the difference between them both and "Jane—whom I adore—" marks all the distance between ecstasy and heartache. "No iron can pierce the heart with such force as a period put at just the right place," in Isaac Babel's lovely words;

a comma can let us hear a voice break, or a heart. Punctuation, in fact, is a labor of love. Which brings us back, in a way, to gods.

## QUESTIONS ON CONTENT

1. What is the point of puncuation, according to Iyer?
2. What gives words their human voice?
3. What are some of the functions of punctuation?

## QUESTIONS ON RHETORIC

1. Look at the organization of the essay. How many metaphors does Iyer have for discussing punctuation?
2. What examples does Iyer use to illustrate these metaphors?
3. Look at the beginning and ending of the essay. What commonality do they share?

## VOCABULARY

(4) inscrutability

(6) menace, ignominy

(7) aesthetics, subtlety

(9) nuances, cadence

## WRITING PROMPTS

1. How does punctuation keep law and order?
2. Write sentences whose meaning could be drastically changed by punctuation.
3. How does the use of punctuation become the "signature of a culture"?
4. Write about punctuation as the human voice.

# Full Circle Lessons

## Mary E. Mitchell

Maureen Ferris belonged to one of those families who never raised their venetian blinds. Every room in her house looked like dusk. Maureen's light-blue eyes were the brightest, most extravagant things in the house. Of all my third-grade friends, she was the best, and this is why I sometimes accompanied her to her sad split level after school.

We would try to avoid her mother. It wasn't that Mrs. Ferris was a bad person. She was stern, however, and colorless. At dinner at her house, each person got one hamburger. If you were still hungry, you could eat more salad.

Dinner at my house was a free-flowing affair with lots of chatter and baby noises and teasing, with globs of mashed potatoes tap, tap, tapping onto plates and gleaming forks flying at the meat platter. My mother was a living palette of color, with red sauce stains on her striped apron and cheeks flushed pink from the stove. Maureen loved her.

She loved our messy house as well, the way scuffed sneakers lined each tread of the staircase, and clean, folded underwear sat in sorted piles along the top of the sofa.

In the midst of all the laundry and bustle, my mother took time each day to read. Afternoons, when the baby napped, she sat in the floral armchair by the picture window, a bevy of half-dead houseplants on the sill behind her, a romance novel or a magazine in her hands. This was her time, stolen from endless hours of child care and housework. Unironed school blouses and dirty kitchen floors might make her feel guilty, but her midafternoon reading never did.

One day, as I played in Maureen's clean house, Mrs. Ferris fixed me with her cool gray eyes and said, "Your mother's nice, but she reads too much." I was stunned.

The next time I caught my mother reading in her little patch of sunlight, I studied her in the doorway and decided her apron could use a washing. Shame flushed through me. Reading was the cause—pleasure-reading in broad daylight. Silently, I made vows that would keep me from sharing my mother's fate.

I didn't know it was already too late for me, that the way I lovingly handled the pages of my Nancy Drew books, the hours I spent with the *National Geographic* behind locked bathroom doors, revealed the extent to which I already was cut from the same flawed cloth. The years passed in a blur of covertly turned pages until I was a grown-up schoolteacher with a husband and children of my own. I struggled mightily with my own desire to open a novel in brazen daylight, or spend five extra minutes over a morning newspaper. My only guiltless reading occurred at night, when the dishes were rattling in the dishwasher, the kids were in bed and my husband sat with a pile of bills or watched television.

Off I'd go to work each day, passing on the gift of reading to others. I'd start with my students as early as kindergarten, helping them memorize lists of rhyming words that I then put together into sentences for them to read: "Dan the man ran over a can with his van." "Draw this," I'd say, and the pictures were awesome, wild things infused with the broad strokes and bright colors of a child who'd discovered that he could read, could make sense of the letters and the words on a page. All over the world there was agreement that this was important, as important as eating or thinking or working. And then one day, I finally understood what my mother had tried to show us, that reading was housework of the very best kind.

She called yesterday, and I described an Anne Tyler book about a woman who runs away from home and leaves her husband and kids to clean up their own messes.

"Would you like to read it?" I asked.

"Sure," she said, "as soon as I'm done with Danielle Steel." I picture her in her floral armchair, the houseplants behind her gasping for water, the smile on her face serene.

## QUESTIONS ON CONTENT

1. Why was the Ferris house described as "sad"?
2. What did Mrs. Ferris say about Mrs. Mitchell?
3. What vocation did Mitchell follow?

## QUESTIONS ON RHETORIC

1. Compare the description of Maureen's house to the Mitchell's house.
2. What cultural expectations of women are addressed?
3. Compare/contrast the two mothers.
4. What lessons did Mitchell learn about reading from her mother? From Mrs. Ferris?

## VOCABULARY

(8) covertly, brazen

(9) infused

## WRITING PROMPTS

1. Describe yourself as a reader.
2. What messages about reading did you learn from your family? From school?
3. Write about a book that you could not put down.
4. Write about a life lesson you learned as a child.

# INTERNATIONAL RELATIONS

## MOHSIN HAMID

Before I'm allowed to see my girlfriend, I must offer proof of my love—to a consulate official.

The passport I hand through the slit in her glass shield runs suspiciously backward, the right-hand cover its front, and above the curved swords of its Urdu lettering she reads, "Islamic Republic of Pakistan." Words to make a visa officer tremble. The scene is the Italian Consulate in New York, the back entrance, a subterranean room staffed by three polite sentries. They are charged with the defense of a wall that runs around wealthy democracies, and their post is less tense than many because it lies inside the fortifications of an ally.

I am well dressed. A navy suit, pinstriped, three-buttoned. White shirt, blue tie, brown face, brown eyes. I shaved this morning but missed a patch beside my chin. The stubble there, though short, is dense. Fundamentalist stubble. Ayatollah, Hezbollah stubble. Fighting in the heights of Kashmir stubble. But just a hint.

In uncalloused hands, marred only by cuticles in need of a lesson, I hold my remaining documents: letter from employer, bank statement, proof of insurance, recent pay stub, airline ticket, hotel booking. A mother could arrange marriage with less information than I am asked to present. My eyes are shadowed with stress or lack of sleep. I am sweating slightly, despite the coolness of this day, and my scalp glistens where the hair has forsaken it.

My smile is dishonest, the smile of a man who hopes his smile will make it easier for him, insincere as attempts at sincerity tend to be. She is almost friendly in return. We are both young, after all, healthy members of the same species and of breeding age.

There are only 101 points to the inspection a Pakistani must pass to be deemed travel-worthy. I fail—because I have succeeded in the past. I have traveled to Italy too often.

Why so many trips over so short a period? she asks.

Love, I say. My girlfriend is Italian.

She pauses, not eager to do this. But she must: it is her duty. The wall is only as strong as its weakest gate.

Yes, that is a very good reason, she says. But I am afraid we will need proof: a notarized letter and a copy of her passport.

You need a letter from a woman saying she is my lover? I ask.

The visa officer is human. Humane. She blushes. I am afraid so, she says. But I will approve your application now so you do not have to make an extra trip. Just bring the letter with you when you come to pick up your visa. Please do not forget: you will be asked for it.

I know I am fortunate. She could, at her discretion, have turned me down. Other visa officers in other consulates, especially in American consulates, regularly reject my kind for far less. Still, I am not pleased.

My colleagues in our business-casual office were amused that I wore a suit that day, but I was ashamed. It tacitly acknowledged an accusation I would have liked proudly to ignore. But what exactly is the accusation?

Race has become too clumsy a shorthand for the legal boundaries that divide liberal democracies like the United States. Nationality, unless overcome by wealth, is a far more acceptable proxy. Nations deemed prone to poverty and violence are walled off to consume themselves, to fester. And national discrimination has taken its place alongside racial discrimination, denying both our common humanity and our unbelievably varied individuality as it frisks us at the border.

Here, in cosmopolitan New York, I am able to reside only at the sufferance of my employer, halfway through a six-year H-1B work visa, which binds the legality of my presence in the United States to my job. The Labor Department and the I.N.S. are kept so understaffed that it currently takes several years for most green card applications to be processed. I could face eventual deportation even if I submit my petition today. Like much of the indentured work force, I feel insecure. I must produce notarized love letters at checkpoints. My category is not a desirable one.

But I do as I am told, and I am given my Italian visa.

I get into a cab and head back to my office. My driver looks like a terrorist: steady eyes, thick beard, the reserved watchfulness of the devout. A verse of the Koran dangles beneath his rearview. He could be my uncle.

Where are you coming from? he asks me in Urdu.

I was applying for a visa, I tell him.

You have had a hard morning, brother, he says, turning off the meter. This ride is on me.

## QUESTIONS ON CONTENT

1. What is the author trying to obtain?
2. Why is he having difficulty obtaining it?
3. Where does Hamid live?
4. What does the taxi driver do for Hamid?

## QUESTIONS ON RHETORIC

1. List the words in the beginning of the essay that relate to war. Why do you think the author uses war terms for description?
2. Why does Hamid say "My smile is dishonest"? What effect does this dishonesty have?
3. In cosmopolitan New York City, would you expect "national discrimination"?

4. Why would the cab driver offer a free ride to Hamid?

5. Are these people living the American Dream?

## VOCABULARY

(2) fortifications

(3) fundamentalist

(14) tacitly

(15) proxy

(16) cosmopolitan, deportation, indentured

## WRITING PROMPTS

1. Can love be validated?

2. Have you ever traveled in another country? What were your feelings there?

3. Look at America through a foreigner's eyes.

4. Write about "legal boundaries that divide liberal democracies."

# Soul Disposed

## Cynthia Williams

As a child I feared garbage. Out comes a memory from the waste-basket of my soul: me, age 6, a solitary, skinny Irish Catholic girl dashing through the dark tunnel that runs beneath our San Francisco flat. I am clutching a soggy bag of trash and running for a black, chthonic alcove reeking of earth and mold. In this foul corner squats, like an idol, a scrofulous metal can. My awe-full duty: to offer it our trash.

The worst moment is the blind lifting of the lid, for always I feel sure that, this time, something will leap out. Not a rat or a cock-roach, but a being sprung of the garbage itself: some creature that has assembled itself out of our leavings, wild with rage at being imprisoned in a dungeon-dark metal can. Breathless with panic, I ram the bag into the can, jam down the lid, and run back down the tunnel—fleeing our angry trash.

And so it went for the next two years. By the age of 8 I had devel-oped freckled arms and a tendency to hide after school in Golden Gate Park. One frigid March afternoon found me wandering in the foggy pines behind the botanical gardens. The wind from the Pacific, a quarter mile west, kicked up, and something blew across my feet. Garbage: an empty potato chip bag. Frito-Lay's Barbecued Potato Chips, as I recall. The orange plastic-coated bag clung with a kind of desperation to my saddle shoes, as if pleading for mercy. I found

myself imagining this bag blowing around later that night, lost and
frightened in the darkness of the damp, gothic park. Suddenly, I saw
garbage in another way—it was lonely. Overwhelmed by pity, I
picked up the bag and took it home, to rest under my bed. I even
named it: George.

Kids see the world animistically. In a limited way, we tolerate it.
How cute if baby Ashley tries to feed that head-shaped hunk of
basalt her applesauce; how sweet that little Jonathan imagines the
elm is talking to him. Even adults believe that great buildings or
paintings or statues have a kind of soul. We semi-jokingly admit the
possibility of consciousness in favorite cars or old teddy bears. And
pagans are in favor of wood nymphs, wind sprites, and spirits living in rock formations.

But in scraps of PVC piping? Ripped-up sofas? Dove Bar
wrappers?

My mother found the potato chip bag under the bed and tried
to discard it.

"Don't throw him out!"

"What? Why?"

"He's sad."

My mother gaped. "Sad? The bag?" She was a patient woman,
but the drudgery of impoverished single mother-hood had left her
as worn down as an old tire.

"What in God's name are you talking about?"

I couldn't explain; I just knew that he—the bag—was pitiful.
Though I, like little Ashley and Jonathan, also felt that basalt and elms
had souls. I didn't feel sorry for those sorts of things. They didn't seem
bereft to me. They didn't seem solitary and pathetic, didn't seem like
orphans, like riders on the storm. They lived in their own world, the
world of rocks and elms. But what world did the potato chip bag
belong to? It belonged to us, the world of people. The bag had been
created by us like parents create children. And then, abandoned. The
way parents sometimes abandon children. The potato chip bag blowing forlornly around the dark park—it was like seeing a lost child.
It scared me.

"I'm not throwing him out!"

My mother shrugged wearily and put George back under the bed. My newfound compassion for garbage didn't go away; it grew, like a landfill. I began to pick up all sorts of refuse. Soon I was developing a trash collection. But *collection* isn't really the right word. It was an *orphanage* stuffed into cardboard boxes underneath my bed: a scrap of foil from a chocolate bar, an exploded foam-rubber cushion, an unspooled Petula Clark tape, a fraying, rubber-coated coil of electrical wiring. I gave names to them all: Fred, Marie, José, Deirdre. My mother started to get seriously upset.

"Get rid of this frigging garbage!"

"It's not garbage!" I countered. But it was, of course, and I knew it; I didn't have a (gnawed-up, thrown-out chicken) leg to stand on.

The word *garbage* comes from the Middle English word for chicken guts, but nowadays *garbage* is the inorganic, what cannot rot: broken circuit boards, old mascara wands, empty orange juice cartons, plastic shrink wrap from a CD. When we call cities "dirty" we no longer mean they are heaped with decomposing animal entrails, smashed-up clay pottery, and flea-ridden woven mats. Or, for that matter, dirt. No. We mean that a lot of discarded machine-made objects are lying around. When you think about it, this is strange.

After all, a mere empty potato chip bag is an object of marvelous technical and industrial complexity, in some sense more rare than any diamond. And here it is, lying on the street. And over there, four inches away, a half-inch screw; and there, beneath the tires of that parked car, a flattened tube of children's paint, and next to it, the glitter of an aluminum can; and here, under my feet, the soggy latex conundrum of a condom.

My mother and I argued about my trash collection for the next several years; I eventually began hiding it. Finally, at 12, I lost my empathy for garbage and stopped taking it home. The next seven years are an existential teenage blur: I took to reading Nietzsche and seldom left the house.

In my 20s I left behind the self-absorption of adolescence, went to San Francisco State University as a film student, and once again became emotional about rubbish. I was in the usual bohemian phase—shaved head, illegal pharmaceuticals, artistic pretensions—but my own personal idiosyncrasy flowered anew. I began to collect trash again, but now I called it Dumpster diving.

I hunted up and down the streets and gutters for the leavings of civilization—a thrown-out mattress, a chipped Blue Willow teacup, holey sweaters and shirts and shoes, a waffle iron with a frayed cord. I slept on the mattress, wore the clothes and shoes, made grilled cheese sandwiches in the waffle iron and washed them down with red wine I drank out of the blue teacup. In all this, I was as tensely alert, as primed to opportunity, as any Pleistocene hunter-gatherer. I could spot on the sidewalk a cast-off black bookcase at 50 yards, a broken accordion at three blocks. Once, while I was passing the foyer of an apartment building, I saw a drunken man pleading into the intercom for his ex-girlfriend to take him back. She hung up, and he despairingly dropped his box of candy on the sidewalk and took off, weeping. I ran over while the pavement was still warm from his boots and scooped up this brand-new garbage. Standing on the street corner, I wolfed down the cast-off chocolates—junk food, indeed. Finally, garbage was friendly, not bathetic; now garbage was doing *me* the favor.

In my late 20s I moved to Los Angeles and became a screenwriter. There, garbage again became alien and threatening. It had something to do with driving: Viewed from a car, refuse on the streets looked black and distant, dark piles of matter hunched underneath freeway overpasses that I whizzed by at 70 miles an hour. To stop my car and scavenge street-corner junk seemed inconceivable. I had more money—for a few years, a lot of it—and I bought things. I ordered stuff brand-new from catalogs: chiffon dresses, vibrating toys, midnight-blue towel sets. I began to think back with astonishment and horror on the stained mattress I'd slept on, the battered sweater I'd worn, the rusted cast-iron pan in which I had fried my *huevos rancheros*. It was like guys you can no longer believe you were fool enough to sleep with. Me? I actually touched that trash?

In my mid 30s I moved back to San Francisco. It was much dirtier now, and the city was filled with homeless men and women—garbage people. Some of the more energetic of these dregs of society managed to eke out a living from the nonhuman dregs of society: They stole recyclables. Vietnam vets with shopping carts and Vietnamese families in decrepit trucks hit the streets at 4 a.m. to beat the garbagemen to the bottles, newspapers, and Coke cans other people put out on the sidewalk. My grandmother, Zorka "4E" Asten (elderly, ethnic, extremely eccentric), took personal umbrage at the garbage stealers and became obsessed with defeating them: She disguised her garbage, took it out at odd hours, mixed the bottles and cans up with cold oatmeal and feces from her whippet, Twerpy. The garbage thieves retaliated by flinging her trash all over her driveway. Zorka got up at three to sit in the living room in the dark, waiting to shout out the window things like "You no-good bums!" and "You damned dirty Chinamen!" But they were too tenacious for her, like an army of carpenter ants scavenging a corpse, they just kept on coming. Defeated, Zorka gave up and let the resolute garbage stealers have their way.

There were people on the streets selling garbage, too. Entrepreneurial homeless people set up little illegal "shops," as defined by discarded squares of carpeting on the sidewalk, and sold, for a quarter or 50 cents, scavenged trash: '70s Matt Helm paperbacks with a page or two missing, flaking patent-leather platform boots, chipped ballerina statuettes, kind-of-broken toasters. One day my friend Jeanine and I walked by a woman with no legs, a wild shock of white hair, and a face like a wasted Beata Virgo Maria who was sitting on the corner of 20th and Capp Streets trying to sell little bits of broken glass.

"How offal," I heard myself joke. I immediately felt ashamed, but my friend hadn't even noticed; she was worrying aloud how she was going to make ends meet that month. She kept complaining that she couldn't afford to pay the garbage bill.

We walked by a half-burned rowing machine someone had tossed in the gutter, but I felt no greed, no curiosity, nothing. Trash wasn't fun anymore. It was too serious.

Now I'm in my late 30s and, owing to the flotsam of events, I live in a desert resort town. It is very clean here. A platoon of Hispanic men in large brown trucks spend their days under the fiery

Sonoran sun, sweeping, blowing, and carrying away any stray bit of refuse that manages to make it onto the white, blazing streets. Sometimes, like a prisoner breaking free, a brown, twiggy ball of Russian thistle—tumbleweed—will blow onto the road. The men quickly take it away. Occasionally I hear them singing a snatch of some Mexican rock 'n' roll song, but mostly they are subdued and silent, as if they don't want to draw attention to themselves.

I also have an 8-month-old child now, and we seem unable to teach him the difference between toys and garbage. As far as he is concerned, they are of equal interest. Yesterday, I pried out of his mouth a scrap of discarded newspaper, he was chewing it with exactly the same quiet pleasure with which he mouths his nice new plastic rattle. The soggy piece of paper, I saw, was the tail end of an article from the local paper. The state wants to build a giant landfill nearby, it said, at a place called Eagle Mountain. Environmentalists are trying to stop the landfill, since the decaying garbage will leach heavy metals and petrochemicals directly into our aquifer, and it will damage the habitat of a local tortoise. But the state wants to go ahead. The garbage must go somewhere, officials say.

Someone else once said there is a great weight of sadness on the world. Maybe there is. Maybe it consists of millions upon millions of tons of trash, inside of which, perhaps, is trapped a flicker of consciousness. Is it possible our garbage is suffering?

As are we, of course. It's commonplace, but worth repeating. We are drowning in the urban bilge of civilization, suffocating under the rags and bones of technoindustrialism. The air is heavy with cast-off carbon particles, the water scummy with discarded oil; plants and animals groan under the chemical grime of estrogen disruptors and PCBs. In the pesticide-and herbicide-drenched cornfields, even the *dirt* has become dirty.

I look at my baby boy, chortling with pleasure in his bath, and think: My son, what if I were to discard you on the street as if you were nothing, as if you meant nothing to me, as if I myself had not created you? Wouldn't such wickedness demand punishment? And so if our rubbish does indeed have a spirit, do not we, a stinkard civilization that has trashed its trash, soon have to prepare to suffer some very bad garbage karma?

But back to the rotting compost of memory and my trash-terrified, 6-year-old self: On Wednesday mornings at 5 a.m., when it was still very dark, the garbagemen of the San Francisco Scavenger Company would come and take away our fearsome refuse. They were cheery, burly Italian men with green uniforms, and they loudly sang opera as they picked up the cans. They always woke me up. I would lie in my narrow bed in my dark bedroom, massaging my jumpy stomach (I was worrying about school, where a little girl said I was white trash) and listening to the men yell out riotous songs from *Carmen* and *Rigoletto*. People in San Francisco had romantic theories of esprit de corps to explain the opera singing, but as it happened, my mother had a family friend who was a garbageman, a large, balding man named Frank Vucci. He said they sang so that no one would think they were burglars, and shoot them. But I thought they sang because they were alone in the darkness of the trash tunnels and because they, too, feared the garbage.

## QUESTIONS ON CONTENT

1. Why was Williams afraid to take out the garbage as a child?
2. What bit of garbage did she first keep under her bed?
3. What does the word *garbage* mean in Middle English?
4. Why did the garbage men in her neighborhood sing opera?

## QUESTIONS ON RHETORIC

1. How does the author come full circle with her topic?
2. Who do you think is the audience for this essay?
3. What tone does the essay have? Does the tone change as the narrative unfolds?
4. Why does Williams have an obsession with garbage?

## VOCABULARY

(1) chthonic, scrofulous

(3) gothic

(4) animistically

(12) bereft

(20) empathy, existential, Nietzsche

(21) bohemian, idiosyncrasy

(22) Pleistocene, despairingly

(24) eccentric, umbrage, tenacious

(28) flotsam

(29) aquifer

## WRITING PROMPTS

1. Write about garbage as "creation..., an object of marvelous technical and industrial complexity."
2. Write about "Dumpster diving."
3. Have you ever seen a homeless person eating from trash bins? How did you react?
4. What are the effects of the garbage problem in our country? Write about "the *dirt* has become dirty."
5. Write about "garbage karma."

# 3

# STUDENT ESSAYS

# LEAP OF FAITH

## BRANDI GRADY-GROSZ

Two of the most troubling concepts I have had to deal with throughout my life are success and failure. So much of what we do, if not
all of what we do, is focused on gaining success and avoiding failure. If one is consumed with being successful, yet has a warped or
untrue understanding of what being successful means, he is in a lot
of trouble. Taking a step back to look at my own perception of what
this term means brought me to the conclusion that I was in trouble.

I don't want to say that I've always been competitive because I
can think of countless times where I've been the most apathetic person in the room, but in general, I've only tried things a second time
if I were really good at them the first time. To me, success meant
being natural at something—good at it the first time you tried it. If
first attempts weren't fruitful I wasn't going to try anymore. Practice would have only made me average and to me average meant failure. I have held to this little theory of mine as though it were law
and it has kept me tied to the floor for a very long time.

Sad to say, I have been that way since day one and now I have
a huge battle on my hands in changing a behavior that has come to
make life joylessly comfortable. I've never been a chance taker.
Through the few experiences I've had (as such limited living makes
them few) I have come to feel that safety is found in comfort and

comfort is found in the known. No doubt, I have lost a great deal by running my life focused on safety and comfort.

I can no longer live by such an hilarious falsehood. There are too many things that I want now where I proved to be less than average at first. In fact, in all reality most people are only going to have about a handful of things at which they could possibly be above average. I don't have a scale or standard to tell me what about average, below average or just plain average means, so in my youth and immaturity, I have left the answer in the amount of effort one must take to achieve the results desired. In other words, I perceived a person to be above average when he or she achieved something with little effort, as naturally as possible; like the kid who can shoot the three-pointer from the beginning, with little practice behind her.

Because I've struggled for so long with the concepts of "success" and "failure" I believe others might be struggling with the same things. As I said, I have lost so much due to this struggle. So many experiences and joys were never fulfilled because I wasn't prepared to be average. Highland dancing, acting, singing, piano, speaking different languages, sewing, writing, drawing and designing—the list could go on and on of all the things I was interested in doing but missed out on because I wasn't the best at them, and therefore thought that I shouldn't continue with them. This makes me wonder how many others there are with this inane sense of what it means to be successful and what it means to be a failure. I have come to understand how wrong I was in my thinking and I feel this strong need to help others not make the same mistakes.

This is a part of why I've pursued education as a career. What better place could I spread such valuable lessons? Lessons about life that seem to make or break the kind of life one will lead. So many of us look back with regret. It seems almost impossible to not have any regrets at all. But if one can limit them with a wiser understanding of the goals she sets and the true achievement of those goals, then she's on her way to a richer, more fulfilling life.

I want my future students to live much more freely than I ever did. I know that a good majority would never dream of believing in the silly laws of success and failure that I believed in, but many will have the tendency to stay in their comfort zones where they will take few chances and end up unfulfilled in their lives. A central goal of mine in a future classroom will be to make chance takers of my students. To do this I have to come up with what feels like a magical formula that is somehow going to wipe away all that has been programmed into my students' heads. Every comment made by a parent, commercial, friend, movie or song will have to be removed, so the students can use their own hearts and brains to find truths. Yet, once they've been contaminated, it's difficult to turn back and so the job ahead of me is a tough one. I may only reach a few, but you never know, those few that I reach might turn around and reach a few more.

I want to help my students to become more daring, willing to fall and then not even see their fall as an actual fall. I hope they can put learning and experience before most everything else. The more I can get them to experience or try, the more they will come to know themselves and come to know what brings them joy—which will eventually leave them with success. I hope to do this through example. Students in my class will see first hand that stepping out has consequences. But they will also see that those consequences, more often than not, are going to be less severe than the ones that await the person who sits stagnant in the comfy chair fearfully watching all that personally interests him twirl down the drain. I will need to set up an environment that provokes action, almost to the extreme where the old saying of "look before you leap" will no longer hold. Experiences and learning will be of the utmost priority, not just to me, the teacher, but to each individual student.

My goal here is to have my future students leave school with more than the Pythagorean Theorem, or a memorization of the Declaration of Independence. We constantly hear the talk of lifelong learners; well it seems to me that a path like this could make such talk become realistic. How can one learn if he doesn't try or experience new things? And if so many are walking around jilted by the fear of failure, few will ever reach the heights of success that education as an institution so badly wants them to reach.

## QUESTIONS ON CONTENT

1. What two concepts does the author address?
2. What career has the author chosen?
3. What lesson does she want to instill in her students?
4. What is the author's definition of success?

## QUESTIONS ON RHETORIC

1. How does the title connect to the essay?
2. What examples of success and failure does the author include?
3. Grady-Grosz writes about mental contamination. What exactly does she mean?

## VOCABULARY

(2) apathetic

(5) inane

(7) contaminated

(8) stagnant

(9) Pythagorean Theorem

## WRITING PROMPTS

1. Describe your comfort zone. How does it affect your behavior?
2. Are there things you have not tried because you were afraid to fail? What would happen if you tried them and did fail? Succeed?
3. Write about a chance you desperately want to take. How will it affect your life if you do? If you don't?

# COON HUNT

## BRENDA SALAZAR

"Come on kids, let's go hunting." We are all bundled up and ready to go. Ray and Cheryl and I are going in the woods with Dad, to go hunting.

It is September and the leaves are beginning to fall off of the trees. The air is not too brisk; it is a perfect Indian summer day. The sun filters to the ground and leaves shadows between the popples.

It is fun tromping behind Dad through the woods. We are explorers! Or . . . early settlers. We go past the place where Lloyd had his house at one time. All that is left is the foundation. My little legs really have to move to keep up.

Finally we get to stop and rest! I lie on the ground and watch the clouds float by, letting the sun absorb into my skin. It is a wonderful day. The rest is over.

It is my turn to carry the gun. I have listened very carefully. I know the rules. Carry it over your shoulder; point the barrel down. Do not point it at anyone else; set it down if going over a fence. Always check the safety! I am so proud now. I am a grown up just like everyone else.

My arm is getting tired from carrying this heavy gun so I switch to the other shoulder. Soon it is getting tired also. I do not dare to complain. That would only be looking for trouble. I just try to keep up. The sticks are slapping me in the face because I don't have time enough

to grab them and move them out of my way. I do not want to get lost.
I would be lost forever. I don't think anyone would come look for me.

I catch up to where Dad is waiting. He has spotted a raccoon in
a tree.

"Brenda, let's see how good a shot you are."

Oh no! I am going to have to kill a raccoon! How am I supposed
to tell Dad that I can't kill anything. I can't confront him and tell
him that, so I quickly form a plan...

I will close my eyes and shoot.

My arms are shaking as I point the gun up at this beautiful creature that is shaking because I am pointing a gun at it. It is looking
down at me with fear in its eyes. I know how it feels. I have felt that
look in my eyes when dad is looking down at me. I want to tell this
poor little creature that I would never do anything to hurt it because
I know what it feels like to be hurt.

I close my eyes and pull the trigger.

Please God let me have missed.

I open my eyes. Dad is smiling, "Good shot."

How could I have hit him with my eyes closed?

This poor creature is stuck up in a tree because I shot him. When
I hit him he grabbed on with his claws and now he can't let go.

Dad makes me shoot him again, and again. Finally he falls to
the ground.

I want to throw up.

## QUESTIONS ON CONTENT

1. What is the group hunting?
2. What happens when it is Brenda's turn to carry the gun?
3. What was Brenda's plan for missing the animal?

## QUESTIONS ON RHETORIC

1. Salazar uses very short sentences throughout her essay. What
   effect does this have?

2. Seven of the last eight paragraphs are one sentence in length. Was this a conscious decision? How does it affect the essay?
3. Look at paragraphs 6 and 11. Why are they so much longer than the others?

## VOCABULARY

(2) Indian summer

## WRITING PROMPTS

1. Have you ever wanted to belong to a group so badly that you compromised your beliefs? Write about your feelings on both sides of the issue.
2. Do members of your family have beliefs that are different than yours? How do you compromise? Do you have to?
3. Write about a tough lesson you have learned.

# In the Garden

## Deb Sullivan

There is a definite hint of spring in the air. Nothing blatant—no budding of the trees or daffodils peeping through the soil—I have yet to see the first robin. Yet, there is a lightness in the air and strength in the sun's rays. In a burst of hopeful energy, I walk out to my garden. I plan to make note of the things that need to be done in preparation for the new season. My intention is simply to make a brief inspection and become reacquainted with my old friend. The crisp, clean breeze guides me on my way.

Some people find it odd that I refer to my garden as a friend. It makes perfect sense to me. Many times I have found a solace in working the soil that had previously been elusive. The rhythmic pulling of weeds relaxes me. Each turn of the spade brings a sense of release. Gardening is not exacting work, at least not for me. It doesn't require deep concentration or precise movement. It is this aspect that I love the most, for with my hands at work on familiar tasks, my mind is freed.

I decide that maybe I should rake up the leaves that have blown in ridges along the fencing. Soon after I set to work, I begin to think about my need to nurture—animals, humans, the plants in my garden. People who know my husband and I have asked me why we don't have children, "You would make great parents." My answer is always the same, "I guess we can't." Biologically speaking, that is. We have given thought to adoption, but the years continue to slip past. Maybe someday—we are both still young. There are times when the desire to become a parent is almost overwhelming. It is as if I can hear the ticking of my biological clock.

As I bend over to repair the garden gate, my thoughts turn to two of my nephews, Jake and Ben. I often think of them when I feel maternal. They are identical twins, just fifteen years old. Oh, how I love them! From the time they were born, I have loved them with a passion that sometimes surprises me. They were my first nephews— the first babies in our family—and much anticipated. I was young and single at the time of their birth and spent hours with them as their ever-ready babysitter. As the boys matured and my life expanded to include my husband, the four of us have created terrific memories: camping trips, boating, Minnesota Twins games. The bond we have formed is unbreakable.

A couple of years ago, tragedy struck. Their parents, my brother and his wife of fourteen years, divorced. Certainly not a new phenomenon, but I had no idea the change and tremendous pain that divorce can bring. Life for Jake and Ben, from my perspective, has been shattered. Bitter words and ugly fights were the norm in their house during the divorce. I learned the meaning of "egocentricity" as I struggled to understand how two adults, who I thought I knew, could endeavor to destroy each other and inadvertently their children. Although I continue to see Jake and Ben whenever possible, and talk with them on the phone at least weekly, it is not the same. They have been forced prematurely into adulthood and hide the scars of their pain under layers of affected indifference.

The cool breeze calls attention to the moisture of tears on my face as I stand and stretch my back. I marvel at the fact that I still cry over this sad situation. I was certain that I was "okay" with things—had worked through my feelings. I had spent hours trying to decide how I could help the boys and only recently became resigned to the fact that I could not fix things for them. I have learned to force thoughts of the two of them wandering the streets with their other "latch-key" friends from my mind. I won't reach to the anger I feel toward their parents for becoming wrapped up in their new single lifestyles and seeming to forget about their children. Just the other day, my mother and I both agreed (again) that although my husband and I would love to have Jake and Ben live with us, and the rest of the family thinks we should take them, this is not the answer. So why the tears?

As I wipe my sleeve across my face, I notice the dirt on my hand. I am brought back to the present—back to my garden. Perhaps this explains the tide of emotion. The strong internal pull of my womanhood, my instinct to care for all things vulnerable reacted to this, my most special place. I realize that I want to do for Jake and Ben as I do for the plants in my garden. I want to plant them in my world and tenderly care for them, helping them to grow healthy and strong. I want to build a fence around them and protect them from the harsh elements of life. I want them to thrive.

The wind, for it is no longer a breeze, has a sharp sting. It is after all, only March. As I leave my garden I feel a sense of peace. I have helped these two boys whom I care for so deeply. I have showered them with love. Now I will pray that the seeds of love I have sown will flourish. I hope that, by example, I have helped them to develop the integrity to make the right choices and "weed out" the negatives of life. I have done as much as I can, and must stand back and let them grow. For now, I will get back to the business at hand and plan my garden, waiting for spring.

## QUESTIONS ON CONTENT

1. What time of year is it?
2. What does Sullivan call her garden?
3. Who are Jake and Ben?
4. Why does the divorce bother Sullivan so much?

## QUESTIONS ON RHETORIC

1. Sullivan uses the breeze as a transition in her essay. Find each mention and note the mood each time. How does the mood change with the breeze?

2. What device does the dirt on Sullivan's hand provide?
3. How does Sullivan use the garden as a metaphor?

## VOCABULARY

(5) egocentricity, inadvertently, affected, indifference
(8) integrity

## WRITING PROMPTS

1. Do you feel you are running out of time to achieve a certain goal? Why? What can or should you do about it?
2. Is divorce always bad?
3. Why do we ask people why they have no children? Are we just curious—or perhaps envious?
4. What in our nature makes us want to make everything all right? Is there something you want to fix for someone but know you can't? How are you dealing with it?

# Time Keeps on Slipping

## Eric Ostrowski

It's real old. I'm not sure how old, but real old. My grandma gave it to me when I was five. I found it on one of my expeditions in one of her many cupboards. I remember the day vividly; it was raining outside and my parents forced us kids to stay in. They were well aware that rain, kids and puddles are a dangerous combination so inside we played. I remember my grandmother grabbing me by my socks and pulling me from the cupboard I was exploring with the hourglass in hand. She picked me up from the floor, after dragging me half way across it to the table, and sat me down in a hard wooden chair. She quickly took the seat next to me, sealing off my escape route. She plucked the hourglass from my hand and took a long hard stare at it and then at me.

"You know where I found this hourglass," she said. I shook my head, waiting in anticipation for one of Grandma's stories, knowing the sooner it was told the sooner I could go back to exploring.

"I found that when I was walking along the ocean many years ago. The waves carried it in right to my feet." I sat in awe. My mouth hung wide open while I concentrated on the shape of the hourglass still in Grandma's hand, its smooth lines sending me into a trance.

"I think it was from a pirate ship," she continued.

"Can I have it?" I spouted.

"I'll let you have this hourglass, if you promise not to dig through the cupboards any more." Grandma said this while dangling the hourglass over my head just out of reach of my pudgy five-year-old fingers.

"I promise," I said and plucked it from her hands as soon as they were low enough for me to reach. After a drop to the floor, I ran off toward the basement to tell my brother and sister of the pirate treasure that I had obtained from grandma.

Three metal spindles hung down vertically, collapsing on two metal plates that held the glass inside, which in turn held the sand. It looked like an exact duplicate of the hourglass that appears at the beginning of that soap opera, *Days of Our Lives,* but my hourglass had one major discrepancy from that one. Mine had hot pink sand flowing inside.

It's amazing how hourglasses hold up over the years—better than grandmas do. She was so young back then. Actually, looking back, she was in her mid sixties, but still sharp as the needle she darned with. Today she is in her mid eighties and dull as a spoon. She doesn't even take the time to color her hair anymore. I've heard if you're a woman that's a sign of acknowledging your old age.

When you flip the hourglass upside down the sand comes pouring from one end draining into the other. Every grain of sand can almost be counted as it slides through the tiny opening in the middle and falls onto the pile that starts to form on the other side. I'm reminded of a lyric from the Steve Miller Band: Time keeps on slipping...Into the future." I flip the hourglass back over thinking for some reason that this inversion is going to stop the flow of sand, but it doesn't. It just keeps flowing into the other side. No matter what, I can't stop the sand from flowing completely out into the lower basin and emptying the top.

I asked my grandma once about a year ago where she really got the hourglass. She didn't know what I was talking about.

"So how old are you now?" Grandma asked.

"I'm the same age as I was when you asked me last week, Grandma." Of course I didn't tell her that. You still have to respect your elders even in senility.

"How's your sister doing? Is she out of school yet?"

"She's good. She's been out of school now for three years. She got married six months ago. You were there right next to me at the wedding." I turned and mumbled so she couldn't make out the last part of my reply.

I turn my hourglass over again once more and watch the sand empty out as it had before. My mother informed me a few months back that my hourglass was really an egg timer. I told her the story of pirate treasure. In turn, she pointed out the stamp on the bottom that said, "Made in the USA." From hourglass to egg timer. From dark haired Grandma to white haired old woman. Sand slips away through the tiny opening, slowly at first and then faster.

## QUESTIONS ON CONTENT

1. How old was Ostrowski in this essay?
2. Where did he find the hourglass?
3. What did the hourglass look like? What color was the sand?
4. Where did his grandmother say she got the hourglass?
5. Where is his grandmother at the end of the essay?

## QUESTIONS ON RHETORIC

1. Describe Ostrowski's grandmother through five-year-old eyes. Describe his grandmother through his grown-up eyes.
2. What tone does the phrase "found it on one of my expeditions in one of her many cupboards" set? Where does the tone change? Why?
3. Look at the two sections of dialogue between the child and the grandmother. What differences do you note in the grandmother? In the child?
4. Look at the title. Who is losing time?

## VOCABULARY

(1) expeditions, hourglass

(3) awe

(13) senility

## WRITING PROMPTS

1. Write about a story that a grandparent told you.
2. Write about going back to a childhood place as an adult.
3. How do you think you will age?
4. Write about the way elders are viewed in our society.

# THE KEY

JEFF HANSEN

There is an object I possess, or, more properly, have been the keeper of, for a number of years, having held it since I was all of fourteen years old. The object is a well worn but original key to a 1953 pan-head Harley I used to own, which is now scrap metal or possibly only in separate parts on many different bikes. That is not the important part of this tale, just a worthy side note on the original purpose this object fulfilled. It fulfills a wider purpose now, as it represents a knotted mass of memories and concepts which to me range from the stark realities of life to things sublime and indiscernible at first glimpse.

One such stark reality is the memory of the bike for which the key was ground—the first object ever to have the effect of binding my father to myself. I had acquired the bike from a man I worked for, and subsequently poured two years of blood, sweat and tears into it until it was perfect. My father was active in the project as well, although his role was more subtle, more the sounding board and reference source than the active participant. He did occasionally provide some mechanical parts, hard won by the sweat of my back, laboring at some ancillary task he had no time to do himself. The true feeling of pure joy coursed through me at the end, when I inserted said key and the beast rumbled to life, earning from my father a single phrase: "Nice job."

Another thing brought to mind by the key is the events it is tied to by the strings of memory, the threads connecting past to present and weaving the future. I look upon it and remember the sweetness of youth, the innocence of that first love (a girl fascinated by bikes), and the loss of that innocence: an exchange of the act of physical love punctuated by her father attempting to kick my ass for being biker trash that had deflowered his princess. The key enabled my escape by allowing me to ride away, smarting from his words.

I envision freedom in this key, the ability to just escape to the wide road and go, leaving everything behind in the name of enjoying the wind in my face. This does not preclude the freedom of the mental break I get when the key stirs some long forgotten memory, or sparks imagining of new things the future may hold. Yet more sublime is the freedom that it gives me by reminding me to be myself, which is to say I am reminded of what I am, biker trash or laborer or father myself, and the truth that entails.

To leave out the future this key may be helping to weave is not an option—for without that part, the structure of my life may fall. The visions of the future that are called forth by the key are those of continued freedom and new things to be built, perhaps as a son, but more likely as a father or a teacher. I see myself watching others, younger than I am now, find their own keys, ground to their purpose but connected to mine through time and the concept of keys.

## QUESTIONS ON CONTENT

1. What is the key to?
2. How long did it take to rebuild the bike?
3. Why was Hansen considered "biker trash"?
4. What happened to the bike?

## QUESTIONS ON RHETORIC

1. Consider the organizational pattern of the essay. Would a different pattern be more effective? Why or why not?

2. Where in the essay would you like more detail? Less detail?
3. Find the metaphors for the bike and the key. How effective are they? What images do they conjure?
4. What effect on you, the reader, does the last sentence have?

## VOCABULARY

(1) sublime, indiscernible

(2) subtle, ancillary

(4) preclude

## WRITING PROMPTS

1. Write about a bonding experience you've had. Who was it with? How did it happen? Why?
2. Consider an object you have that is tied to many memories. Write about some of them.
3. What is your definition of *freedom*?

# WHEELS OF PERSPECTIVE

## JOSEPH MARTHALER

I took a ride in a wheelchair the other day. It was a humbling experience for me to try a maneuver myself around the campus in that four-wheeled contraption. I bumped into doors and walls. I got stuck trying to make it up over a curb that was supposed to be handicapped accessible. While traveling down hills, I had to maintain constant pressure on the right wheel, for my chair pulled slightly to the left. Failure to compensate for that pull would have sent ass-over-teakettle, and quite possibly left me needing a wheelchair for real. At other times it would have slammed me into the walls of buildings. It was burdensome, but I wasn't going to allow these minor problems to discourage me, for I knew that when my three hours in this chair were up, I could once again stand and carry myself about via my own two feet.

Sitting on the other side of the street, across from the Education Arts building, I could hear the shuffling of sneakers on the concrete walkway I had just traveled. As I waited for the traffic to clear completely, the person behind me caught up and stood next to me, also waiting for the opportunity to cross the road with minimal danger.

The student did a double take as did I when we both realize at the same time that we know each other. It was Doug Prazak, a fellow student who attended Sino-Summer with me in June of 1998. His eyes widened and jaw dropped as he stared at the chair that now confined me. It was probably quite a shock for him to see the man who was the first to make it to the top of both the Great Wall and the Thousand Peaks Mountain, sitting so casually in a wheelchair, staring back at him with my shit-eating grin. An air of relief fell over him as I explained that I was in the chair as an assignment for one of my education classes. We talked about our summer and the things we had done since coming back from China. As the time passed, Doug had to get running to class. He offered to help me cross the street, but I had to decline. I appreciated his offer but I needed to complete this assignment without his or anyone else's assistance. I wanted to do this on my own.

After the run-in with Doug, I got to thinking. I sure do take my legs, feet, and ability to walk for granted. I knew in the back of my mind that if some part of my wheelchair experience got too rough, I could cheat and use my legs, but what about those that can't cheat? To them, a wheelchair is a way of life, not an assignment. This got me to thinking about an experience I had several years earlier.

Sam was a junior when I entered the seventh grade. He was short for a junior—really short. I, in my scrawny seventh grade body, stood a good four inches above him. For this I think he hated me. On more occasions than I care to count Sam would steal my pencils while I walked down the halls in between classes. If I had no pencil, he would knock my books and papers out of my arms and kick them like hockey pucks till my assignments cluttered the entire second floor hallway. For this I despised him. He made every day in school a living hell.

I made it through that year by avoiding Sam at all possible costs. If I saw him coming my way down the halls, I would change my direction even if it meant getting a tardy slip. I didn't let Sam get to me, however. I knew that he would get his someday and I would be happy when he did. At the end of June, following my seventh grade year, Effie, my hometown, held its 3rd annual Mosquito Festival. It was a fairly new tradition started by the business people of the town to promote tourism. For me it was a day to check out flea markets and enjoy games where one could win money. It came as a great day of excitement in a town where nothing ever seemed to happen that was even remotely interesting. There was the Frog Race, the Spider Race, and the dunk tank. There was a contest to see who had the most mosquito bites. There was the Bigfork vs. Effie tug-of-war. Tons of other games and activities filled the day, but for me the most exciting activity was the Boiling Water contest. I had taken first place in the previous two Mosquito Fests and this year I was going to make it a hat trick.

As the day wound down to a close; I was at home regaling my family with the tale of how I masterfully got my water to boil faster than anyone else's when I saw a black Chevy truck speed past my house headed towards Togo. Fifteen minutes later an Itasca County Deputy screamed past with his sirens blaring.

The next day, talk of the accident dominated the conversation of my town. The boys in the black Chevy had been drinking and getting a little too rowdy. While they were screwing around on the old Busty road the driver lost control and rolled his truck down one of the steep banks that ran along the dirt-covered road way. The young man who was sitting in the passenger seat was thrown from the vehicle and into a tree. That boy was Sam. He was air lifted from Bigfork to St. Mary's down in Duluth. Sam's life was forever changed.

The next school year I didn't have any problems with Sam. The accident had cost him the use of his legs and confined him to a wheelchair. It had also changed his attitude toward life. He was no longer the bully that went out of his way to torture seventh graders. His humbling experience made him a better man. He would talk with people about the dangers of drinking and driving. He would say that people shouldn't take anything for granted, for in the flash of a moment it could all be taken away and there would be nothing to do about it. I forgave Sam for all the crap he put me through during my seventh grade year. Even though I wanted him to get his own I never wanted him to lose the power to walk. It saddened me to know it took an accident like that to change the person he was to the great man he is today.

Life looks different when you're staring from a chair that has wheels. Minor hills become a difficult challenge when trying to make your way around. Unless many years of experience accompany a person in a wheelchair, stairs are impossible. Just trying to get into a bathroom that doesn't have one of those automatic doors is a formidable task. Nevertheless, millions of people are faced with these challenges everyday, and they can't cheat by using their legs as I could. Taking that ride in the wheelchair changed me a little for the better. I was offered a tiny glimpse of what life is like for those who cannot walk. Life will never look the same since I had the chance to look at it from another person's wheels.

## QUESTIONS ON CONTENT

1. Why was Marthaler using a wheelchair?
2. Why did Marthaler dislike his classmate Sam?
3. What happened to Sam?

## QUESTIONS ON RHETORIC

1. What organizational pattern does Marthaler use? Is it effective?
2. Why is the title appropriate?
3. Look at the conclusion. Are the examples Marthaler uses really important issues for wheelchair users? Why or why not?

## VOCABULARY

(1) handicapped
(9) formidable

## WRITING PROMPTS

1. Write about the assignment of using a wheelchair for three hours. Can someone really get a true perspective of what life is like for wheelchair users in three hours?
2. Imagine life without the use of your hands.
3. Write about an event that changed your perspective on something.

# A THOUSAND WORDS

## JULIE STUARD

They haunt me, these pictures. I find them in basement rooms of antique stores or in the stairways going down. They are forgotten pictures of forgotten people, bought and sold for grainy tones or their antique frames. I've often wondered if I could buy one, remove the picture and replace it with mirrored glass. So far I cannot.

I think of them often. Not in conscious ways, not in rational ways. They occupy my attention, a sort of daydream. I wonder what it's like to be without a name. Somewhere the name exists, in some county records office or on a tombstone, but separate from likeness. I wonder how this could happen. If this family—the stiff moustached man, the woman with her bunned hair and cameo at her throat—were of any national or international fame, they would not hang here. They would hang in a museum or some house of state. If the photographer were of note, they would be reproduced in some anthology. If they had family—that's the one that sticks in my throat—if they had family, could they be this forgotten, this neglected? Who was it that sold a family treasure, a link with their own past? Was it auctioned by a stranger at an estate sale? Or by a relative who cannot name the face or family?

I am thirty-three and childless and may always be. This may explain my attention. Will I be the forgotten aunt in some antique store while my sister passes down studio pictures of a wedding, a birth, and a family? It's the downhill slide after years of schooling, travel and career. It's the proverbial biological clock.

But should I have five or ten children, still possible, I think the pictures would haunt me. I think of my own pictures. My grandmother in her homemade dresses, corsetted and heavy on her black orthopedic shoes. She holds hands with my grandfather. He's in his green work clothes, tall and lanky, his gray hair cut close, his black heavy-rimmed glasses tucked in a pocket. They sit each in their respective lazyboys in front of their trailer house windows, the old wash house in the distance.

My five or ten children can pass this picture down, but I'm the last generation to be able to associate memories to these two. My son will never taste the sour cream cookies or the homemade donuts that always lay in coffee cans next to the stove. He will never smell like bacon when he returns from great-grandma's house. My daughter will never comb my grandma's hair in exchange for a dime, or try parting it on the other side.

These things happened outside the frame, behind the photographer, beneath the two dimensions. My grandparents are dead and reduced to a flat surface, and they will matter as much to onlookers as some other family's vacation pictures matter to me. Four children, fourteen grandchildren, and countless great-grandchildren could not stop the eroding memory, the eroding tie.

As I began a new relationship with a man whose family never ends, I first met an endless string of pictures. His mother's real sister, then her half siblings, then her step siblings. None mattered to me until I began to meet them in person, until I began a relationship with the faces in the snapshots. They began to belong to me.

And my family has its own pictures, grainy toned and framed, or pasted to black pages in ancient albums. We've lost our matriarch, and no one can remember.

When the Gulf War was going on, I watched the screen, just like everyone else, and I felt for soldiers on both sides. Having just returned from overseas, I felt multiple perspectives. I could sense the Iraqi side; I could feel the international viewpoint. But I never felt at all, not until a soldier in my class read of his experience. From him, I became aware of context. I had a sense of each participant on either side of the war, on either side of the camera, on either side of the TV screen, on either side of involvement, possessing his or her own universe, so each frame of every reel became a flat representation of a universe, a universe other than mine.

I remember seeing pictures of both London and Washington, D.C. before I had ever visited. I saw the same or similar pictures afterward. The afterviews meant something, not only because I could say I had been there, but because now I could see a universe in that shot. I could see the White House in relation to the Capitol building. I knew how to get from Westminster Abby to Big Ben.

So in these antique stores, I don't see lost faces, I see lost universes without relation which no one can enter. I am stopped at the frame.

## QUESTIONS ON CONTENT

1. Where does Stuard find the pictures she writes about?
2. What three reasons does Stuard find for these pictures hanging there?
3. What does Stuard refer to when she writes of "afterviews"?

## QUESTIONS OF RHETORIC

1. Look at the description of the people in the photograph in paragraph 2 and compare it with the description of Stuard's grandparents in paragraph 4.
2. What does Stuard mean when she writes about "things outside the frame"?
3. Why does experience color the way Stuard sees photographs?

## VOCABULARY

(8) matriarch

# Writing Prompts

1. Think about a favorite photograph. What story would a stranger see in that photograph?
2. Imagine your family dividing your things after you are gone. What would they keep? What would they sell? What would they trash?
3. What is the most haunting photograph you can remember seeing? Describe it in full detail. Why did it haunt you?

# A Girl Needs to Know How to Defend Herself

## Karen Krueger

There was never any doubt that my dad loved his daughters but his desire to have a son manifested itself by his insistence in teaching us "boy things." Boxing was one of those things. He considered it a necessary skill for girls.

The lessons took place in the garage or his workroom, away from the disapproving eyes of my mother. Boxing wasn't something girls did and she reminded Dad of this often. My dad, instructor, punching bag and sparring partner, watched for times when we could sneak in a lesson. We practiced when Mom was on the phone, doing the dishes, taking a nap, or turning her back on us in the grocery store. She caught us once and sent us to the car; we boxed in the parking lot. I could dodge, duck, jab, fake with left, hit with right, fake with right, hit with left and deliver a nasty uppercut. I practiced in front of a mirror. I was Jack Dempsey and I couldn't wait to try out my skills.

My chance came the spring of sixth grade. I was the only girl in my neighborhood, except for my prissy niece, three months younger than me, who wore dresses and played Barbies. I chose to hang with the guys. Erich and Carl Belz lived one house down from mine. Carl was the closest to my age. He was a big 7th grader and a bully who liked to pick on smaller kids and girls, though he pretty much left me alone.

The fight happened one morning while we were waiting at the bus stop. I don't recall how it started, but I remember how it ended. I faked with a left and jabbed with my right, my fist landing, just as Daddy taught me, squarely into Carl's right eye. I had taken him by surprise. Suddenly, he found himself on the opposite end of bully. He ran home crying.

In the speed of a punch I became a hero. Word got around I had punched out the school bully. Congratulations came in the form of gum, candy and cuts in line. His brother even picked me up at school that day in his car and took me for ice cream. I saw the look of envy on the other girls' faces as we sped away.

I was pretty full of myself, a legend in my own mind, until I got home. Mom met me at the door with her hands on her hips and a dish towel thrown over her shoulder. No amount of explaining could shield me from her wrath. "Doesn't matter if he started it. You're a girl," she explained. "Girls don't hit, girls don't fight and for that matter girls don't do anything boys do." She told me it was high time that I adjusted to being a girl and that I should spend time playing with my niece, who was a fine example of a girl, instead of those boys, one of which I was not! She grounded me to my room until my father came home. As I walked past, I heard her questioning God about not giving her a boy to keep *her* husband from ruining *her* girls. When my dad got home she dished him the same lecture I'd had plus seconds for teaching me to box.

Dinner was quiet that evening. While Mom finished the dishes, Dad and I retreated to his workroom. He patted me on the head and had me show him exactly how it happened. I saw the smile on his face as I recited my embellished story and reenacted my moves in the air. He said that even though the kid had had it coming, I should, for my mom's sake, apologize to him. He also said, "There is nothing a boy can do that you can't. It's just gonna be a little harder, because you are a girl." I apologized the next day.

I only boxed one more time after that. It was in the narrow hallway of our house in Illinois when I was fourteen. Dad walked by me, turned, and "put up his dukes." I instinctively responded with

a fake and a jab. He bobbed forward a little farther than I anticipated. My fist connected. The soft tip of his nose collapsed back into
the hard bone of his face. Blood poured from his nose. I stood frozen
as he ran for the bathroom. My hand throbbed, but I didn't move
to rub it. Mom came to my father's first aid. As she walked past, she
said quietly, "Wouldn't want to be you right now."

I was still frozen in place when he finally came out, Mom trail-
ing behind with an armful of bloody bath linens. He looked pretty
serious as he took me by the hand. Dad was not prone to fits of
anger, nor was he in the habit of punishing me, but then I'd never
punched him in the face before. Mom watched as I was escorted
to the garage and placed in the car. We headed toward town in
silence. I glanced at him but he kept his eyes forward in a stone-
faced stare. I lowered my eyes and stared at my bruised knuckles.
The car slowed, made a turn and stopped. The Dairy Queen? He
winked as he told me I could have anything I wanted! Just don't
tell Mom. She thought we were having a serious chat. He said how
impressed he was that his little girl could throw a punch like that,
even told the guy at the counter as he pointed to his own nose and
my fist.

My urge to box died that day. It wasn't fun anymore. Dad must
have understood as well, for he never asked me to put up my dukes
again and he quit calling me "Lil Jackie D." He never quit telling
me that there was nothing I couldn't do.

## Questions on Content

1. What "boy thing" did Krueger learn from her dad?
2. What happened at the bus stop?
3. Who did her mother want Krueger to be like?
4. What "punishment" did Krueger receive for punching out her dad?

## Questions on Rhetoric

1. Every paragraph begins with the subject-verb sentence pattern.
   What effect does this have on the tone of the essay?

2. Look at the gender-based arguments. How are they supported? Refuted?
3. What effect does the phrase "his little girl" have in paragraph 9?

## VOCABULARY

(1) manifested

(2) sparring

## WRITING PROMPTS

1. What gender-identifying things, events, or toys did you grow up with? What message did they instill in you?
2. Should girls be taught "boy things," and should boys be allowed to play with "girl things"? How much of a child's identity is wrapped up in these early messages?
3. Is there ever a need to physically fight? What methods of defense were you taught?

# WRITING RAPE

## KATHERINE FLUKE

Writing had never been a personal experience for me. I always wrote for different reasons, but never to seek personal release or reflection. My parents must have agreed that writing was not really important, because they saved all of my kindergarten artwork, but none of my writing. Since the day I blissfully wrote the word "pizza" in three-year old writing, I saw writing as a way to prove my intelligence and win my teacher's love.

I was lucky to be in an excellent grade school with the goals to teach children how to read, write, and think. We had projects where we had to invent a meal, then write out the ingredients and preparation instructions. It was made clear that penmanship didn't matter, but creativity was vital. My "Spring Pie" was made out of my mother's scarf, sunshine, bubble wrap and my best friend, Alexandra. Because I was working to improve my imagination, not grammar or penmanship, I learned how to think and create. Though the benefits of that school lay dormant throughout most of my high school experience, I believe that the elementary school's attitude helped me begin to change my opinion of writing to something more than a homework assignment.

I was doing very well in class, happy to be in third grade with Alex and my favorite teacher, Mrs. King. Mrs. King had a story project for every occasion. We always read during the first part of class and always wrote towards the end. Also, for every holiday, we would have to write a story in relation to that holiday. For Halloween, the instructions were simple: write a page-long story to read in front of the class. I went home and wrote my story, which I thought was extremely scary and well-written. I illustrated all of my sentences and stapled the pages together to make it a real book. When I gave my story to Mrs King, however, instead of smiles and praise, she gave me a hard look. She told me to sit in the principal's office and wait for my parents. About 15 minutes later, my dad came into the office with my story in his hand. "Now Katie, I know you like to be a good student and I know that you want Mrs. King to like you. But it is very wrong to copy another student's work. Who did you get help from, Katie?" Mrs. King was standing next to him, waiting to hear my excuse. It seemed to me that it would be easier to lie and admit I had copied someone else, but I refused to give the credit of my story to someone else. It was a matter of chance that my sister came in from recess to get a Band-Aid, and settled the matter by affirming that she had watched me write the assignment. While I listened to their justifications for calling an honest child a liar, I never forgave Mrs. King, and it was a long time before I felt like reading in front of the class.

In Junior high, the emphasis of writing assignments shifted from creativity to clarity and the ability to state facts. It was a great deal easier for me than it was for Alex to make the transition. She and I had different opinions about writing facts and writing imagination. I felt that as long as I could substantiate whatever I wrote with someone else's writing (such as a textbook), the teacher couldn't arbitrarily grade homework. I felt it was much easier than trying to create something new, and as long as I followed the necessary grammar rules the teacher would give me a good grade. When Alex muttered, "But I don't write for the teacher," I did not understand what she meant. "Why else would you write?" I wondered. The school still encouraged creativity, but I got in trouble for wearing green lipstick, and others got in trouble for trying to write. Invention, we were told, was for art class and free-time.

I was lucky to be recommended by my seventh grade teacher to join the school's smart and gifted program. Two history and English teachers joined to form the Humanities program, and except for science, PE, and lunch, we never left those two teachers. As the topic was the middle ages and renaissance, the teachers taught by making us live in the time. The class came to school and dressed in costume. I was made a knight when I earned enough "chivalry points" to kneel in front of Queen Gillespie and be tapped by a sword in the light of the stained glass stencils that the class made together. The class learned the dances performed by royalty, and every week we had a different dish of food that was once eaten by kings. For the writing aspect, we had to keep a diary for the character we had chosen to be, narrating events of war, new knowledge, and daily life. I was Lucretia Borgia, and I loved writing her "journal." I wrote about corruption, poison, and how rich I was, all the while learning about the real Lucretia. The class was also divided by different countries, clans, and tribes, and we had to keep peace and diplomacy. To do so, my group in Italy dispatched frequent letters to the other countries to offer our praise and wish for peace, as well as strategic marriages and gifts. Everything we did, we wrote about in a report or project. I have never written so much in one class, and I most certainly have never learned as much in two months. When school ended in the eighth grade, I was promised a place in the program that had taught me so much. All summer, I looked forward to school and learning, but when I got to high school, I learned that funding for the smart and gifted program was cut, and my two teachers had to teach their own classes in their own subject.

In spite of losing the smart and gifted program, I was lucky to have wonderful English and theater teachers. While I rarely wrote in my theater class, it is important to mention the influence Mrs. Stuart had on my general outlook. That teacher broke all the rules of convention and structure, and she had an amazing class. Because Mrs. Stuart patiently broke down all of my shyness and seriousness, I was able to better succeed in English. From her, I learned that a good teacher improves the student's entire education, not just the immediate subject.

My English teacher was a new teacher, and at that point unaffected by the importance of grammar. The first semester was great; both Alex and I had fun when Mr. Curry had us re-write Romeo and Juliet with characters replaced by students in the class. I had Greg be a fastidious, uptight Romeo who really didn't want Juliet, but she was the only girl in town who would let him polish her car. Mr. Curry was the king, and I wrote him as acting only for the explicit approval of his mother. I rearranged the play to take place at a homecoming dance, and everyone wound up marrying each other. The students were all friends in that class, and the day we read or acted the stories was full of laughter. Both Alex and I got A's that semester, along with an option to be in the honors English class. I knew that the honors class had more structure, but I wanted the weighted grade and the approval of my parents, so I switched classes. Alex stayed with Mr. Curry.

I quickly learned in honors that I had to support every thought I wrote with a quote from the book. Every paper had to be formed by five paragraphs within four pages. Grammar had to be precise, but I could rewrite papers as many times as I needed to. The words "I, my, me," or "mine" were to be studiously omitted from everything I wrote, even if it was my original thought. Though we were learning about the influence of the American Dream in terms of individual importance, it was clear to me that my ideas were not welcome. This system was fine with me, and even easier than the assignments I had in Mr. Curry's class. I had to read many more books, and write many more papers, but I had the process down. I could manipulate any book to mean what I wanted it to, and prove that by quoting the book. I was quite comfortable writing mediocre papers that got a satisfactory grade. Writing continued to be only homework, and nothing more.

I kept on writing only for my teacher's pleasure and the grades I received justified that writing was only for repeating other's work. Any part of myself in the paper, unless proven by the book, was frowned upon. Tenth grade passed without much incident, although Alex and I noticed we were not that alike anymore. She had continued to choose teachers that gave her the freedom to learn, while

I chose teachers that would give me easy grades and weight on my college applications. The difference was noticeable, though we stayed friends.

Then, by Christmas of my junior year in high school, my world changed. I was violently raped by the most popular boy in school, who was also my boyfriend of nine months. It was clear to me that no one would believe my word over his, and certainly no one could understand what I was feeling. In response to the shock and fear and turmoil I had inside of me, I simply stopped everything I was doing. I quit speaking entirely, even to my friends and teachers. Homework lost all importance and meaning to me, and I didn't even try to do it. When I went to school, I gazed out the window and waited for the bell to ring. My grades soon dropped from a 4.3 to a 2.5, and they were getting worse. The only activity I stayed in was swimming, and my parents made me quit when my grades suffered so. Indeed, my parents and teachers never asked what was wrong with me, only demanded that I get my act together and quit slacking off.

Alex was the only one of my friends to make an effort to talk to me, at least once every day. Although I had no voice to tell her, it meant something that she talked to me without expecting a response. It was the only thing that meant anything to me at that time. One day, Alex brought a book and gave it to me, explaining that it was mine to do whatever I wanted to. When she left, I opened the book, expecting to find the same mundane self-help and motivation that my parents had tried to press on to me. Instead, I discovered that it was a blank book, every five pages having a quote selected by Alex. The first page had a verse that made me understand exactly what I was holding in my hand:

> Something we were withholding made us weak
> Until we found it was ourselves we were withholding
> From our land of living
> And forthwith found salvation in surrender.

It was from Frost's poem at Kennedy's inauguration, of course. I once had to write a book report on it, but I never actually heard the poem. The way I saw it now, my silence was withholding me from my land of living, and by surrendering myself to the blank pages in the book, I might find salvation. For the first time, I began to write for myself. I started by writing everything that happened the night I was raped in extreme detail. I made it real to me, so I couldn't escape from the truth I tried so hard to hide from. I wrote for hours, stopping only to change pens or sleep.

The writing exhausted me, but I could not stop. I wrote whatever came into my mind, and filled pages about the day, other poems I had read, and other odd bits of thought. Alex noticed I was writing, and gave me another journal when she saw I was running out of pages.

My parents were close to giving up on me, and my teachers were getting frustrated. In a last effort to pep talk me into committing myself to grades and speaking again, I had to join a meeting with my parents, the guidance counselor, the principal, and my advisor. Again they discussed every fault I had from stubbornness to laziness. They contributed more solutions to solve my slacker problem and a few suggestions to solve my mental problem of stubbornness. Tutoring was again advised, as well as a possible visit to a "rest home" so I could perhaps be inspired to get fixed enough to go back to school and succeed as I had once done so easily. In the midst of all the solutions and quick fixes, I stood up. Ripping the pages out of the first journal that testified what my problem really was, I threw page after page of the violence that took four hours of my life away. "Did any one realize that not one of you ever asked me what was wrong?" I stepped on the pages I had thrown at them and walked out the door. That was another surrender, I thought. Now it is time to look for the salvation.

Alex was waiting outside for me. "I think I want to switch to your English class," is what I wanted to tell her. Instead, we linked arms and went to find sunshine and sea air. I think she understood perfectly when I mentioned later that I didn't want to write for a teacher or a grade anymore. I finally grasped what Alex had always understood: writing makes us and our experiences real, and there is healing to be found in the words and pages we write.

I have come so far since Alex's first lesson. I still loathe it when a teacher discourages original thought and insists on a five paragraph format, but it does not really matter. I write for myself in my journals, or if I am lucky, in the classes that allow my personality and individuality. I write throughout the entire spectrum of emotions, and I learn some truth about myself every time I write. With a pen and a piece of paper, I have granted myself permission to be free.

## QUESTIONS ON CONTENT

1. What was the first word that Fluke learned to write?
2. Who was Alex?
3. What influence did Fluke's theater teacher have on her education?
4. What event happened to Fluke to change her attitude toward school?
5. What gift did Alex give Fluke that turned her life around?

## QUESTIONS ON RHETORIC

1. Fluke wrote for teachers and Alex wrote for herself. What is the difference?
2. Fluke's essay follows a chronological organization pattern. How does this affect the essay's main point?
3. Look at Fluke's last sentence. What does she mean?

## VOCABULARY

(2) dormant

(4) substantiate, arbitrarily

(5) Humanities, renaissance

(7) fastidious, explicit

(8) studiously, manipulate, mediocre

(16) loathe, spectrum

# WRITING PROMPTS

1. Write a case study of your writing memories from over the years.
2. How would you teach writing to elementary school students? To high schoolers? To college students? To adults?
3. Write about a traumatic event in your own life. How did it affect you? Does it still?
4. Write about a teacher who influenced you—either positively or negatively.

# ANOTHER ROAD.
# OTHER FISH TO FRY

## KATRINA PINK

I have a collection of undergraduate catalogues. Their pages are torn, penciled, and highlighted. I think they have been opened as many times as my telephone directory. I have looked at these catalogs as if I were shopping for something—and I am. We all are. We want to choose an occupation that will suit our interests and match our desired work atmosphere. We ponder where our jobs might take us. We make conscious or subconscious pros and cons lists while reading the possible career directions under each field of study.

We have taken personality tests, interest tests, tests that will supposedly navigate us to an ultimate career destination. We have talked the talk, and walked the walk from academic building to academic building. We feel the frustration of knowing today, and not knowing tomorrow, of our alarm clocks ringing—their bright red numbers poking fun at the passing of time and the scattered eternity of still not knowing. The numbers illuminate some sort of foreign yet familiar language, the repetitive and constant: know, not know, know, not know.

Then there are the decisions that we make and attempt to make. We wonder if our tires are leaving tracks on the right road, or if we missed a turn or two. Is all of this necessary? Why are we demanding answers for things that we cannot yet answer? We can't find the answers because we are not in the future. Is it not frustrating, trying to arrive at a destination when there is no way of getting there?

Our humanness has given us the diabolic ability to look back to the past, to analyze and dissect the decisions that we have made. But how can we be efficient judges, how can we make good decisions, when the evidence, the situations, the food that was on our plates is no longer there? The plate is still there, but we cannot feel the texture of that same cake, nor can we see the same greenness of the lettuce leaves from that first garden.

We need to realize that with the exception of Tinsel Town and its shining silver screen, we can only be in one place at one time. We must stop causing ourselves grief by attempting to be in three different places: the past, the present, and the future. It's absolutely, positively, and quite undeniably impossible.

After five years of going backward and forward for answers, after wondering, turning in tests, running to make class on time and trying to tell my parents what exactly my loans were paying for, I realized something. Something that made me stop trying to catch fish in the sky, something that made the shovel fall out of my hands as I dug deeper and deeper for answers.

My realization was no revelation, no prize-winning innovation, no Einstein in the brain, or cure for every pain; rather, a sigh of relief, a glimpse of hope, a star in a starless sky.

Of course, I wish that this wisdom had come a bit sooner, but these are the things we that we sometimes learn after the fact. These are the things we learn after chasing our tail around once, then a thousand times more. These are the things we learn when our ship is almost at bay, when we can almost see a tree line, or the wings of some song bird gently on its way.

So what is this new wisdom that seems so grand? What was this realization that put a star in a starless sky? The realization is that we don't have to ponder whether we are on the right road. We just have to be on a road. For some reason, we have acquired the tendency to feel as if the degree we choose, and the choices we make, will become strapped upon our shoulders for all of eternity. That is probably why we fret so: the fear of drowning in quicksand, of being stuck in some job, in some way of life that doesn't suit us as much as we thought it would.

But we won't become stuck. There are hands to pull us up and out; there are branches to cling on to. There is freedom, there are endless roads to travel, and stumps to sit upon along the path of life. If we tire of one road, of one career, there are mile signs to remind us that there are other destinations, other dreams to pursue, and other wings to help us fly.

Life is a journey that begins when we take our first breath, and ends when we take our last. Life is becoming, exploring, and experiencing. Our college years are a time to gather supplies for our journey and a time of self-discovery. So let your enjoyment for writing, theater, history, or whatever it may be, carry you where it will. Don't think of your future diploma as an identity card, but as a passport that shows the marks of where you've been, and the empty spaces of where you'd like to go.

I don't know my final destination, and you may not either, but I'll walk on the road for a while, or journey on an ocean breeze. I'll try out my degree; I'll talk the talk and walk the walk. Maybe I'll drop anchor or maybe I'll realize that I have other fish to fry, but as the age old saying goes; you will never know unless you try.

## QUESTIONS ON CONTENT

1. What does Pink have a collection of?
2. How long has Pink been a college student?
3. What is Pink pursuing a degree in?

## QUESTIONS ON RHETORIC

1. Find examples of clichés in the essay. What effect do they have?
2. Look at the organizational pattern. Arrange the essay differently. Does the new arrangement matter?

3. List the questions Pink asks. Does she answer these questions? If so, what are her answers?
4. Pink compares life to a road. Find examples that explain what she finds on this road.

## VOCABULARY

(4) diabolic
(8) tree line

## WRITING PROMPTS

1. Choose a metaphor for your life's journey. Describe it.
2. Write about your college experience. What lessons have you learned? What lessons do you need to learn?
3. Write about a decision you made that made a difference in your life.

# One Hour

## Kim Dennig

It was daybreak on a day that would go down in the history of my life. It was a beautiful day. The sun was shining, the sky was blue, and there were a few of my favorite kinds of clouds in the sky, the wispy ones that look like feathers. There were three generations in the car, my grandmother, my mother, and myself. We drove in utter silence. This was a day I had never imagined would come. This was something I couldn't even fathom.

We were the first ones to arrive, but my grandpa was half-awake and waiting for us. This was a day he had been waiting for, a day he needed. My grandpa and grandma's five sons started arriving next, with their wives and some of the grandkids, too. Of course my mom and I were there as well. We all got the chance to go in and talk to him alone. It was the last time we could tell him how important he was to all of us. That he was the pillar of our family. That he was the one who taught us how to love, that without each other we were alone, and that he was the father I never had.

My father has lived in either Colorado or Texas all my life. He would call for my birthday and for Christmas. That was usually only to see what I wanted. A lot of times he would call and talk to my mom for a while to see how and what I was doing. We never really talked much. That is how I remember it. I felt abandoned and fatherless.

Well, I felt biologically fatherless. My own dad didn't even want to be in my life. That is how I rationalized it. I never knew what I did wrong but I always blamed myself. I know now that he wasn't ready to be a father, but the effort he did make made it worse. It made me feel like I was only worthy sometimes. He didn't understand what I was going through nor did he seem to care. He didn't know how to be a father. He was miles away and maybe thought that checking up on me through my mother was enough. It wasn't. Gifts don't heal wounds of the heart. Although I didn't have a "real" father I had my grandpa.

He was the neatest man. He loved everyone and everything. I was the first grandchild raised in the family. My grandpa was one of the few men that I respected and didn't dare disobey. I never wanted to disappoint him. Maybe I was afraid he would leave too. I knew that was absurd because he loved me in a way that my father could never do. The uncles I had were the men that I played with and had fun with. I would listen to them, but it was more of a brotherly and carefree relationship. My grandpa was all of those carefree and fun things; but he was a father figure, as well.

I only realize looking back how much I craved and needed that father "authority" figure. He treated me like gold but he never let me get away with anything. He didn't let me disrespect my mother or raise my voice unless it was justified, which was never. It was so funny the way he would tell us to quit yelling at each other. He would say something like, "you two...will you stop?" or, "come on...quit?" I loved him and he loved me. Of course he loved everyone, but there was something special between us, something more. We shared a bond that was unlike any other. The place he filled in my heart can never be filled again. No one could measure up to those standards. That is my grandpa's spot and will be his forever.

My grandpa was a special man. He was a carpenter until his final days. His workshop was in the basement and he went up and down those steps until he couldn't walk any more. After that happened we moved his workshop to the garage so he could work on his last projects for all of us. He made some of his best work in those final days. For the Christmas twelve days after his death we all got elves climbing up ladders. He wanted to do more with them but that is as far as he got. That was good enough for us. He thought of his family up until the end.

His work in his garage workshop lasted until he couldn't hold onto anything anymore. Even then he never gave up. He never let it get him down. When my grandma had to cut his meat, he just made jokes about getting waited on and how it was about time. He never stopped smiling. I knew his illness was serious, but by looking at him, he wouldn't seem to be bothered by it, except when he was in pain, and that wasn't a conscious decision. He never once let it defeat him. His spirit was as strong as it had ever been if not stronger in those last months of his life. He was amazing. He never let us get down about it either. He would say something about that is just the way the ball bounced. That was life and they had to make the best of it and every situation because that was just the way it was. Nothing would have changed the circumstances had we found out it was ALS and not diabetes from the beginning, except that we would have had to deal with the fact that he was dying sooner.

He pulled us all together even on his last day. Even on that last day he was smiling and telling us how much he loved us. We knew that he wouldn't be in pain any more and that helped. I think we wanted the best of both worlds: for him not to be in pain and for him to be able to stay with us. That couldn't happen. We gathered around his bed and sang "Silent Night," recited the Lord's Prayer, and held hands. I had his right, my grandma his left. My grandma never let go of his hand. I did only to run to the bathroom. I think that took me only fifteen seconds.

Then, at 1:45 p.m., the doctor came in and turned the machines off. The ventilator was one of the most important. Having ALS, or Lou Gehrig's disease, his muscles stopped working and deteriorated. His lungs did just that too, and he needed the ventilator. Without his lungs working, he couldn't make it. That is exactly what finally took his life—his inability to breathe and then his heart stopping.

We watched, and waited, and tried to tell stories. But his breathing was so shallow. I wanted to be selfish and make him stay. But this is what he wanted, what he needed and I couldn't justify keeping him in pain. So I did all that I could to help him be comfortable.

I held his hand and he held mine, my tears running down my cheeks. Then he opened that big mouth of his under that big hooknose and his back arched as much as it could and he took his last breath at 2:45 on December 12, 1993. His pain is over.

## QUESTIONS ON CONTENT

1. Where was the family going?
2. What illness did Dennig's grandfather have?
3. Why was his relationship with his grandfather so special?
4. Who held the old man's hands as he died?

## QUESTIONS ON RHETORIC

1. Does Dennig's tangent about his biological father enhance or distract from the main story line?
2. Consider telling this story from a different viewpoint: Dennig's mother, the grandmother, or the grandfather. How would that change the story?
3. Where in the story would you like to know more?

## VOCABULARY

(7) ALS (amyotrophic lateral sclerosis), Lou Gehrig's disease
(9) ventilator

## WRITING PROMPTS

1. Write about one of your grandparents and a lesson he or she taught you.
2. Write about being a prisoner in your own body and having to have everything done for you.
3. Write about having a fatal disease.
4. Write about death rituals in our culture and in other cultures.

# Hush! Hush!

## Liu Wei

It is already six in the afternoon. Having stepped into my home hastily after school, I immerse my mind in a love story by a Taiwan writer who is now very popular in my hometown—Chongqing, China. I can read it merely before my parents show up after office time because they will confiscate it at the first glance. Only in the next thirty stolen minutes can I peek at a world quite different from my present one and send my present entire lesson into limbo.

When the bell of six thirty tolls, I tear myself away from the beautiful love story with great reluctance, and hide it in the recess of my drawer. Then the dismaying memory of the math examination just now recurs in my mind. The last several pages of the examination are actually superfluous for me because the questions on them demand the mastery of the bewildering math formulas, and I have left them all blank.

The more vivid scene happened in my math exercise book. One day, a conspicuous comment on it from my math teacher caught my eye: "Do you have ears during my class?" Do I have ears? Yes, I have. In her class, my ears always hear her patient, her passionate, her threatening addresses about how important her subject—math—is, how useful her math formula is and how useless my story reading is. "I heard some of you were reading stories. These dopes are still dreaming in the present crucial time. You dopes should bear in your minds that math is your principal subject. Spend the time of your reading junk on the formulas. If you do not master them, next year you cannot find a door to enter college. In addition, now you need not hurry in reciting the liberal subjects such as politics and English...." How long does she want me to deal with her formulas in a day? Every night, her formulas exhaust almost all my energy derived from my supper. Now she has relentlessly trampled my only spiritual morsel in an overloaded day.

Moreover, the subjects pinching my mind are not limited to math. In the subject of politics—Marxism—our teacher requires us to begin each of our answers with the fundamentals. And he often admonishes us, "Your own words do not count in your score. You'd better use the original sentences in the textbook." How can this be? I know that Marxism belongs to philosophy, but according to his words it seems to be composed of formulas like math. OK, I recite that textbook. This time there is a flunk mark on my politics examination.

In English, I do not feel at ease, either. We are given a prescription by our teacher to use a beginning paragraph, a middle paragraph and a conclusion paragraph for each of our compositions. Further, she advises us to begin each of our compositions with the word "nowadays," to wit, the first word of our composition should be "nowadays." Even the should-be flexible subject is bound with a straitjacket and is manipulated by the formulas.

In my present world, all my subjects are tormenting my mind by their numerous formulas. I wish I could have another mind so as to spare one for those formulas to abuse. If a formula cannot be found in my textbook, then it is formulated by my teachers. All the formulas from either of the two origins have the same force upon the minds of us kids.

Further, those formulas are not only formulas but also laws. If they do not possess us, then they will outlaw us. During the class we kids are frequently trapped by the questions launched from the teacher. When that happens, the teacher is always able to ascribe our mistake to our oblivion or misuse of some formula. At that time, the broadside upon the trapped kid will characterize the teacher's comment.

"Do you have a head? I have emphasized this formula again and again in class. You fool, listen to me carefully. If you can enter college by just teaching yourself, I will use my hand as the utensil to cook fish for you to eat," sputtered our math teacher with a glowing face to a kid in class one day. The wretched kid was sitting silent on his stool with a red face and a drooped head. We knew he dared not utter even some grumble sound because that would trigger much more formidable penalties upon him from the teacher. Nor did the rest of us have the courage to produce any sound audible in the classroom, not to mention interposing a different voice.

At that time, I imagined: Standing high, stern on the platform, she looks like a sergeant standing on a glade trying to detect some criminals in the jungle. Yeah, I bet she can be an excellent sergeant because she is able to execute her punishment with no mercy. And we kids sitting low on our stools look just like those hidden criminals in the jungle. Hush! Hush! We are safe if we do not make any sound for that sergeant to discover us.

In my vision, my present world appears to be all formulas, all laws, all sergeants and all criminals. Our teachers seem to have the obdurate purpose of molding our minds by their formulas. They would use a photocopy machine made of their formulas to duplicate each of our minds if they could find such a machine. I admit that I am afraid of the low score on my examination from my teachers and also their castigation upon my unapproved behavior. Month by month, year by year, I see the minds of us kids yield to those formulas.

But, I bet their purpose can never be realized. Why? Just look at that comment on my math exercise book: "Do you have ears?" Of course, that math teacher is blaming me. But besides that, she is doing what? She is using language! It's not only language. She is using rhetoric! A rhetorical combination of rhetorical question and metonymy! Can she use a cosine formula to blame me? When the time comes that her formula is most needed to mold my mind, she is utterly unable to use any of her formulas. Instead, she resorts to language, to the rhetoric that she often devaluates in class. How useless her formula is! In my wretched mind, she is all exaggerations, all pretentiousness, all hollowness.

She always asserts that we kids are naive and are in dreams. How about herself? Month by month, year by year, she has been nourishing a dream of molding our minds by her formulas. For her dream, myriad disagreeable comments are in array. But, we'd better not bother to wake her. Hush! Hush! Let her indulge in her millennial dream that shall never come true.

## QUESTIONS ON CONTENT

1. Why does Wei hide the book she is reading?
2. What question does Wei's math teacher ask her?
3. Why is Wei uncomfortable with formulas for everything?
4. What does Wei compare her math teacher to?

## QUESTIONS ON RHETORIC

1. Wei writes of subjects that "pinch her mind." What does she mean by this? What examples does she give?
2. When Wei compares her teacher to a sergeant, what images does she use to achieve the comparison? Is she successful?
3. What is ironic about her math teacher's complaint?

## VOCABULARY

(1) confiscate, limbo

(2) superfluous

(3) conspicuous

(4) Marxism

(7) oblivion

(8) formidable, interposing

(10) obdurate, castigation

(11) rhetorical, metonymy, cosine, pretentiousness

(12) naive, myriad

## WRITING PROMPTS

1. Write about a time that someone tried to "mold your mind" with a prescribed argument.
2. Does the American education system try to "photocopy" its students?
3. What is the most important thing for a student to learn: math, science, language, or philosophy? What has been your most valued subject?

# Feeling Out of Place

## Ronald Markovich

The date, August 27, 1967, finally came and I was on a plane leaving the Republic of Viet Nam. I was on my way home from serving one year in a poor war torn country that I had never even heard of three years previously. I would be coming home—to the country that I loved.

The Braniff Airlines 747 roared down the runway of the Cam Ranh Bay Air Force Base. We were on our way. The cheers and excitement from the three hundred GIs as the wheels of the plane left the ground was deafening. It was a great feeling to be a part of this happiness that so many men felt. It was finally over.

After the plane reached cruising altitude the cheers and excitement started to diminish and the silence started to take over the plane. There was some conversation here and there, but overall the reality of the long ride was claiming our thoughts and minds. This left most of us to our own reflections. I thought about the past 365 days and about what home would be like; I'm sure the others did the same. I thought a lot about the ones we had left behind—the ones that hadn't made it.

I realized for the first time that there were going to be many new things in my life. I would have to get a job, I would have to continue getting my welding degree, and, most importantly, I would be seeing my three-month-old daughter. I would be a father. Having seen pictures of her had kept me going, especially on those days when I didn't care if I lived or died. She was the biggest reason that I made it through.

The flight was very serene. With the deep blue water and green landscape below, things almost seemed normal, like I was on a trip, not the nightmare that it had really been. This had not really hit me yet.

There was an announcement that broke the unsettling silence. The voice on the intercom announced our descent into Tokyo, Japan. This would be our only stop before going on to the United States. I was tired, but did not fall asleep. I don't remember much about the descent. I was in a semi-hazy state; yet my mind was racing out of control. It was playing the same record over and over. Forget this, forget this, forget this.

As the plane landed and taxied up to the terminal building, there was another announcement that we would be here for two to three hours, and to check in after two hours. It was the longest two hours of my life. Things seemed to move in slow motion. I did not want to be there; I wanted to move on. As the sounds of happy men heading for the bars to celebrate reached me, I could not bring myself to join them. I wanted to save my celebration for home.

Eventually, we got back onto the plane and as before there were cheers and an air of excitement in the cabin. The engines roared and the hubbub came to a crescendo. When in the air the chatter and laughter subsided into a weak murmur, once again. Hours, days, years, seemed to go by. Spokane, Washington, was our next and last stop.

My thoughts bounced back and forth in my head. I was going home, and had changed, this I knew. I was not the same person that my family had bid farewell to one year ago, and I did not know how to act anymore. My emotions were not the same, after I had experienced war and knew what it was really all about. I kept thinking about the ones left behind, both dead and alive.

The intercom clicked on, with the big announcement that we would be arriving in the U.S. in approximately one hour. The flight officer, who was in charge of us, gave a sarcastic speech. He informed us that protesters would most likely greet us, and there was to be no confrontation by us as a group. He threatened military legal action if it did happen. We were ordered to remain in a group, and buses would pick us up to proceed to Fort Lewis, Washington, to "clear the county," which meant that we would get papers for our next assignment.

The flight crew appeared with sprayers. They fumigated the plane so insects from the Orient would not enter the country. Fumes from the spray were so strong that I could hardly breathe. I was not aware that this going to happen and did not bother to cover my face or mouth. Now that I look back, it was just one small thing that the government had failed to tell us. There would be many more unpleasant surprises in the following months and years. Would I have changed things at all had I known better? I have asked myself this many times.

My mind was now focused on the protesters. We had heard very little about this while we were in Viet Nam. My opinion, at the time, was simply put. Why would the people not want us back in America? After all we were the same citizens that left. We had been out there fighting a war for them. Yes, it was true. I really was not sure that communism was at my back door, but I had done what my dad had done and what was expected of me.

Coming into view was land; the soil that we all loved so much was finally in sight. The giant plane's nose was sloping down, and soon we would be in Spokane. The wheels came down with a thud and the runway appeared. There was an outcry of joy that was like a thunder.

After taxing to the terminal, doors of the plane were not opened until we had the warning repeated to us by the flight officer. No encounters or we would be seeing the inside of Leavenworth Prison.

The doors opened with a creak and people started to jump out of their seats. When I started to disembark from the walkway, I remembered to step out with my left foot first. One year ago I had exited with my right foot. I didn't want to lose a step in my life and had kept this little thought to myself for the entire year.

Coming into the main terminal I saw the protesters we were told about. They were on both sides of the two lines that were told to form. People were chanting at us in loud hostile voices. "Go back to the jungle, animal," "baby killer," "we hate you," but worst of all, "this is not your home anymore!" Spit was being directed our way and they were beginning to throw things at us. We proceeded to the buses in silence. I only hoped that the people in my community did not feel the same as what I had just experienced.

At Fort Lewis, we were issued our new uniforms, airline tickets and the papers we would need to bring with us to our next assignment. Having less than ninety days of my two years commitment, the papers I carried were to be handed over to the Selective Service Office, to become my discharge orders.

Returning to Spokane for my next flight, which would be arriving in Minnesota, was my ultimate dream. I had visions of this many times while alone with my thoughts. I only had to wait one hour.

The flight to Minneapolis seemed much like the flight across the ocean. My mind overflowed, like a river. Am I a baby killer? Am I an animal? Am I not wanted anymore in my own country? I knew that I would be accepted by my family, and hoped my good friends hadn't changed.

Arriving in Minneapolis, I called my sister-in-law, and asked her to pick me up at the Greyhound Bus Terminal, in Grand Rapids, at six-thirty that evening. The ride seemed endless.

I saw things that I had missed about Minnesota, which I had not even realized. There were farms and fields, colors and sounds, and even my senses seemed to be different than they were one year ago.

Thoughts of the protesters we met at our first stop in Washington were still swimming in my mind, and were stinging me like a hot knife going through me. All I could think of, at this time, was that I didn't start this damn war, and I would not accept the blame for what had happened. I was confused and hoped I still had a home.

As the bus shifted gears coming into Grand Rapids, I looked out of the window and saw Wynetta, my sister-in-law, standing in a crowd of people. I eagerly greeted her. It was someone from my family and I felt better already.

We drove through the familiar streets of the town and out onto the highway toward my parent's home in the country. They still did not know that I was home, because I had wanted it to be a surprise. Pulling into the driveway and seeing the house almost took my breath away. I knew my daughter would be there and I still couldn't believe I had survived the past year.

My mother met me at the door. She had the most surprised look on her face, as tears streamed down her cheeks. My wife greeted me also and she cried too. It felt like I was in a dream world. They were clinging to me and hugging me. The emotion was so overwhelming. As my father approached me, I knew that he would not hug me; he never was much for that. He shook my hand and smiled as he welcomed me home.

The moment had come that I was looking forward to the most. We stepped into the living room and there was my beautiful daughter. She had big round eyes and I just couldn't wait to pick her up to give her that first hug. With all of the emotion running through me at the moment, all of a sudden it struck me. Am I a baby killer? This flash in my mind made me feel strange. Why in the world had this thought come into my head right now? This was supposed to be a happy time.

We spent an hour or so at my parents' home and then it was time to go to see my wife's parents. This was a visit that I was dreading. I was worried about this encounter and had thought about it often. My wife was only eighteen and while in Viet Nam I had received letters from them that were not pleasant. It had been a "shotgun" wedding, in Hawaii, while I was on R and R. Things had started on a bad note and this relationship seemed to be the hardest to handle for me. Now I was about to face the music and their scorn once again. I knew what they thought of me.

Arriving at my in-laws' bar/resort, we strolled into the bar where they were working. It got so quiet that it was like the jukebox stopped playing in mid-song. My father-in-law came over and gave me a hug, to my surprise. He was not very talkative. Next my mother-in-law approached me and also hugged me. To this day, I suspect that this was all for the benefit of the local patrons, who were in the bar drinking.

My father-in-law went behind the bar and came back with two beers in his hands, and asked me to join him for a welcome home drink. This took me by surprise, because I had expected him to rebuke me with a lecture about his daughter and my lack of responsibility. I didn't want a lecture or any speeches and luckily the rest of the night went well.

For the rest of that week I followed the news at six o'clock, on the local station. I was stunned by how much coverage was broadcast about the war—it was almost like being there all over again. There was a lot of footage about protesters and demonstrations and this awakened me to the fact that there were people in America that did not appreciate the soldier's effort. It seemed to me that these people were taking it out on the soldiers and that they should have been angrier with the government that had sent these young men there.

I realized then and there that I had to be very careful about who I was going to talk to about my experiences. I knew that there were people that wished that I had not made it home, that I was thought of by some as a "dirty killer." This was so confusing and wrong, but it was the reality and I would have to stuff my feelings and keep my mouth shut.

As the weeks turned into months, the arrival of cold weather brought the annual deer season. I had lived for this as a kid. Everyone in the family hunted as a group. I could feel my apprehension about this particular season. I didn't feel the same about shooting guns and hunting. I bought my license, as usual, and readied myself for opening day.

As we walked through the woods on opening morning, I was nervous. On the first deer drive shots were fired from the standers and I froze. All I could see before my eyes was another gun battle. It was my first flash back. People were getting killed and I needed to get out of there right away. I did not belong here. My family was very understanding as I picked up my gear and left to go home. No one pushed me to hunt anymore that year.

As the years have unfolded, I have put much of these war experiences behind me and hopefully to rest, but I still have a problem with the feeling of being out of place in certain situations. I had always hoped that this feeling would go away, but now I have just come to accept its being there. When I hear the cliché, "time heals all wounds," I know how false this statement can be.

I am back to hunting deer and doing the things that I have enjoyed over a lifetime. I must go on and not dwell in the dark places of my mind. I must not embrace the negative feelings that still cling inside my mind, like bats in a cave.

It has been thirty-two years since I stepped into the plane that changed me forever. Still I do not feel accepted as a soldier who fought for his country, a soldier that was too young to know what it was all about. I hold the government responsible for my feelings of frustration and rage. I feel deceived and feel like I was in a big war game, but I was not aware of the rules or why I was playing. Deception is the most hurtful feeling that can befall a man.

While talking politics or history, I think about what happened to all of us boys back then. Some of us will be forever young, and in my mind I envision the past and all of its pain. It is at these times that I have to really struggle to let things go. I have to look to the new day then.

One day I was discussing Viet Nam with my twenty-something students. Yes, I know that this was a long time ago to them, but I was appalled by the lack of knowledge that they displayed. I was saddened and angered both, to find out that America's public school system does not study the Viet Nam War and very little is known about what really happened. The government, I'm sure, has chosen not to enlighten these young people about the fact that we lost this war, in a big way. America never loses, in the history books. Top Gun and Rambo are the fantasies of today. Maybe, it will take another generation for the truth to be told. It will be tragic, because many of us will go to our graves still feeling lonely, confused, misunderstood, and out of place in our own country.

## QUESTIONS ON CONTENT

1. Where was Markovich flying to?
2. What had he been doing the previous year?

3. What did the flight crew spray in the plane? Why?
4. Who met Markovich at the plane? Why?
5. How did Markovich's father-in-law greet him? Why did it surprise him?

## QUESTIONS ON RHETORIC

1. The essay is arranged chronologically. Look at the time span involved.
2. What questions did Markovich ask himself? At what points in the essay did these questions come?
3. What impact does the deer hunting have in the essay?
4. Markovich could have ended the essay with the next-to-last paragraph. How does it change the essay to include the last paragraph?

## VOCABULARY

(8) crescendo

(10) sarcastic

(11) fumigated

(27) "shotgun" wedding

(33) flashback

(38) appalled, enlighten

## WRITING PROMPTS

1. Markovich wrote that his three-month-old daughter was the biggest reason he made it through this experience. Write about a struggle you had to make it through. What thoughts kept you going?
2. The war experience has become a "dark place" of Markovich's mind. Write about a dark place in your mind.

3. Many young soldiers died in Vietnam, and Markovich says they will be "forever young." Write about someone you know (personally or through the media) who died too young.
4. Write about the statement "America never loses in the history books."

# Dear Shelley,

## Sheree Kiser

I know, I know. You can't believe I'm writing after all these years. I hardly acknowledge your existence and now, when I'm troubled, I turn to you.

There is a reason for this. One of my professors suggested writing a letter to someone to help us through a certain assignment.

Yes. I said "professor." I'm back in school after all these years. It's always been my dream, but it was put on hold while I raised my other dreams.

So now I'm at an awesome place in my life—seeing the wonderful results of twenty-three years of work and doing something I totally enjoy.

So why am I turning to you? I can't focus. There are so many things happening that I am losing track of my dream. I try to work and my mind quits. This year has been hard for me. My youngest is graduating. When you've had a house full of teens for years, reaching the end is very difficult. Trying to think of a huge party when you are going through so many 'lasts' is not easy.

On top of that, my oldest is also graduating—from college. We are also trying to put together a small celebration for that. These things have been weighing heavily on my mind.

Then I have all the normal worries of my life: Will Rusty's tux fit? Are Ronnie and Chris going to make it? Will Roxie get in the social work program? Will Reg and Laura survive marriage preparations? Is Luke going to leave and, for God's sake, what's for supper?

Whew! That was a lot of ranting and raving. But I'm not done. That's why I chose you to write to. I think you kind of know all and see all and would understand what I'm going through—especially this next part.

I've been struggling with the graduation thing all year. I knew it would be hard. The end of something is usually hard. But within this last month, I've seen the end of something much more important. Two of my best friends lost a parent.

I've never been good with death. When I was young, I would avoid it or any talk of it at all costs. Now I'm at the age where it is in my face constantly. There is no hiding. My own mortality and the mortality of those I love sometimes seem to loom in front of me. It makes every aspect of life seem so important and so fleeting.

Now I realize that these heavy, oppressive feelings are not here to stay. What seems so huge today will eventually settle back in my mind to its appropriate size. But what do I do in the meantime? What would I do if I were teaching right now? Everyone goes through these times, they survive, they go on. But how?

Just writing this letter is a great help to me. Even picking you to write to, which seemed almost morbid at first, now seems appropriate. It helps put things back in context. After all, I have these people to care about. I'm going to school to learn to do something I love. You never had a chance to do any of these things. I am so lucky and I do know that. I guess sometimes we just get mired down in sad thoughts—almost need to wallow in them—and then we come back to the reality of how good life is.

Thanks for letting me purge myself. I like to picture you in Heaven, watching over us, your family, smiling at all we've become and guiding us in the right directions.

I wish I could have known you.

Love,

Your Sis,

Sheree

## QUESTIONS ON CONTENT

1. Why is Kiser writing the letter?
2. Who is Shelley?
3. What is bothering Kiser?

## QUESTIONS ON RHETORIC

1. The format of this essay is a letter. Does that make it any less an essay?
2. Look at the repetitions in the letter. Are they effective? Why or why not?
3. When is the first indication that Shelley is dead? Why does Kiser wait so long to tell you?
4. What impact does the closing of the letter have?

## VOCABULARY

(1) acknowledge

(5) focus

(12) morbid

(13) purge

## WRITING PROMPTS

1. Write a letter to someone you were close to who is now dead. Tell them anything you wished you had told them before they died.
2. Write a letter to someone who is still living but that you don't communicate with very often. How does this letter differ from the first?
3. Write about the mundane stuff that steals your energy.

# Picnics and Milk

## Stacy Jurgens

When I was five years old, my father quit his job as a mechanic to help my grandfather with his farm full time. My earliest and best childhood memories come from this farm and what life was like depending on it to keep us fed. My grandparents were dairy farmers and my family lived in a trailer house at the edge of one of their fields. My days were spent exploring the farm and the fields surrounding it. Occasionally, I could earn a dollar by helping my grandfather clean out the calf barn or bottle-feed the calves. These were things that I loved to do regardless, but the dollar was always nice. As good as my days were, the memories that stand out in my mind are the mealtimes. Everybody would stop what they were doing and join together not only for a meal but a deserved rest and chance to catch up with each other's doings. Although I didn't realize this then, those meals did more than fill our stomachs.

During the summer, my mother would send my older sister and I down the hill to the milking parlor to draw milk from the bulk tank for supper. I still remember the path leading through the field, past the garden, and through Grandpa and Grandma's yard to the milking parlor. Often, Grandpa and Dad would still be in the milking room, finishing up the evening milking, and Dad would yell and ask what mom was making for supper. We always lied and yelled back pizza because we knew he didn't like it, and then Grandpa would jokingly tell us to set an extra plate for him. I guess Grandpa liked pizza.

After my sister and I had filled the milk jug from the tank we would begin the task of carrying it up the path to the trailer. This was never easy, as we were two young girls trying to carry a large, round jug full of milk up a rather long path. We managed though, often stopping to rest and sneak sips from the jug. Although I drink skim milk today, I still remember the cool thickness of those stolen sips of whole milk. The milk was also perfect for making legitimate milk mustaches, and Shannon and I could have been poster girls for today's Got Milk campaign. There we were, two young girls in faded cut-offs and feathered hair, splashing milk out of the jug and onto our bare feet as we struggled to carry the milk up the hill.

It was only rarely that we had to carry the jug the entire way back to the trailer house. Most nights my dad would finish the milking and catch up to us before we made it past the garden and carry the jug for us, teasing us all the way. By the time we got to the trailer and Dad had washed up, we would have supper on the table and a large, cool glass of milk setting at each place. I don't remember much of what we ate, but I remember the milk, I think because I knew I had helped put it there.

Lunchtime was different than suppertime in that my father did not come back to the house to eat. Instead, he either took a lunch with him or (my favorite) we took a picnic lunch to him. We never knew when these picnics would occur, but sometimes Mom would pull out the old wicker picnic basket and send us girls to the garden for fresh tomatoes and cucumbers. We knew then that we were going to go find Dad in the fields.

After getting the food ready we would pile into the car and take off on the endless gravel roads that ran through our county. It was almost a game to see who would spot Dad's tractor first. Once we did, we would pull into the nearest approach and wait for him to come around. My mother would flag him down and then put out our picnic blanket and the food while he finished his lap. Then we would eat, all of us sitting there on a blanket in the middle of nowhere, hidden from the world by waves of grain or rows of corn.

There was no buzz of a radio or whine of traffic, just my family catching up on our day. Time stood still during lunches like that.

After the food was gone and the remains packed away, our parents would send us off on some silly errand to find a certain rock or a special flower so that they could have some time alone. We would take off down the rows of corn knowing full well what our parents were up to. We saw no problem with our parents sneaking some afternoon loving into their busy days. There's a good feeling you get, even at the age of five, when you see your parents madly in love with each other. I consider myself a very lucky person that I have experienced that feeling so many times, standing there with my sisters peeking at my kissing parents through the long grass.

These memories from my childhood embody everything that I want for my children someday. I want them to appreciate what they have and work for what they get, just as my sister and I did with the milk. I want them to be thrilled at the slightest event, just as I was at the thought of a picnic. I want them to experience the timelessness of a summer afternoon, alone with the people you love and surrounded by swaying grass. Finally, I want them to know the comfort and security, along with curiosity and wonder, that I knew watching my parents steal kisses on a blanket in the middle of the day.

## Questions on Content

1. What kind of farm did Jurgens grow up on?
2. What did the girls always tell their dad they were having for supper? Why?
3. During the summer, what was the girls' job each night for supper?
4. What did the wicker basket signify?

## Questions on Rhetoric

1. Look at the imagery in paragraph 3. What is Jurgens referring to when she says "legitimate milk mustaches"?

2. What details does Jurgens use to make time stand still during the picnics?
3. Look at the last sentence of paragraph 1. What does Jurgens mean and how does she make her point?

## WRITING PROMPTS

1. Write about mealtimes in your family.
2. Write about the relationship between your parents that you perceived as a child. How does it compare to what you now perceive?
3. Choose an ordinary day from your childhood and capture every essence of it.

# CREDITS

JOHN HOCKENBERRY

"Limited Seating on Broadway" by John Hockenberry from*The New York Times*, April 13, 1992. Copyright © 1992 by the New York Times Co. Reprinted by permission.

ALICE HOFFMAN

"The Perfect Family" by Alice Hoffman from*The New York Times Magazine*, November 1, 1992. Copyright © 1992 by The New York Times Co. Reprinted by permission.

ZORA NEALE HURSTON

"I Get Born" from *Dust Tracks on a Road* by Zora Neale Hurston. Copyright 1942 by Zora Neale Hurston. Copyright renewed 1970 by John C. Hurston. Reprinted by permission of HarperCollins Publishers, Inc.

PICO IYER

"In Praise of the Humble Comma" by Pico Iyer from *Time*, June 13, 1988. Copyright © 1988 Time Inc. Reprinted by permission.

MARTIN LUTHER KING, JR.

"I Have a Dream" by Martin Luther King, Jr. Reprinted by arrangement with The Heirs to the Estate of Martin Luther King, Jr., c/o Writers House as agent for the proprietor. Copyright 1963 Martin Luther King, Jr., renewed 1991 by Coretta Scott King.

ELAINE TYLER MAY

"Women in the Wild Blue Yonder" by Elaine Tyler May from *The New York Times*, August 7, 1991. Copyright © 1991 by The New York Times Co. Reprinted by permission.

MARY E. MITCHELL

"Full Circle Lessons" by Mary E. Mitchell from *Family Circle*, September 1, 1997, p. 124. Reprinted with the permission of Family Circle Magazine.

## N. SCOTT MOMADAY

"A Kiowa Grandmother" from *The Way To Rainy Mountain* by N. Scott Momaday, published by University of New Mexico Press. Reprinted by permission.

## DOROTHY NOYES

"Senior-Teener. A New Hybrid" by Dorothy Noyes from *Newsweek*, September 5, 1994. Copyright © 1994. All rights reserved. Reprinted by permission.

## GEORGE ORWELL

"A Hanging" from *Shooting An Elephant and Other Essays* by George Orwell, copyright 1950 by Sonia Brownell Orwell and renewed 1978 by Sonia Pitt-Rivers, reprinted by permission of Harcourt, Inc. and Bill Hamilton as the Literary Executor of the Estate of the Late Sonia Brownell Orwell and Secker & Warburg Ltd.

## ANNA QUINDLEN

"Our Animal Rites" by Anna Quindlen from*The New York Times*, August 5, 1990. Copyright © 1990 by the New York Times Co. Reprinted by permission.

## SCOTT RUSSELL SANDERS

"News of the Wild," copyright © 1994 by Scott Russell Sanders; first appeared in *1995 Sierra Club Wilderness Calendar*; collected in the author's *Writing from the Center* (Indiana University Press, 1995); reprinted by permisison of the author.

## MAY SARTON

"The Rewards of Living a Solitary Life" by May Sarton from *The New York Times*, April 8, 1974. Copyright © 1974 by The New York Times Co. Reprinted by permission.

## ANNA MAE HALGRIM SEAVER

"My World Now" by Anna Mae Halgrim Seaver as appeared in *Newsweek*, June 1994. Reprinted by permission from an article compiled from notes found in a drawer after Mrs. Seaver passed on.

BRENT STAPLES
"Black Men and Public Space" by Brent Staples. Reprinted by permission of the author.

LINCOLN STEFFENS
"A Miserable Merry Christmas" from *The Autobiography of Lincoln Steffens* by Lincoln Steffens, copyright 1931 by Harcourt, Inc. and renewed 1959 by Peter Steffens, reprinted by permission of the publisher.

DEBORAH TANNEN
"The Triumph of the Yell" by Deborah Tannen from *The New York Times,* January 14, 1994. Copyright © 1994 by the New York Times Co. Reprinted by permission.

SUSAN ALLEN TOTH
"Boyfriends" from *Blooming: A Small-Town Girlhood* by Susan Allen Toth. Introduction copyright © 1998 by Susan Allen Toth. Copright © 1978, 1981 by Susan Allen Toth. Used by permission of Ballantine Books, a division of Random House, Inc.

JUDITH VIORST
"What me? Showing off?" by Judith Viorst. Copyright © 1982 by Judith Viorst. Originally appeared in *Redbook*. This usage granted by permission.

EUDORA WELTY
Reprinted by permission of the publisher from "Listening" in *One Writer's Beginnings* by Eudora Welty, Cambridge, Mass.: Harvard University Press, Copyright © 1983, 1984 by Eudora Welty.

E.B. WHITE
"The Family Which Dwelt Apart" from *Quo vadimus?* by E.B. White. Copyright 1937 by E.B. White, renewed © 1965 by E. B. White. This essay originally appeared in *The New Yorker.* Reprinted by permission of HarperCollins Publishers, Inc.

CYNTHIA WILLIAMS

"Garbage Karma" by Cynthia Williams as appeared in *Northern Lights*. Reprinted by permission of the author. Cynthia Williams is currently working on a book called *Personal Ad*, a tragi-comic memoir about trying to find a mate in the modern world.

VIRGINIA WOOLF

"The Death of the Moth" from *The Death Of The Moth And Other Essays* by Virginia Woolf, copyright 1942 by Harcourt, Inc. and renewed 1970 by Marjorie T. Parsons, Executrix, reprinted by permission of the publisher.

STANTON L. WORMLEY, JR.

"Fight Back" by Stanton L. Wormley, Jr. from *The New York Times Magazine*, March 10, 1985. Copyright © 1985 by the New York Times Co. Reprinted by permission.

WILLIAM ZINSSER

Chapter 3, "Clutter" by William Zinsser from *On Writing Well*, 6th Edition. Copyright © 1976, 1980, 1985, 1988, 1990, 1994, 1998 by William K. Zinsser. Reprinted by permission of the author.